Jo-Anne Nadler entered broadcasting with a bang – making pop music programmes on national radio – but she gave up the rock 'n' roll lifestyle to work for the Conservative Party. In the dog-days of the Major government she returned to the BBC as a producer and reporter with political programmes and now works as a freelance writer and commentator, making regular appearances on television and radio. She has contributed to a range of newspapers and magazines and is the author of *In His Own Right*, a biography of former Conservative leader William Hague.

TOO NICE
TO BE A TORY

TOO NICE TO BE A TORY

It's My Party and I'll Cry If I Want To

JO-ANNE NADLER

**SIMON &
SCHUSTER**

London · New York · Sydney · Toronto · Dublin

A VIACOM COMPANY

First published in Great Britain by Simon & Schuster UK Ltd, 2004
A Viacom company

1 3 5 7 9 10 8 6 4 2

Simon & Schuster UK Ltd
Africa House
64–78 Kingsway
London WC2B 6AH

www.simonsays.co.uk

Simon & Schuster Australia
Sydney

A CIP catalogue record for this book
is available from the British Library

ISBN 0-7432-2076-5

Typeset by M Rules
Printed and bound in Great Britain
by Mackays of Chatham plc, Chatham, Kent

For my sister, Helena

CONTENTS

TOO NICE
TO BE A TORY

PREFACE

I'M A CONSERVATIVE – GET ME OUT OF HERE!

A few years ago I was drinking with some friends in a popular bar in Portobello Road. We had met straight from work. The bar was, as always, packed with a typical Notting Hill clientele: young, stylish, creative, black, white and all shades in between. The air was hot and smoky. Loud house music was the backbeat for our attempts at a shouted conversation.

Just as we edged our way up to the bar disaster struck. My bag burst open and its contents spilt all over the floor, or at least over the feet of the rest of the people in the immediate throng. I caught the expression of sheer horror on the face of my friend who was already juggling drinks. As I dropped down to the floor to collect up the papers a gust of wind from the open door made a discreet exit even harder. Within seconds Conservative Party press releases, complete with deep blue torch logo, were wafting through the whole room. In those days I worked for the Tory Party but there, in the heart of the chic metropolis, I was none too comfortable about advertising it. It wasn't the most obvious place to start a recruitment drive. I understood why my friend in the bar did not want our cover blown.

Conservatism and I go back a long way. As you will see, further back even than I can remember. But my relationship with the party has been rather up and down over the years; sometimes it has been active and supportive, at others rather more estranged and critical. Not that I've ever doubted that I am on the right. I believe that the tools of the right, the market, enterprise and liberal economics, overwhelmingly beat the tools of the left, government control, high taxation and bureaucracy in improving life for most people most of the time. Call me old-fashioned but I still think that if you believe in free markets, privatisation, competition, and wealth creation you are of the right whatever you chose to call yourself in these postmodern times. And despite having to share the label with some people I'd sooner not go drinking with, I persist in calling myself a Conservative because the party of the same name has done the most to champion these ideas and to put them into action. But at times, it has also done a lot to make that label less than always desirable.

Over the years I've done my stint as an activist, I've worked at the party's HQ and I've studied it up close but with the detachment of a journalist. I've seen it at its best and worst, from the bottom and the top, from the inside and the outside. I have joined it, I have worked for it and I've voted for it and it has left me at turns amused, bemused and confused. As with family I feel entitled to criticise the party but if someone else does I feel I have to spring to its defence.

I remember the last time the Conservative Party was out of power – but only just. I grew up with Maggie, grew indifferent with Major and now I've grown used to the merry-go-round of leadership elections and power struggles that have become part of the party's soap opera. When I was writing a book about William Hague it was widely taken for granted that he was a nerd. This was broadly deemed indisputable because as a teenager he had not only joined the Young Conservatives but he had also decorated his bedroom with posters of Margaret Thatcher. If these were the defining characteristics of nerdhood I knew I was in trouble because, truth be told, so had I.

As a self-styled woman about town I wasn't sure I was completely comfortable about this shared secret bond with William Hague, but it forced me to look at the reasons for my ambivalence. After all, it's only looking back on it now that I cringe with embarrassment at having been a Tory tot. It seemed perfectly reasonable at the time. Adult experience has showed me that admitting to a Conservative habit remains one of sophisticated society's last remaining taboos. Most of my friends and media colleagues tolerate my Conservatism but even now they'd rather not know too much about it. They treat it as an amusing aberration. But before I was susceptible to such mores I was completely unselfconscious and totally unapologetic about my convictions. Has the party changed or have I? I was going to have to go back a long way, further even than I had imagined, to find out.

PART 1

BORN TO BE BLUE

2 May 1979

Dear diary:
Went into school late today after morning off with period pains
(Ugg). Went to dance club extra practice lunch time – getting quite
nervous about the show. After school Helena and I went back to
Jacci's as Mum teaching. General Election tomorrow. After supper
popped in to see Wendy as having trouble with Latin homework.
Tried to get Wendy to persuade her mum to vote Conservative.

1

VELOCITY AND PRECOCITY

Spring 1979

A school performance, south-west London

Suddenly the spotlight cut a dramatic shaft of light through the
dusty air and across the gloom of the makeshift stage. In the audience there were proud parents, anxious teachers and awkward,
amused siblings shuffling and coughing. It was the stuff of school
performances everywhere with flash photography and the odd cine
camera poised to capture the big moment. Then came the click of
the tape recorder switch and the hiss as the cassette whirred into
action. And suddenly music! An unlikely figure waddled into the
light. A plump, prepubescent prima donna had taken to the stage
with precious little grace but absolutely no embarrassment. You
would have thought that the costume alone would have induced
awkwardness – head to toe in white leotard and tights with a white
tutu, a feathered hat and a yellow beak. In a show that had featured

a variety of original talents this contribution, more Daffy Duck than *Swan Lake*, still managed to surprise.

It was May 1979 and I was giving the performance of my life, well certainly of my twelve-year-old life. My school dance club had never been set for international acclaim but it was our inaugural performance and the first time we had had an audience after weeks of after-school rehearsals. That Saturday afternoon I had spent hours in the wings poking my beak around the edge of the stage watching as the rest of the team perfected an all girls' version of 'Summer Nights' and the rather more exotic 'Red Weed' from Jeff Wayne's *War of the Worlds*.

My friends and I were just a couple of years too young and certainly too prissy to have understood punk, which had erupted in the middle of an otherwise moribund decade, but later the pop hits of *Saturday Night Fever* and *Grease* were instant successes and the inspiration for our amateur efforts. At ten I had been greatly troubled by a *Sunday Times* colour supplement on punk rock. I sat on the stairs of our comfortable three-bedroomed house in Wimbledon and stared in disbelief, and a fair bit of horror, at photos of mohican-cut, safety-pinned boys and parakeet-haired women with multiple piercings parading up and down the Kings Road. After all, Chelsea was familiar territory for little girls like me because Peter Jones, as well as being the defining shopping experience of the practical middle class, stocked my school uniform. My sister Helena, younger by four years, and I had for years made regular trips to the top floor for our regulation sports kit, navy blue knickers (which had to reach the waist) and pale green aertex shirts. The rest of the uniform was similarly plain and utilitarian – navy pleated skirts and white shirts. The best of it had been the bowler hats but these were later phased out by the time I reached junior school and oddly, or so I thought at seven, I was the only one who missed them.

Our Friday after-school practice sessions were the closest thing Wimbledon High School came to *Fame* (and that was still some way off). In the late 1970s WHS was a worthy but dull establishment, perfectly good at getting its 'gals' through exams but generally very conservative. That is with a small 'c' as politics along with death and sex were never explicitly referred to even by the time we pupils probably knew considerably more about any of them than the staff. In fact, the school symbol was an apple: an Old-Testament warning against the dangers of temptation.

I had a straightforward school career. At the age of five I joined the prep school, hanging my blazer and bowler up in the stark first-year cloakroom of the imposing Victorian house at the bottom of Wimbledon Hill. From there, without too many hiccups, I progressed to the 1950s low-rise junior school at the back of the site and, at eleven, on to the grand pile of the senior school with its rather impressive science-block extension. Unfortunately these modern facilities were wasted on me as I was no good at science or indeed anything remotely numerate, preferring instead touchy-feely things like painting and religious studies. In the senior school my favourite teacher was the English mistress, Mrs Kershaw, who best epitomised the ubiquitous pleated-skirted, K-shoed, tan-stockinged and mauve-jerseyed (always jerseys – never the more suggestive sounding sweaters) style of the high school teachers. It was a well-behaved, rather quaint school on which passing whims of fashion or social change seemed to have made little mark. This was the decade after the closing of the 1960s but there was little indication that if anything had swung in the 60s it had swung anywhere close to this school.

Set against this strait-laced, though not severe, ethos our modern dance club was a daring innovation. The school had eventually allowed our non-conformist swimming teacher the use of the assembly hall to teach dance lessons in the hope that she might be able to bring exercise to those of us who had no aptitude for netball or hockey. So there we were, various shapes and sizes of well-brought-up young ladies in footless tights and legwarmers, rather pleased that our extra-curricular activities cast us as exotic free spirits in an otherwise conventional, academic school. Each week we had one hour in which we set aside our neat pleats and green-and-white-striped ties for T-shirts and leggings and a record player that provided the soundtrack for several leaps of imagination, both for the participants and the audience.

Through our exertions we were transformed not into elegant dancers but in most cases into sweaty little dumplings. In our minds, however, we were cool and never more so than in May 1979 as we were preparing for our inaugural show. Practice sessions were a great free show for the boys from King's College School making their way home down Wimbledon Hill, able to catch a glimpse of pubescent wobble if they craned hard enough past the right tree. On the big night I think that straining flesh stirred more than a healthy interest in some of the attendant fathers and brought out a rush of handkerchiefs to mop the brows of concerned school staff whose worst fears were being confirmed. There were some more raunchy numbers from older members of the cast on whom the Kate Bush-style white leotards were rather more appropriate. Compared with the regular diet of discordant chamber concerts and choir practice it was shocking stuff. What with the make-up, the lighting and the dried ice we all brushed up quite well and it was probably hardly surprising that the following year we had no problem recruiting male volunteers to help behind the scenes.

I had been nervous about the show for weeks but according to my diary it was only one of two things playing particularly heavily on my mind in the spring of 1979. Our impending performance was a normal, indeed positively healthy, preoccupation for a twelve-year-old schoolgirl. The other was perhaps less predictable. The overly neat joined-up handwriting chronicles mostly ephemera, each week carefully noting the number one single and the progress of the dance routines, but scattered in among the daily trivia are the occasional, unknowing references to history in the making. With a complete lack of irony I note my heroes and influences, my loves and my hates. In May 1979, alongside Olivia Newton John and John Travolta, Margaret Thatcher makes a first appearance, casually referenced alongside the homework problems and pressing choreographic dilemmas.

Our all-consuming premiere coincided with the week of the general election and Maggie's own premiere at Number 10. In the run-up to this dramatic week my friends and I had been mainly pre-occupied with balancing on points and the lunch queue while all around adults had been preoccupied with the balance of payments and the job queues. Two days after Mrs T had swept to power on a landslide our very mixed bag of a dance troupe had swept across the high school stage mostly on our backsides. Although we had taken the rehearsals seriously, the dance group was also a way to have fun. Even to a child's limited world-view, it also seemed a necessary rebellion against the atmosphere of the time: in the 1970s it was grim, even down south.

Whilst I would not claim that life was exactly tough for a middle-class child at a private school in leafy Wimbledon, no one was completely immune to the pervasive gloom that characterised a decade blighted by 'stoppages', terrorist attacks, IMF loans, stagflation, exchange controls, ILEA, power cuts, inefficiency, man-made fibres and the Bay City Rollers. It wasn't that I felt under special threat but it was clear that the country had big problems even if I didn't completely understand what they were.

Adult conversations overheard, brief attention paid to the TV news and *Weekend World*, and to the gloom-laden headlines in the dense, colourless pages of the pre-Murdoch broadsheets only seemed to confirm the prevailing climate of despondency. Constant references to the 'British disease', the 'sick man of Europe', and the daunting sounding 'brain drain' reinforced my naive but vivid sense that, beyond the safe world of school, things were troubled and uneasy. Puberty and exams were bad enough but in the encroaching world of adulthood it seemed that there was even more to worry our parents. Low-level grumbles certainly confirmed the idea that nothing ever seemed to work: the trains, the electricity supply, the Water Board, the ill-fated Austin Allegro (of which ours, in ubiquitous brown, was constantly off the road) and as I understood it, quite a lot of the workforce. In fact as the arresting billboard posters confirmed even, or perhaps especially,

Labour was not working. Phone calls to the Gas Board were met with otherwise uncharacteristic expletives from my mother. Appointments made were never kept, spare parts were never available. Visits to the local GP took for ever as tonsillitis-infected kids coughed all over each other in fidgety queues. Televisions which hummed for ages after being switched off brought news of a biblical sounding 'winter of discontent'. We were constantly reminded to turn off the lights and save power, to watch out for suspicious packages, to clunk-click every trip and to prepare for another sugar shortage by stockpiling those little packets from the brand new McDonald's fast-food restaurant.

The recent taste for recycling history would have us now believe that there is such a thing as '70s chic' but seen at the time, without the benefit of soft focus revisionism or overused postmodern irony, flared trousers and teak furniture were simply ugly, beef Wellington was just a giant sausage roll and Britain in the pre-greed era was not some quaint idyll since lost to progress and globalisation, but merely a badly run, frustrating place that was intent on kissing goodbye to a glorious past in a fairly inglorious fashion.

In May 1979 an election set to break the failing consensus was necessarily a big event for the adult population, unavoidably politicised by the daily grind of economic failure. The biggest things in my life should have been perfecting my dance routines and moving out of the lowest stream for maths. And so they were really, but something else had filtered through the screen of my immediate preoccupations.

In our house *Nationwide* and *The Nine O'Clock News* were a nightly ritual. I did not always watch with rapt attention but the unavoidable impression was that Britain was a grey place. Grey reporters stood in Downing Street with news of grey haired men in slack grey suits attending endless dull meetings with beer and greying sandwiches. Into this monotone world had stepped a more colourful figure.

On aesthetic grounds alone Maggie demanded attention. Her

blonde hair and electric blue suits marked her out from the flabby chopped chaps. She was something new. I was interested to chart her progress with the same sort of anorakish scrutiny I had thus far paid to the pop charts and the Eurovision Song Contest. Since about the age of six I had followed the annual song festival with close attention, through from the first round 'primaries' to the excitement of the night and the nail-biting voting procedures. So a much trailed general election, with its dramas played out nightly on the television and its potential for a far more complex pattern of voting and results, was bound to stir some kind of interest in someone who was perhaps a burgeoning psephologist. And certainly that is all there in the diary. I had started a chart detailing the number of seats needed for a Conservative victory, the swings required, the geographical dispersal. But given that I was a girl who hated numbers this interest must have been fired by something more than the challenge of an arithmetical puzzle.

My parents were relaxed people who had never preached politics or indeed anything else, but my father's work for the BBC had always brought current affairs into the house and had sparked an interest in the world beyond our front door. The only things I can ever remember my mother telling me in the way of advice for life were not to eat in the street and to wear a hat. Useful though this advice has proven it hardly constituted a coherent philosophy and was not the making of a political indoctrination. Although Conservative voters, my parents were not party members and seldom referred to party politics, but I can remember how the sheer inefficiency of the 1970s provoked their constant murmurs of disapproval of the government. As a journalist and a design lecturer they had busy working lives. Their friends were artists, writers and broadcasters, all ideally qualified for the liberal elite – all, as I later found out, desperate for something, or someone, to turn the tide against the postwar consensus.

Our home, a 1950s detached house, was very comfortable by many people's standards, but in terms of suburban London, nothing grand. Sending my sister and me to a private school throughout the period when direct grants were being removed was about their most explicit political statement and when I had on occasion queried the decision, ('Was it fair,' I might ask, 'to pay for a better education?') I was rebuked. They were doing their best to give us the best they could and we had a responsibility to make the best of it. With a demanding full-time job my mother barely had time to take off her own hat before rushing in to make supper and oversee homework for two demanding daughters, let alone polishing us up as potential recruits for the Young Conservatives.

The rest of my small family comprised a selection of sweet but dull great aunts who considered spaghetti Bolognese a daring foreign dish. They were definitely conservatives with a small 'c' but equally they came from a generation of hard-working women for whom the effects of two wars had hastened the pace of emancipation. They were living proof that women had had to be independent long before the 1960s had made it fashionable. Theirs was a different strain of Toryism from my parents though they certainly were not political proselytisers either. Nevertheless, as my diary testifies, I had absorbed and distilled enough to declare my own sympathies with the same degree of naive enthusiasm I had for my dancing and my dubious pop heroes.

My sense of excitement in the build-up to election day rated alongside the sense of anticipation ahead of the dance show. I had developed something of a compulsion that often kept me awake for long into the night. I was addicted to late night radio chat shows. I would lie in bed in the dark with the radio chattering away under the duvet. Beneath the gaze of Sandy and Danny staring down from the *Smash Hits* posters that covered the brown floral walls, I would curl up determined to listen a little longer each night. I was absorbed in a world of discovery that crackled its way via medium wave into my consciousness, and later subconscious, as I eventually drifted off to sleep. LBC's 'agony uncle' later became a vital source of information for my otherwise non-existent sex education, but on Thursday 3 May 1979 the radio was tuned for news of Maggie from Grantham, rather than Mark from Greenwich with a personal

problem or Martha from Greenhayes asking about the best conditions for growing pot plants. With zeal appropriate to someone
who harboured hopes of one day being a head girl, I had started out
by making notes.

'We all hope Maggie will win!' I jotted down the results of the
exit polls but never made it to the real ones, as by twenty to twelve
I had fallen asleep pen in hand leaving a scrawl of blue ink running
down the side of the page. So much for the marathon radio listening session. It was left until the next day, Friday 4 May, for me to
fill in the details.

> *Well I woke up at 6.30 finding I'd left the radio on all night. Was
> so excited went to school early – I know I'm mad! Someone had
> tied a King's Boy to one of the parking meters outside the school
> and put a sack over his head. We are all very pleased that Mrs
> Thatcher has won, the country will be much better off with the
> Conservatives.*

2

LONDON CALLING

Kensington Young Conservatives, 19 December 1949

Young couples were revolving around the dance floor with rather more enthusiasm than elegance. Clean-cut chaps in evening dress sporting freshly barbered hair optimistically led their pretty, taffeta-wrapped girlfriends in routines they had not quite mastered. Satin toes were in danger of being stubbed by premature twirlers but as the evening drew on English self-consciousness and stiff-upper-limbed formality relaxed to the rhythm of the band and the effects of the limited selection of drinks. By ten o'clock the decorous two-step had given way to a relatively risqué rumba, and couples sitting by the side of the dance floor chattered and giggled through a gauze of smoke, the tempo of their conversations seemingly conducted by the baton-like cigarette-holders.

Unlike many of the surrounding streets in Kensington, Stratford Road had emerged from the ravages of the war with relative dignity. Its railings were still intact and the original street lamps illuminated once again stood proud, though only ineffectively spreading small pools of custard light through the dense, cold air and across the dirty faces of the Victorian houses. Exactly halfway between Kensington High Street and Earls Court, Stratford Road was in the heart of bedsit land but with its irregular gardens, ageing trees and quaint run of corner shops the street was somehow less intimidating than many of its lofty neighbours. The Conservative Association at number 23 had a large extension built on the back. The room was impressive, with four wide sash windows over-looking the street, and though not grand it was considered fine enough by those eagerly arriving for the Christmas dance.

That evening Hilary had a double celebration in mind. The fes-tive dance was a party in itself, as well as falling on the evening of her twentieth birthday. The everyday deprivations of the war had been subsiding gradually but its effects were still evident in many ways. Since 1945 relief and celebration had been tempered by the quiet acceptance that recovery would require patience and another big push, the war effort having been replaced by the rather more nebulous postwar effort. In a few short years the enthusiasm and goodwill that had greeted the ambitious intentions of the Labour government were straining and disappointment threatened to cor-rode the famed national spirit in a way Hitler had failed to do. Britain had won the war but increasingly people were asking at what cost to its economy and place in the world?

London was wounded and weary but resolute. Gradually its broken bones were being reset, but buildings that had stood at the heart of an empire were being repaired for an uncertain and less glorious future. It was a period of tangible readjustment; everyone knew from what, few were certain where to. But despite and because of anxieties real and exaggerated there was a hunger for vitality and fun, a need to grab at those frivolities and pleasures so recently restricted and which now seemed especially vivid and desirable. There was a yearning for recovery.

That Christmas the enterprising spirit that had pulsed through the capital's history and its people was much in evidence even

though rationing still meant that Christmas staples were scarce. For
the very few who could afford to eat out and work their way round
the restaurant restrictions Mayfair's Bagatelle was licensed until
2.30 in the morning and for Christmas featured Winifred Atwell,
the Dusky Queen of Swing. But champagne and chanteuse were
not typical of London's nightlife, particularly as 'youth' would
take at least another two decades to come into its own. There
were limited options for dating. A few smoky cafés offered opportunities for conversation eked out over weak coffee in Pyrex cups.
The fug of nicotine and the windows etched with condensation created intimate caverns insulated from London's layers of grey.

Against that background a party at Kensington Young
Conservatives was really quite a glamorous affair, especially for a
girl new to London. The new organisation was proving a hit with
young people keen to meet like-minded, or like-backgrounded
people. And my mother, though hardly the twin set and pearled
type who flourished in Kensington Conservatives, had thought
joining was an obvious step on coming to London. Her move to
the capital after her teenage years in Sussex had followed when she
had become the first member of the family to be awarded a place
at university. But she did not consider herself especially political,
if at all, although that, if nothing else, would have made her a typical Conservative. She knew that her own parents had always
voted Conservative and she had seen the way in which they had
lived, their unfailing work ethic, their dignity and civility, their
loyalty and common sense, their kindness, and she had taken for
granted their seldom stated politics as a way of life. She had sensed
the suspicion and the scepticism with which her father and
mother, although working people, had viewed socialism. They
thought that was all about politics with a capital P, about new-
fangled ideas that did not really accord with history or with life as
people lived it. When Labour really was new the forces of
Conservatism keenly believed that socialism was treacherous. In
spite of the trend towards greater political consensus that developed out of the depression and the war, the still waters of tribal

politics still ran deep in their aftermath and without a great deal of reasoning Hilary knew her tribe was blue. But most of all, Hilary was just looking forward to getting out and having some fun and as for most members that was the appeal of the Young Conservatives.

Through the haze that swayed across the coloured party lights a familiar and dependable face drifted in and out of view. The framed photograph of Churchill that coolly surveyed a room of Christmas merrymakers was one reason to feel allied to this tribe. Of course no one would claim that the war effort had been anything but cross-party, in spirit and in organisation, but Churchill's charisma and determination had made him an enduring figurehead that spoke to many on the right about the qualities they wished were somehow theirs particularly. Despite the nation's desire for a new broom in 1945, Churchill would always command loyalty and affection that in part continued to rub off on and benefit his party. In that unflinching gaze cast over the dance floor the face of Churchill radiated a brand of resolution, a steadfast commitment to the worthy battle which the victors of a terrible war could reasonably claim was peculiarly British; others grateful for that victory could happily ascribe it to the best of British values.

Hilary was not the only newcomer to London who had come to dance that night. James had recently arrived from Exeter where he had been studying. He had noticed Hilary before he had noticed Churchill, but was momentarily distracted and transported by the photograph and what it meant to him. In the picture of this British hero, hanging in this particular setting, he hoped that he saw the culmination of his odyssey. To be there that evening James had come a great deal further than from Devon and to play the part he intended he still had a great way to go, but standing there amid the music and the chatter he did not feel like an alien. He didn't care whether other people there were privileged. His privilege was merely to be there. Here in London they could dance and drink and talk about anything. It was Christmas; they were young, single and most of all free. James smiled as he took off his coat, and tucking his copy of the evening paper into his pocket he sensed it was going to be a good night.

Mum had been nearly ten when war was declared. On 3 September 1939 she had been visiting her grandparents in Derby. Her parents, Dora and Stanley, had taken her to lunch at Anchorage House, the seemingly impregnable, stone-built villa that was home to her mother's family. Hilary was an only child but the rest of the family, although disparate, was large so she had many aunts and uncles. Dora's family had a military background and a certain bearing drawn from that, which gave them a sense of place in the world that their otherwise indefinite class would not have offered. They considered themselves slightly superior to her father's family. Stanley, like his father before him, had been a policeman. He had fought in the trenches in the First World War (although this was never spoken of) and entered the police force on his return to civvy street. He was in his late thirties, Dora in her late twenties, when they met and married in Newcastle. Dora, like all her three sisters, worked. She was a sales rep and as one of only a few women to drive a car, travelled the country for Lever Brothers. She was a striking woman, always immaculate, industrious and self-sufficient. She and her husband were hard workers. Theirs were hard-working families, with a strong sense of patriotism, duty and responsibility, to each other and to their country – although not to an abstract 'state'. Despite being warm and affectionate people, they were nonetheless touched by a northern stoicism. Stanley and Dora Vickers were not the sort of people to put their faith in anything they could not effect themselves so they were sceptical about grand gestures from politicians, and the unlikely promises of religion. They had ideals without being idealistic, standards without being dogmatic and convictions without ideology. They were sensible and cautious although enterprising and conscientious. They were conservative but not reactionary. When necessary they got on their bikes.

That Sunday afternoon Hilary's feet were clattering up and

down the hallway as she played hopscotch, jumping in and out of
the patterns made by the black and white tiles that ran the length
of the ground floor. Her carefree exuberance was cut short by a
sombre message. Peace in their time had proved as flimsy as the
piece of paper on which it had been written. The tense culpable
voice of Chamberlain crackled through the walnut wireless set, in
a few short seconds delivering the news that would change the lifetime of everyone who heard it, the destinies of many who did not.
Germany had invaded Poland, the trigger to send Britain to war
against the dictator she had tried to appease. Through the BBC the
Cabinet Room at Downing Street had merged with thousands of
living rooms around the country on an otherwise ordinary Sunday
afternoon. The news though not unexpected was nonetheless
shocking, yet in households like these across the country this was
no time for panic. Although there was no mistaking the anxiety
that hovered in the air as tangibly as the fading cooking smells,
Hilary was not at all sure what was meant by this curious turn of
events.

Hundreds of miles away in the heart of Poland, the country whose
honour Hilary had heard the prime minister pledge to defend, the
outbreak of war was already disrupting the lives of thousands of
people and one little boy in particular. Thirteen-year-old Jashu
and his parents were planning to flee the Polish city they loved.
Lvov (now Lviv in the Ukraine) was in the heart of a continent and
at the crossroads of so many different cultures. Throughout Jashu's
childhood it had crackled with energy fired by competing beliefs
and passions, each trying to make sense of the aftermath of the
Great War. Much of the time these had been creative tensions
reflecting the relative sophistication of a city that had been a
common home to Poles, Jews, Ukrainians, Hungarians, Russians,
Austrians and all shades of Christian denomination. Although Lvov
had been Polish throughout Jashu's childhood it was a city where
ideas of nationality and identity were complicated and nuanced.
From the hill where once had stood a medieval castle long since

ruined by various sieges, Jashu could take in the whole of the city's skyline, from the extravagant Baroque churches to the newer town hall and university, buildings that evoked the power and ambitions of Hapsburg rule. The First World War had changed Lvov yet again and in recent years it had become a cultural and political delicatessen with various political movements and ideas struggling to take hold. The view, with its mixed heritage, revealed a contradictory personality, a city whose setting and architecture spoke of solidity, progress and evolution yet whose governance and politics revealed inconstancy and conflict.

It was the city from which Jashu's family had been forced to flee a few days before the events that had led to Neville Chamberlain's broadcast announcing the start of the war. Until the day that his family had packed their lives into suitcases and headed for the Romanian border Jashu had enjoyed life and the hot summers spent in his perfect garden where, surrounded by the fresh scent of honeysuckle and the hypnotic vibrato of insects, things had seemed settled and comfortable. Jashu was living in a Polish town. His language was Polish. He considered himself a Polish boy, and he also knew that like a third of Lvov's population he was a Jew. It was a dual but indivisible identity about which he had had little reason to be concerned. But the garden was a child's playground, sheltered from the shadows cast from the east by the violent extremism of the Soviets, and from the malignancy that was taking hold several hundred miles to the west in Germany. And most of the time it was also a sanctuary from tensions closer to home, a self-contained idyll that filtered out the sometimes barely suppressed and vicious hatreds that were the ancient and unavoidable by-product of life in such a mixed community. Jashu's parents, particularly his mother, Genia, a journalist and translator, took a keen interest in political events; it was hard not to, given the potency of the times. Although Germany had signed a non-aggression pact with Poland in 1934 Jashu's father and mother could see beyond the garden and the portents were stormy. As much as the Nadlers tried to shield their son, as news worsened throughout the 1930s, he was not completely immune to tensions at home and abroad.

Jashu had his own induction into the enmities beyond the garden wall. One afternoon he had returned from school in tears but he had refused to tell his mother the reason. He felt instinctively that the truth would upset her even more than it had him. He also felt a little ashamed although he was not sure why. Suddenly his perspective had been widened, his view of the world altered and he had learned something of the reasons why the adults around him often seemed nervous. On his way home from school a stranger had turned on him. The Pole shouted, 'You know what you are, you are a filthy Jew. You bloody Jews you should leave us to ourselves, leave Poland for the Poles!'

Rather than worry his mother further Jashu went up to his room to read the day's news. When he later appeared for dinner he was happy again. Genia was pleased although she did not really understand why he had cheered up so quickly, even when he explained. 'I was reading the newspaper,' he said, 'and I found a story about an English man who has just died. He was the Marquis of Reading. The obituary said that he had been the Viceroy of India.' It seemed an unlikely source of consolation, but Genia assumed that the newspaper had distracted him from whatever had upset him by taking his imagination to foreign and exotic lands. That day had broadened Jashu's horizons; it had been a certain rite of passage, but Genia was unable to appreciate the significance of it until much later.

For the Vickers family in Derby the outbreak of war that Sunday afternoon was met with a typically practical response and within minutes of Chamberlain's broadcast they were heading down to the cellar to clear out the coal. Hilary's father knew that he was too old to be conscripted and he worried that he had not yet been able to provide a permanent home for his wife and daughter. His work as a policeman had provided a living and accommodation that had insulated them from the worst of the depression but since having a daughter he had been determined to find a way to buy a family home. The onset of war might make the manufacturing town of Derby a particular target. He and Dora wondered what would be best for their daughter and they soon decided that a move to the relative safety of the countryside and the much aspired-to 'South' would be best for their small family. By the end of 1941 the Vickers had mounted their metaphorical tandem and arrived in Sussex for a different kind of life.

Growing up in a pub was a mixed blessing. Hilary did not see very much of her parents, who were committed to working seven days a week, but as the daughter of publicans she did at least feel at the centre of things. No need for theme pubs when there was a war on, hers was the real thing: a community centre, a mustering point, an oasis of mild and bitter in the midst of uncertainty and change.

The Cock Inn, Southwater, was traditional with oak beams sur-rounding the one bar, horse brasses and sawdust. It was the only place for any sort of social life in the small town and became ever more pivotal as the war dragged on. Rumours about troop move-ments swirled around the bar along with gossip about the villagers. Chatter would filter through the ceiling to the flat above where Hilary was working on homework and her first love, painting. The studying and the painting paid off. An art foundation course in Sussex led Hilary to a place for a teaching diploma at London University. Her experience of the war had not been traumatic. With relatives too old to fight and a move to the comparative safety of the countryside, Hilary and her family had not suffered the losses, dramas and daily upsets of so many other families. Although they had known that their country was fighting a terrible phenomenon, like all Britons they could barely have imagined the worst of the excesses being inflicted on the continent. When these were later revealed, their own lives, in comparison, seemed par-ticularly secure and civilised, a world away from those of the millions who had been deemed expendable.

However much they appreciated their own universe, hard graft had taken its own kind of toll on Stanley and his wife, precipitating another change of pace and location for the family. The constant demands of running a pub had left them exhausted and eager for some sort of break. With the war over and Hilary set for her studies, Dora and Stanley decided that they too would head for a new life and new challenges in the capital.

The year 1949 brought a move to London for the whole family. The pub was traded in for something barely less demanding – running a bed and breakfast in Earls Court, but it did allow some evenings and weekends off with the chance of outings, the occasional film or tea and buns at Lyons Corner House. This came rather late for Hilary, who, nearly twenty, was hoping for more of her own social life. The Young Conservatives seemed the perfect vehicle. It proved to be a shrewd idea by the Tory Party at a time when there was a general desire for social activity and little else on offer. Without being particularly aware of it Hilary had absorbed the political messages implicit in her upbringing. On the evening of the Christmas party she too had glanced up at the photograph of Churchill overseeing his latest acolytes at play, and felt a certain reassuring familiarity. Her parents had remained steadfastly loyal to his leadership, heeding particularly his sceptical warnings about the ambitious plans of Mr Attlee.

In those ten years between 1939 and 1949 Hilary's journey had taken her from childhood to adulthood through the course of a war and across her country to a new home in London. In the same ten years Jashu's more traumatic journey had taken him back and forth across countries and a continent until he too had the chance to set down roots in London. But viewed from September 1939 London was just a distant dream for him, the capital of an empire that was the stuff of his school textbooks. Perhaps the empire that he had come to admire, because of its respect for civility and law, could help his family with a chance of asylum in Palestine? That was the hope of his desperate family as they struggled to get visas that would allow them to enter the British protectorate where Jewish immigration had been increasingly limited throughout the 1930s.

With German troops approaching Lvov, the family were forced to leave even though they had not secured their visas. They took a handful of possessions – as much as they could fit in their car – but had to leave behind the only things that really mattered. Genia was unable to persuade her sister Stefa and her husband to make this dangerous journey with their baby, Helena, and her ageing mother, so the rest of the family stayed on to make alternative arrangements.

Their tortuous journey among the growing columns of refugees took them past the Carpathian Mountains where they had holidayed in happier times. At the border the sight of Romanians standing in rows with buckets of soup and fruit as offerings to their new if temporary compatriots was welcome indeed. Less welcome was the news that Lvov had been overrun already, but by Russian not German forces. Was this a lesser evil? Perhaps for the immediate moment it seemed so and they briefly considered returning, but the threats though less acute were hardly more appealing. They knew that either prospect spelt oppression. They believed there was more that united their common enemies than divided them, two shades of inhumane ideology. Genia knew that being Jewish meant they stood no chance at the hands of the Nazis. But Jews had hardly had a great time of it in Russia where the threat of pogroms often had been realised. And being bourgeois Jews did not make them obvious friends of the communists, whose Jewish advocates had either chosen to or found their own identity submerged in the cause of class revolution. It was not a cause close to the hearts of this family.

So there was no choice but to continue, although to rely on gaining entry into Palestine was optimistic and threatened to strain a boy's idealistic enthusiasm for its British rulers. Eventually, after first reaching Palestine by ship and being sent back, Jashu was granted a student's visa. He travelled on alone to Tel Aviv. Within weeks he was reunited with his parents who had successfully found a route in with a group of refugees sponsored by the British Council. It was spring 1940, Warsaw had been overrun by the Germans and Lvov was still in the hands of the Russians. As long as that remained the case the family hoped that eventually they might be reunited with their loved ones back in Poland. But by the following year, when Germany attacked Russia, they had already heard the last news from those they had left behind.

Throughout the war Jashu followed the news as closely as he could, riveted by English language broadcasts. In Tel Aviv it was the language he studied most avidly. To a boy engaged on a romantic quest for decency and stability to counter the upheaval that had so far uprooted his life London was calling.

In 1946, Jashu, aged twenty, made the next and most important journey of his life. After a determined effort he had been accepted for a place at the University of Exeter. With his family standing on the harbourside at Haifa, Jashu mounted the steps to his future on a ship called *Providence*. As they watched the boat gradually fade to a silhouette and then to a dot, Jashu's mother knew that he was sailing towards the fulfilment of a childhood dream, Britain. Of course she had her doubts. Could it possibly live up to the expectations Jashu had of it?

Sometime later, on a visit to England, she had the chance to ask him. Jashu was studying at the London School of Economics, they went walking in Kensington. There a friend of hers had similarly found a haven for her middle European sensibilities, her home a cool and elegant Victorian house filled with beautiful continental antiques, a testament to the richness of the union. It was a warm, still evening decked with the colours of a sunset muted by London's stagnant air.

'Do you feel at home here, darling?' she asked her son.

'I am at home here,' he replied, going on to answer for the first time the riddle of the childhood tears that had disturbed her so many years before. Jashu explained how his walk home from school had been disturbed by the racist chants of an ignorant brute and how he had been cheered by the news he had seen in the paper that afternoon. On reading the obituary of the Marquis of Reading he had promised himself that he would study and live in the country where a Jew could be a viceroy.

The newspaper that Jashu had left folded in his coat pocket detailed yet another reason why he was in so good a mood on the night of the Conservative Association's Christmas dance on 19 December 1949. Although his walk to Stratford Street had been on a harsh winter night James had no quarrel with the weather. The permanent foggy quilt that obscured most of London unmistakably typified the city and as such held an unlikely romance for him. London, home to the mother of parliaments, the BBC and to Turnbull & Asser, bespoke outfitters to the English gentleman, was a city of such fundamental delights it could hardly be made less splendid by a bit of smog. The air he breathed in London was dirty but for him it had the unmistakably heady scent of freedom. Here he was free, as he no longer could be in the town of his childhood, to take coffee and plum-filled doughnuts in the colourful Polish café on the corner of Thurloe Square. 'Good evening, Jashu' they had greeted him in Café Daquise earlier that evening when he had gone to read the paper before changing for the evening's events. Here he was both Jashu and James, as he was to his British friends. This was not a rejection of his roots but he felt a natural evolution.

As the heat from the coffee cup had thawed his hands James turned the pages of the *Evening Standard* and he once again felt particularly grateful to be in this very particular corner of the world. The headline had revealed that the commander of Hitler's armies in Poland and Russia had been jailed for eighteen years by a British military court in Hamburg. This marked the end of the long series of post-war trials. Another chapter in recent world events was closing.

Jashu had been a boy forced to flee oppression. He had been the child who had dreamed of reaching a place that was strong, proud and free, that stood for laws which required the state to make itself accountable to the individual rather than demanding the individual should account to it. The view over Polish hills from his

Lvov house had been replaced in his mind's eye with a hoped-for vision of such a place which he had come to believe was called Britain. He had studied and admired its history, which seemed to have evolved relatively free of the violent eruptions that had beset peoples across the continent, and which seemed established and rooted, less vulnerable to sudden dramatic changes of leaders, religion and ideology. Even if he had not been forced to flee his home, this history would have always impressed him and seduced him into the romantic idea that being an Englishman was particularly civilised.

Others had sought their freedom in the United States, but for all its many virtues it did not hold quite the same appeal for him as Britain. Jashu knew that if his family had travelled to America they would perhaps have had the chance to become citizens, they could have claimed their equal place in the classless polyglot, and he admired and respected the decision to move to the US and that way of life. He knew also that the process of becoming British would demand more of him, literally and emotionally, than becoming an American. He was Polish, he was Jewish and if he had the opportunity he wanted to be British. Perhaps he would never be an Englishman – but British naturalisation would get him as close to his romantic ideal as was possible for someone who had not been born or brought up in England. He appreciated that, aside from the legal process ahead, the degree of assimilation required for that transition would strike some as too great a compromise. Could an immigrant ever be truly British? But Jashu did not see the two as mutually exclusive, for in the stories that had moved him about Jews who had become British grandees he had seen a trait that was both peculiarly British and also universal. He had seen the way in which outsiders could move to the inside, could be welcomed and rewarded even in the establishment, because of what they did, what they thought, how they contributed.

As an adult, James could see that Britain (and indeed the Conservative Party, which he had come to associate with the traditions he admired), were not faultless and that the record was mixed. He recognised that areas of British society were not immune to prejudice, that there were bigots, reactionaries and anti-Semites, but he wanted to look beyond the individuals to the essential truths he wanted to celebrate. For him, both Britain and the Conservatives stood for freedom, the importance and the dignity of the individual, and the idea that people might be judged by their intellect rather than simply by their race.

James had always defended his views with vigour and charm, and he amused his student friends at Exeter, who found him, like many converts, more passionate in his defence of Britain than they were themselves. As a Jew who had lived through such a time they had expected him to be a socialist. After all, they said, surely the left provided a united front against Nazism? He smiled, almost relishing his apparent eccentricity as he replied that he did not see it that way. For him the argument was not between left and right but between liberty and oppression. In the battle just won Britain had played the key role in defending liberty and defeating one tyrant, but another had been left entrenched and he believed the left, even the democratic left, would not take up the longer fight to come. Rather than being perverse, James saw his political allegiance as the obvious and only choice.

As he finished reading the newspaper he headed off for the Christmas dance in an excellent and expectant mood. That was even before he had laid eyes on Hilary in her burgundy cocktail dress.

3

DOUGHNUTS AND CIRCUSES

As my parents met at Kensington Young Conservatives I guess I must be living proof that in its heyday the YCs did live up to its reputation as the unofficial marriage bureau for the middle classes. Unsurprisingly, this was not a thought that preoccupied me during childhood but later I found it ironic that even in the heart of establishment Kensington my mother had managed to meet someone her parents considered far from suitable. They certainly had not expected her to meet a penniless Jewish student whose prospects and future in this country were far from assured. For a family that had never until then encountered a foreigner he was not an obvious match for their daughter, although after their initial concerns they warmly welcomed him into the family. That it was the 1950s Conservative Party, bastion of convention, that served as the matchmaker for this cross-cultural romance left me with an innate sense that it must be some sort of force for good, and not the hotbed of reactionaries that its detractors would argue. So when I heard stories about how my parents had met it was not a great leap from there to assume, as I did, that all Conservatives must be rather cosmopolitan and interesting people. A naive and idealistic view perhaps, but childhood impressions are built on lesser things.

Perhaps my parents' meeting place could be seen as a portent for my own politics, but far more important was the way in which I was brought up. Party politics held little interest for me until those early entries in my diary but my first explicitly political memory dates back before then to 1974, and the prosaic setting of Putney High Street where the very big idea of democracy first made its mark on me in practical and everyday terms. Whether it was the spring or the autumn campaign I am not sure but it was my first brush with the theatricality of elections. It is easy to be cynical now but as a kid such an event was somehow really exciting. The election's associated rituals lent the whole proceedings an air of grave significance.

It was an otherwise very normal afternoon but as I remember it something very unusual was happening in the half-mile strip of chain stores, budget shoe shops and television rental companies that make up the typical shopping street. The pavements then as now were too narrow to contain the never-ending stream of mums with prams, teenage bargain hunters and smutty faced kids who paraded up and down between the river and back. Impatient lads in Farah trousers jostled and pushed their way through the crush, one foot on the kerb, one in the road. These crowds were normal, it is not a place to browse but just to shop for the everyday essentials, knickers from British Home Stores, groceries from Sainsbury's. As usual everyone looked grey and hassled, the buggies played bumper cars while the wail of sticky fingered toddlers was drowned out by the traffic snaking its way towards the bottleneck at Putney Bridge. But unusually on that particular day the predictable urban treadmill was suddenly disrupted. The traffic stopped, children dropped their Kojak lollies and grannies strained over their tea and iced buns to catch a view. There I was, eight years old, fractious and grumpy in my school uniform, eager to get the groceries and go home but suddenly fascinated and transfixed.

For just a few minutes it seemed as though a circus had come to town . . .

But the circus float that had suddenly brought the traffic to a halt was just a flat-bed lorry — a political circus float, I suppose. No clowns or dancing girls but a Conservative Party candidate, astride his own bandwagon bedecked with posters of Edward Heath. No streamers or steel band but flags and leaflets and a chorus of sorts. This was my first experience of democracy in action and, although hardly the grandest oratory or the most exciting spectacle, it was nevertheless vivid stuff for a child. From a distance the sound and tenor of the megaphone cut through extraneous noise with a sort of ominous rumble, suggesting the imminent arrival of something very significant. It demanded attention. As the lorry rolled into view the amplified chant 'This is your Conservative candidate, vote Conservative, vote Heath' became louder and clearer, punctuating the hum and clatter of the high street with a definite sense of urgency. It was arresting and for a few minutes, or perhaps seconds, I could only hear that instruction. It wasn't the message itself that held my attention, I wasn't being brainwashed, but the sense that we were being involved in something considerably more important than the weekly shopping. Clearly there were more significant choices to be made than what to have for dinner.

Mum explained she and my dad would be voting for Mr Heath, but for me the significance of this event was not as an initiation into my family's political tribe but as an introduction to elections. After that I began to look out for the various coloured posters appearing in windows. I took an interest in seeing the faces of Mr Heath and Mr Wilson appearing on the TV news and examined the leaflets that dropped through the door. I had a growing sense that there was something important underway and that it involved all the adults in the country and it wasn't so much about the campaigning but about the voting itself. That message, rather than any particular political philosophy, was certainly reinforced at home. And ever since I have been able to vote that aspect continues to engage me, despite inevitable bouts of scepticism about politicians. I still take a childlike pleasure in going to vote. I'm charmed by the low-tech nature of the whole proceedings, the blunt pencils to mark an X, the splintered wooden booths, the dented ballot boxes and the creaky old ladies at the counter. Electronic voting just doesn't seem to hold the same appeal. Church halls, nursery schools, community centres, all places where I never go other than to vote, make the whole procedure seem at once both quaint and anachronistic yet timeless and profound.

Despite the clear memory of my parents' backing for Edward Heath, it was not the odd explicit reference to voting intentions that really had much of an influence on my later precocious emergence as a teenage Tory. Far more significant were the unstated but distinct set of values that infused our home, along with the prevailing insecurities that characterised an age when the spectre of an 'evil empire' was much more than a James Bond fantasy and also more specific than today's comparatively amorphous 'axis of evil'. So although we barely discussed party politics I nonetheless found the influence of politics all around me as I became increasingly aware of world events. And that coloured my developing allegiances with far greater effect than if I had been told to take a particular view. My father had fulfilled his childhood ambition to study in Britain. He had gone even further in eventually gaining naturalisation and work, which turned into a career, with the BBC. During his own childhood its motto 'Nation Shall Speak Peace Unto Nation' had become a part of the British iconography that had inspired his journey, and had given his drive to work for the corporation a sense of calling.

He worked as a journalist and broadcaster for the World Service based at Bush House in the Strand. From the outside it just another anonymous, 'official-looking' 1930s building of four apparently unconnected blocks. But once inside the courtyard a labyrinth of underground passages is revealed and, certainly in the 1970s, the whole place was a rabbit warren of tiny, cramped offices piled high with foreign language papers and earnest journalists from across the globe. I thought it was the most enthralling and glamorous place to visit.

It was a real treat to pick up dad from work, or sneak into the office with him over a weekend when he was often working. In those days Bush House had the air of an international intellectuals' club. Nowhere was this cosmopolitanism more obvious than in the vast subterranean canteen, considered then one of London's best kept secrets. Here the array of foods was as mixed and colourful as the multinational community of journalists who ate it. Fortunately it was not a secret for me and my sister and we were always very keen to suggest visits there. Our usually discordant selections of goodies from the help-yourself counter amounted to an early rendition of fusion cuisine long before it became fashionable in exclusive London restaurants, and long before the revolution of the 1980s made cappuccino and Café Rouge commonplace on British high streets.

Apart from indigestion, and the opportunity to hijack the smooth running of Bush House by playing in the big mirrored lifts, what I gained from these much-loved visits was a short cut into an exciting international world. Mr Benn had gone through the back of the changing room in the costume shop. I just had to go through the front door at Bush House. Clutching a tray of global tastes, you could walk from one end of the canteen to the other at any time of the day and catch the unfamiliar sounds of different languages, overlapping and competing in always animated and impassioned dialogues between colleagues and friends. Though I didn't know or understand the details at the time there was plenty of news to arouse these committed journalists. Civil wars in Africa, communist regimes taking hold in Asia, Spain's emergence from dictatorship, tensions in Czechoslovakia and Poland, rounds of nuclear weapons talks, a new American president, wars in the Middle East, and 'defections' to the West. What I did understand, or have at least some sense of, was the way in which these events, of which I would catch snippets, were somehow part of a bigger picture. Their significance was reflected through the prism of

East–West relations, or in childlike terms just a sense of an ominous struggle still being fought across the globe. It was superhero stuff writ large and for real. The 'free world' was an everyday expression. There were signs of rust in the Iron Curtain, but not much metal fatigue. Here I was at the centre of it, gradually understanding the role of London and Britain as a hub for ideas and cultures, as a beacon for the persecuted and those who wanted a base from which to evangelise the truth.

During the war, throughout my parents' childhoods, the BBC's broadcasts had countered the propaganda of oppressive and evil regimes. What I was taught during my own childhood was that through the World Service it was still doing that. While my parents were free to go and vote for Mr Heath or Mr Wilson if they chose, I gathered that elsewhere millions were not. And, of course, the World Service wasn't just somewhere Dad worked. Its presence permeated our household. I can still hear its distinctive sound spilling out of the radio in the bathroom each morning as he shaved, and how its formal narration of a world in which the Cold War was still pretty chilly brought a fundamental political choice right into our comfortable home. That choice was between oppression and liberty, between totalitarianism and democracy. Without being told I understood that our real privilege was to live in a free country and that it was our duty to back liberty. Set against the foreground of Britain in the 1970s and the background of my family, such influences, even if they had been the only ones, virtually guaranteed that I would emerge as a Conservative. I didn't think that a vote for the Labour Party meant the tanks were on the move to Westminster, but as I understood it there were sides, 'they' were left and we were right, they were wrong and we were right, and so the battle lines were drawn. Had I been born ten years later I am sure that the choices would not have seemed quite so straightforward.

The teenage years can be very difficult, on parents as well as kids. With what I later put her through I expect my mother may well have regretted that early conversation about Edward Heath.

Neither of us could have known where it would lead. Later mine became the sort of antisocial behaviour that naturally makes parents worry. First it was the signs of moodiness, the fact I would disappear to my room for ages. I would later emerge, sallow skinned, dark eyed – flagrant signs of book and periodical abuse. The self-absorption, the untidiness, a bedroom strewn with the detritus of private rituals – poster making, letter writing. And then later when I was supposed to be concentrating on O and A levels, bringing all sorts back to the house unannounced. MPs, councillors, she never knew who she might find or where the best china would be. But it is really too much to blame all of that on Ted Heath. Although we all had a rather more kindly attitude to the musical yachtsman in those days, and certainly at seven I was in no position to rebuke him for reneging on his Selsdon Park commitments, I did have an early sense that he was not a particularly inspiring figure. Perhaps if he had stuck to the market-driven direction of policy to which he had committed himself at that now infamous Selsdon Park Hotel meeting, Heath would have rendered Mrs T's premiership unnecessary. But anyway, his successor, as my diary so graphically reveals, was certainly more equipped to capture my young imagination and also more importantly to refire an interest in the Conservative Party among my parents and their friends.

The energy and vitality I sensed at Bush House was often re-created around the dinner table in Wimbledon. These were not conversations I was a part of, it was adults' stuff, but I got a thrill from my own small part as a hostess to these lively evenings. Among my favourite memories as a small child I recall the degree of planning and the mounting sense of excitement in anticipation of a party. My father, being Jewish and continental, was characteristically exacting about the menus. My mother, being English and attentive to detail, was generally concerned with standards, and seemed to spend ages ironing tablecloths and polishing cutlery. As she did have a demanding job and a totally impractical husband she would sometimes have help with the cooking from a family friend who had trained as a cook in Austria. This was all an indulgent combination. In those days everything was full fat, seriously saturated, red blooded and in deference to Martha the cook, 'mit schlag'! Transforming our cramped kitchen into a Viennese patisserie was pretty close to heaven for my sister and me. Sneaking in for a mouthful of cake mix or a dollop of syllabub was the opportunity we waited for. Sometimes we might have a preview tasting of a main course, always something meaty, or a sliver of fish mousse, a spoonful of the red cabbage. At that point, with everything prepared, dad would return from work, add a pinch of salt or a twist of lemon juice and then proceed to take the compliments of all his guests who thought him the active gastronome.

By the time I was eight or nine, I was allowed to meet the guests at the start of the evening. They were generally other journalists, usually visiting from abroad, sometimes diplomats, writers and political advisers. Having been introduced it was quickly time for me to retire to bed although I would try to loiter around the kitchen for as long as possible, sticking my finger in the sauce dishes and the cream jug. Then when I really was in the way of the serving up I would disappear, apparently to my room, only to sit at the top of stairs waiting for the next opportunity to sneak back and snaffle a plate of something yummy. My father's passion for food was infectious but not all of the Polish specialities he favoured were particularly appetising to little girls. The gnarled, peppery sausages and all too recently living ox tongues that often inhabited the fridge would make us screw up our faces in horror. On the other hand the feather-light doughnuts filled with the darkest and stickiest of plum jams always went down well. Helena and I ate them when we went on family outings to Café Daquise, on the corner of Thurloe Square. There we would sit with sugar-coated faces and plump, jam covered fingers looking at the same, though by then faded, colourful woodcuts and the same, though by then fraying, leatherette banquettes that had greeted James and Hilary during their courtship.

From my staircase top perch I would hear James and Hilary, Mummy and Daddy to me, chatting, laughing, debating. I couldn't really know what the dinner party guests were discussing and I was too young to understand the details but I had a sense that these were heady and important conversations. It sounded good-natured but passionate. Without being able to make out the words I would hear the rise and fall of animated voices, occasional table thumping and the unmistakable staccato of heated argument as the dining-chair capitalists took on the odd Soave socialist. The house seemed to vibrate to the rhythm of these discussions, mingling with the layers of cooking smells that filled it with warmth and life. If I listened carefully I might make out the occasional word and recognise the name of a place or a politician. Alongside the references to international political figures I noticed the odd names cropping up repeatedly on the news and in the house: Margaret Thatcher, Keith Joseph, Alfred Sherman. It was two or three years before I would reference them in my pre-election diary but I was beginning to get a sense that there was an alternative to the grey, interchangeable *Weath* and *Hilson*. I gathered that there was a hunger for change.

On the very odd occasion my father would venture an explicit political thought for me to conjure with but it was a bit much for a pop-happy pre-teen to take on board. 'I am very right-wing,' he once told me with a chuckle and a hint of irony it would take me many years to appreciate. 'Any more so and I ought to be careful or they'll be calling me a Jewish fascist.' It was the kind of tasteless yet sophisticated provocation I have often felt inclined to make myself when forced to puncture the politically correct squeamish-ness of the humourless left, but back then it was all rather lost on me. I probably rolled my eyes and went back to reading *Jackie*. What was also far too sophisticated for me to grasp or indeed have any great interest in at the time was the extent to which the bur-geoning Thatcherite revolution was shaped by Jewish and other thinkers from outside the traditional confines of the Tory estab-lishment. Some, not only Jews, had made a profound political conversion from former Marxist pasts. Their motivation had not changed, but their means to an end had in the realisation that the market was a far more effective engine of social change than the state.

During the 1950s my father's right-wing orientation had marked him out as unusual. There were of course traditional small-c conservatives among his colleagues at the *Jewish Chronicle* where he had worked briefly before the BBC, but the 'intelligentsia' was still very much associated with the left. Understandably, during the 1920s and 1930s, Socialism and Communism were seen as bulwarks against Fascism. For many the later emerging reality of the Soviet Union came as alarming confirmation that the two extremes were in practice not so far apart. For him, I think, his early and close proximity to both had thrown their similarities into sharper relief earlier, and then, of course there was his experience in Palestine.

It is hard to believe now that Israel, pariah state to international liberal opinion, was for some years heralded by the left as an example of the socialist brotherhood. The kibbutz spirit and communality of purpose of the fledgling state certainly equates with the best motives of the left, but equally the daily fight for survival accords with almost Pavlovian right-wing impulses about defence, identity and the nation state. Visiting Israel as a child and since is always an extraordinary experience, thought provoking, engaging and, increasingly over the last thirty years, unsettling. I was ten when we first made the trip to visit my grandparents there in 1977. It is the only place I had ever been to before or since that inspired such excitement about arrival that was tangible long before the aircraft touched down at Tel Aviv. First laughter, then singing and clapping when we touched down on the sunny runway, but this was not the reaction of expectant visitors but of Israelis returning home. Part patriotism, part camaraderie, part expression of ancient hopes and expectations, for me it was a vivid encounter with the best of national pride expressed far too openly for British taste but thus a great reminder of the privileges of self-determination.

That family holiday in Israel, in 1977, was one of the last overseas trips the four of us took together. I was eleven when my father died the following year. His heart attack was unexpected and fatal. I've thought a lot about how I might write this section, indeed whether it needs to be written at all. Although my father's early death is central to the story of my family it's hard to say how relevant it is to the story of my politics. But to ignore it, or to treat it as the stuff of a different sort of memoir, could seem disingenuous. The shock and the loss did change the whole experience of growing up. I wanted to be busy, I needed to be busy and I was certainly more earnest than I might have otherwise have been about finding out and understanding where I had come from and the great sweeps of history that had bought my parents together. On a day-to-day level it was of course, simply heartbreaking for all of us and particularly difficult for my mother in her late forties with two young children, a job and other responsibilities. But for us there were so many distractions, school friends, exams, dance classes, choir practices, later boys, and of course, politics. It helped to get lost in these things as gradually the acute pain evolved into something manageable but we always missed my father's wonderful personality, his story telling and wit. As I grew older I was particularly sorry that I could not talk to him about my growing interests. Looking back at it afterwards from a distance and trying to discern the different influences from my parents, I realised that where my father's experiences and views had established the broad parameters of my politics, it was my mother and her values and example that helped me to fill in many of the finer details.

The two of them represented different but allied aspects of the Conservatism I embraced, the principles and the practicalities. Now I see that what I had taken from my father's story reflected in the absolutes and the moral convictions that characterised one side of Thatcherism, and equally the other side of that equation, the common sense, family responsibilities and conscientiousness were there in my mother's example. My father's story was perhaps the more romantic and dramatic but I could not say now that either influence was the more important to me. Back in 1979, only a year after my father's death, I was completely unaware of such nuances as I filled out my election diary without stopping to think what a shame it was that Dad had not lived to see the dawn of those exciting changes anticipated during the unrepeatable dining-table debates.

PART 2

THAT WAS THEN

4

HORMONES, HANGOVERS AND HAYEK

Somewhere in Essex, Spring 1983

Multi-coloured disco lights flashed in time to the beat, sending red, blue and yellow beams across the pale, spotty faces of a stiff and unconvincing group of revellers as Shalimar's number-one hit boomed from across the bar making it a night to remember. The days of disco were supposed to be about glamorous excess, new romantic frivolity, sequins and sexual experimentation, but Dave's Mobile Dance Machine, a pile of scratched vinyl records and a few coloured bulbs just weren't enough to bring the spirit of Studio 54 to Romford. But even so the location was a kind of nirvana to the true believers gathered there that night. Beneath the polystyrene ceiling tiles at the Essex Moat House hotel an inconsistent group of pinstriped young fogies, earnest bespectacled sweater-wearers, stone-washed denim-clad youths and girls with high collars and too much hairspray were jerking across the makeshift dancefloor balancing cider and piña coladas in one hand, campaign literature in the other.

And there I was, all big hair, really big hair, stiletto heels and shoulder pads, shuffling self-consciously at the edge and feeling in more ways than one slightly out of step with this rather motley crew. The Greater London Young Conservatives were on their 1983 weekend conference. It was far more than an excuse for a healthy exchange of views coupled with a potentially unhealthy exchange of bodily fluids. By this stage the Young Conservatives were styling themselves as a radical cell, and Essex was no accidental venue but a place of pilgrimage, a cultural and spiritual home to these children of the Thatcherite revolution. This was the sort of disco where the boys stood in corners, hovering in slightly menacing cabals, their dress indicating which brand of right winger they were (wets in cords, libertarians in jeans, authoritarians in suits, anarcho-capitalists in combat gear), and the girls, few that there were, were more likely to pay homage to Hayek than dance around their handbags.

By the time I made it to Essex I had begun to grasp how highly politicised the Young Conservatives were. Gone was the cosy dating club. In its place was a hotbed of intrigue and plotting, a divisive mixture of new-right zealots, traditional disciplinarians and struggling wets. This dynamic tension had been nowhere in evidence at my local branch in Wimbledon when at fifteen I had made my first tentative enquiries about membership. In fact dynamism of any sort was not the impression given by the whole association, comfortable in the seemingly secure reality that suburban Wimbledon, with its detached houses, its private schools and its glamorous international tennis tournament, was a safe Tory seat surrounded on all sides by a sea of blue. To the west the Surrey stockbroker belt was unflinchingly Conservative. Nearer still the momentum of 1979 had brought David Mellor into neighbouring Putney and Angela Rumbold in a later by-election to Mitcham, erasing uncharacteristic spots of red from the local map.

Since noting my early Maggie enthusiasms in my secret diary aged twelve, my own political journey had slowed. After all, there were other things to think about. By thirteen I was obsessed with clothes and pop. I dreamed of being a fashion designer, an actress or a newsreader. I still loved dancing but didn't cut a sufficiently lithe figure in my leotard and tights to think it could ever be more than a hobby. As I moved into my teens I had begun to slim down but like most of my friends felt constantly torn between the F-Plan diet and Dayvilles ice cream with its thirty-two flavours that winked at us provocatively from the parlour next to the school gates.

At weekends I would take the District Line along to Sloane Square with my tall, blonde friend Wendy and we would walk the whole length of the Kings Road window-shopping, or rifling through the bargain rail at Chelsea Girl. She was long-legged and waif-like with an elfin, wispy haircut. I was, I think the expression is, 'well proportioned', curvy with big kohl-rimmed eyes and a rather unmanageable mop of long dark hair that I refused to cut. She looked good in everything and I found at least that shoes always fitted. Not serious shoppers, we were really only browsers, just taking a break from homework, but we would usually go home with a single or two from Our Price records. Adam and the Ants, The Jam, The Police, Spandau Ballet and Wham! were the sound-track to our schooldays, and I would play them over and over again until the vinyl was scratched and thin. I'd lie in my bedroom gazing up at my latest celebrity crush and pull the lever on the record player to hear that familiar click as the stylus lifted and sat down into the groove, playing until the last note had faded out. Then there was the low mechanical drawl as the needle flicked across the exit lane to the final click that sent the arm back to its resting position, until I started the whole thing going again. 'That's Entertainment' went round and round and round until I just could-n't put the maths project off any more. I'm not sure Paul Weller would have felt that his songs of urban angst were particularly appropriate incidental music in a bedroom that was increasingly studded with the evidence of a growing Tory habit.

During the O level years I took a Sunday job serving teas in the sports club opposite the All England Tennis Club and that gave me the money to buy bigger things on our shopping trips. I went through all the crazes, suffering as only a devoted fashion victim can in thigh-chafing satin trousers, mini kilts, fringed spiky-heeled boots, ruffled shirts, zipped jump-suits and ra-ra skirts. None of them suited me, but when it came to clothes reason held little sway.

Going to an all girls school left me awkward when it came to dealing with boys. And during my early teens I couldn't quite see the point of them. The odd ones I met through joint debates with King's College, the local boys' school, seemed immature and nerdy even to me, hardly the stuff of teenage fantasies. But there was a point between eleven and fifteen, I'm not sure exactly when, that the predictable preoccupations of clothes and music and boys seemed less urgent and the outward signs of my interests changed. Alongside pop stars and fashion magazines politics fitted right back in again. Down came the posters of Starsky and Hutch. Up went the posters of Margaret Thatcher and Norman Tebbit.

My O level history course, a solid grounding in twentieth-century events, confirmed both my academic interest in politics and my leaning to the right drawn from the influences I had already absorbed at home. That was all very well but, I suspected, rather insulated from day-to-day events. I had all these high-minded ideas about freedom and self-determination and about what seemed to me the obvious problems with socialism. So I tried to relate these thoughts to my everyday life. Every time I exchanged my weekend earnings for a new studded belt or a handbag I felt I was making my own little blow for free enterprise. I found a convenient link between my philosophy and my interest in fashion, I'm a capitalist therefore I shop! Even before the anti-globalisation protestors had found their voice I was mounting my own spontaneous pro-capitalism marches – that is marching down the Kings Road and putting my pocket money where my mouth was. But I wasn't really as confident as I appeared. If the Conservatives were so right (as I instinctively felt they were) why were they so unpopular? If I was going to come out as a teenage Tory I felt I needed to know a bit more about it all before I openly admitted to, let alone prose-lytised, my still private predilections. So in the summer of 1981, halfway through my O level years, I decided that fieldwork was a necessity.

Oh, and given my age I'll admit there was another reason, far less worthy although equally pressing, for the decision I took to investigate Wimbledon Young Conservatives: sex — specifically the desire to meet and seduce Nigel Havers.

The honey-toned actor had become an instant hit with the girls of Wimbledon High after his appearance as Lord Andrew Lindsay in the hit film of that year *Chariots of Fire*. The movie seemed designed to render girls of a certain background totally unable to concentrate on their Latin homework. Along with the rousing patriotic theme, the evocation of a stirring competitive spirit and the golden shots of the hallowed halls of Oxbridge there were those slow motion sequences of flaxen-haired, iron-thighed Havers running for his life, and rather more importantly, his country. And the connection to Wimbledon Conservative Association was far from entirely random. It wasn't only wishful thinking that had me fantasising about the possibility of bumping into him jogging past the downtown office. On the contrary, it seemed perfectly logical to me that, given his father, the late Sir Michael Havers, was the Wimbledon MP, Nigel would be a leading light in the local Young Conservatives. So it was with great excitement and a fluttery stomach that I first ventured, considerably over-made-up, to an evening meeting of the Wimbledon YCs.

At first sight Tower Lodge, HQ of the local association, did not seem a venue likely to attract film stars, even if related to our MP. And as is so often the case, those first impressions proved telling. The faded Victorian villa was just over the road from the down-town YMCA, where Wimbledon town centre begins to merge with neighbouring Tooting and Morden. Pushing open the heavy blue door revealed on one side an office piled high with Conservative 'In-Touch' leaflets, old manifestos, local maps, and pictures of Sir Michael grinning in the company of his lovely wife, though disappointingly not his son. Michael Havers, then attorney general, was the personification of a certain type of Tory MP so beloved of the party's safer seats: portly and respectable, reliable though uninspiring, a man who would never be out of place in a golf club or at a Rotary Club luncheon. These chaps (very definitely chaps, sometimes also 'good eggs', but never blokes or guys) meet their apotheosis in middle age. It is almost as if they spend forty-seven years in gestation and emerge from the womb with the receding hairline, the slightly ruddy complexion, the yellowing teeth and the blue rosette that spells regulation Conservative MP. It is impossible to imagine they were ever young, but that is one of the inherent problems in running the words 'young' and 'conservative' together; it is just not a wholly comfortable or convincing combination. Even at fifteen I was uncomfortably aware of that paradox and I felt that such a man, successful though he was, had a responsibility to enhance his and the party's image with frequent and public endorsements from a film-star son. But as I also later came to realise, glamorous celebrity endorsements and the Conservative Party are just as unusual a combination as Tories and Youth.

On the other side of Tower Lodge's narrow hallway was the door to the meeting room. If I was looking to find out more about the Conservative Party what lay on the other side of that door was as revealing an insight into local activism as any documentary (many of which I've since made) could have told me. This was a weekly meeting of the Young Conservatives in one of the wealthiest and safest of seats in the country. Naively I had expected a crowd, but I had yet to learn that success breeds complacency. The big, dusty room was almost empty, and it took only a moment's glance to appreciate that it was not the kind of scene likely to attract Nigel Havers or, more worryingly, anyone with anything better to do. I consoled myself that homework wasn't necessarily a better thing to do and so it was OK for me to be there.

Where I had imagined a gathering of sophisticated young things, chatting animatedly, clinking glasses, debating or listening to a brilliant, incisive speaker who would tell me how to justify the rapidly escalating unemployment figures, there were five people around a trestle table drinking lager and looking at leaflets. The room had a large square bay window in which were stacked piles of metal-framed chairs. In fact there were piles of chairs all around the room giving at least some promise of livelier, busier meetings on other occasions. It was a textbook Tory meeting room, the ever-present faded picture of Churchill on one wall facing on the opposite a badly framed portrait of Maggie. The worn paisley carpet and chipped paintwork revealed that at least the local subs weren't being wasted on anything as frivolous as decorating the HQ.

The rest of the assembled 'youngsters' all seemed closer to the upper end of the YC age range (thirty-something), apart from one. Guy, a pleasant, slightly chinless 'chap' was studying at a crammer to retake A levels. The others were in their mid to late twenties: Colin, the chairman, a spit for the actor Simon Cadell, was an earnest accountant; Angus, a sports-jacketed banker, had a hint of Dickie Davis and a splash of a young Leslie Phillips about him. Later that evening when the meeting had adjourned to the Green Man Angus took a great deal of interest in my other extracurricular activities, particular the dancing. 'What did the high school girls wear?' he wondered out loud. Leotards or sweatpants? Had we modelled ourselves on Hot Gossip or Legs and Co? It was then that I noticed his girlfriend, Heidi, an Alice-banded lawyer, glowering ominously. The fifth and final member of what I assumed to be the executive of the branch, but in fact turned out to be the whole membership, was Geoff, a teacher and enthusiast for the TA. So far I had learned nothing about politics but with a lawyer, a banker, an accountant, a student, a soldier and a schoolgirl, we did at least have the makings of some sort of reasonable endeavour if not the raw material for an Alan Ayckbourn play.

It is fair to say that that first evening hardly lived up to expectations and did not augur well for either of my two aims: it was clear that I was unlikely to lose my virginity to Nigel Havers or, more relevantly, to find the answers to the increasingly puzzling political questions that crossed my mind day to day. The grey, gloomy 1970s were giving way to what was promising to be an increasingly troubled 1980s with industrial discontent, unpopular increases in indirect taxes, despised public expenditure cuts and riots in Liverpool, Manchester and Southall. Even the fairy-tale wedding of Charles and Di, which I had watched with genuine awe, seemed an anachronistic sideshow in a country where the prime minister's election day pledge to bring harmony where there was discord was evidently some way from being achieved.

The quest for more information on my pressing dual concerns of sex and politics led me to furtive sessions at the family book-shelves. There, I think, was an explanation as to why my grasp of these issues did not develop with equal speed. The paltry supply of salacious literature rather guaranteed that I might be a late devel-oper when it came to sex. Although I left *Lady Chatterley's Lover* well thumbed, Lawrence bore about as much relevance to those dis-concerting teenage hormone rushes as did the rather better-stocked supply of political texts to answering practical issues of the day. I was not yet sufficiently politically sophisticated to apply Milton and Rose Friedman, Friedrich Hayek and Robert Nozick to the issues I encountered at school and on the television news. (Besides which they were pretty heavy reading compared to *Just Seventeen*.) I knew that I was a capitalist because I loved shop-ping so much, but I wasn't sure that would wash as a considered political platform. Nor did it seem to me that the limited band who made up the local Young Conservatives, nice though they were, could help me much in answering those questions either, or that these esoteric texts would prove particularly helpful in producing the local Tory newsletters. However, I was soon to discover that the philosophers of the new right were as iconic to many of the Young Conservatives I would encounter beyond sleepy Wimbledon, as their shared high priestess Margaret Thatcher.

Although that first Thursday evening encounter with the YCs

was not a humdinger I was happy to give it a second go. It took only one more meeting to seal my fate, proving that the merest taste of power can be a potent persuader. The following week I returned to Tower Lodge to be greeted by a more professional looking gathering. This time the constituency agent was in attendance. There was also another newcomer, a pleasant looking guy in running gear who, as it happened, did appear to have dropped in mid-jog. Not quite *Chariots of Fire* material, but if the group was averaging a new member per week I could foresee a quorum and, by the end of the year possibly enough for a decent Christmas party.

It was the annual general meeting. I learnt a little about the official role of the group: to assist the 'senior party' with campaigning and leafleting, to encourage a younger membership through word of mouth and holding interesting meetings and parties which would help with fundraising. And let's not forget YCs also had an invaluable role to play in lowering the average age at the regular round of cheese and wine parties. These are, of course, the real function of any constituency Conservative association – politics being merely a cover for frequent sessions of artery hardening indulgence in Wensleydale and Red Leicester, washed down with a nice Lambrusco or a Paul Masson Californian Carafe. I am told that for Labour Party activists sex is a major motivator, but for Conservatives it seems to be canapés or perhaps even more vitally, raffles.

Colin, the chairman, went over the 'successes' of the past year, which seemed mainly to have revolved around leafleting during ward by-elections and extending the list of local pubs in which meetings were adjourned after formal business. We turned to the election of new officers for the branch and suddenly I felt as though all eyes were on me. Apparently there was a vacancy for the role of secretary of the branch. Heidi was standing aside. Before I could muster a defence – something about pressure of homework, approaching O levels, the general trauma of teenage angst – I had been proposed, seconded and elected. A week earlier I had ventured in not really sure if I wanted to join the party, let alone hold office in it. Now seven days on I was an official representative. At that rate I looked set to be in the cabinet by the time I was twenty.

A celebration orange juice was the excuse for a further initiation into the world of grass-roots Torydom. Despite the much-hailed rolling pub policy there was a Conservative Club attached to the offices, the quickest place for a post-AGM drink. Apparently I should have considered myself an honoured guest, because by virtue of sharing the same gender as the prime minister, I still required a man to vouch for my good character before I was allowed to enter the club. Even today the institution that is the Conservative Club remains a weird hybrid; more working man's club than political salon – all cheap beer, dartboards and sticky carpets. The clubs originally founded in the late nineteenth century to encourage the spread of Conservatism among the working class remain associated with, but not run by, the party. They are a curious anachronism and seem particularly so in London. That night I had gained office and then, it seemed, travelled back in time several generations and a couple of hundred miles or so north.

Another poster of Maggie, perilously (or perhaps deliberately) close to the dartboard, reminded us that in name at least this was an outpost of the modern Conservative Party. It also seemed to jog something in the mind of our potential new recruit, whose keenly expressed interest in green issues earlier in the evening had seemed counter-intuitive even to me with my relatively superficial knowledge of party policy. 'Oh God,' he exclaimed as a dart narrowly missed Thatcher's right eye, 'I thought you were the Wimbledon Young *Conservationists*.' With that he was off and we were back to being six. TA Geoff suggested coffee at his place and the preview of some 'rather good videos' he had just acquired from Amsterdam. Perhaps in some respects the YCs was going to prove more instructive than D. H. Lawrence, but it wasn't to gain a better understanding of that section of the Nadler bookshelf that I had been prompted to join. Clearly if this was going to be a worthwhile venture politically I was going to have to change the operation.

I would hardly say I orchestrated a coup in Wimbledon YCs but as secretary it was down to me to organise the programme of meetings, so there was plenty of scope to set my own agenda. It must have been obvious that I wanted to shake up this rather dishevelled operation as the others quickly nicknamed me the 'chalk monitor'. I took it as an affectionate reflection on my youth, educational status and, I'm sure, a precocious inclination towards taking responsibility. Maybe I was just bossy. Anyway, as my O level history was teaching me, political movements required organisation as well as ideas. Schoolwork was proving a crash course in 'isms', communism, capitalism, Marxism, syndicalism, and fascism but so far my experience in the party was suggesting that the most active 'ism' in conservatism might be alcoholism. Perhaps for some fifteen-year-olds, some even destined for premature baldness and party leadership, the offer of a new social circle and the allure of underage drinking might have enhanced the appeal of the YCs. But that didn't strike me as the sufficient basis for a recruitment campaign. Even at that stage I knew deep down that joining the YCs was just not 'cool' and never would be. Whereas it was just about socially acceptable for people to admit to right-wing leanings once they had reached middle age and grown out of a naive and idealistic phase of wearing Che Guevara berets, nothing was more alien to universal assumptions of teenage behaviour than to line up behind the establishment as readily as I was doing. Any teenage politico is considered rather odd, but I knew that if I had joined CND or the Young Socialists I might have scored some points for credibility – particularly given how rebellious this would have seemed in my school. But given the degree of romantic idealism that explained my association with the Conservative Party it was hardly worth worrying that being a YC would not enhance my image. The fact was that I was a conformist with a cause! And having been so swiftly inveigled into the party's high command the doubts I might have had about joining were quickly overtaken.

As an officer of the association I was effectively taking a crash course in the inner workings of the Conservative Party, and the first lesson learned was the degree of distrust and animosity between the voluntary party and the professional operation centred on Smith Square. Ten years later when I went to work for the party professionally I found exactly the same in reverse. To add to this tension, the third element in an unholy triumvirate was the elected party, the MPs, who seemed to hold both the volunteers and the professional organisation in low regard. There was at that stage no formal structure, no constitution, holding these three together so that in legal terms there was no one thing that could be described as the Conservative Party, only this loose association of the three elements. It was only possible to join the party by signing up locally. This meant that the whole organisation was remarkably decentralised and democratic, but that when tensions arose, as they would so spectacularly and often throughout the Major years, there was no mechanism for dealing with unruly members, elected and otherwise. On the plus side it was quaint and organic but a less generous interpretation would be that it was amateurish, an impression that would grow in all my later dealings, personal and professional, with the operation. It was also bureaucratic. It seemed that the Conservative Party was a veritable cottage industry in self-perpetuating elections and self-justifying committees with the ever-present danger of becoming a totally enclosed political eco-system.

For a party that eschewed the politics of the special interest group I found a surprising tendency towards subdivision, and in the political hall of mirrors that the party sometimes seems to be, the apparently 'progressive' concept of the Women's Organisation was really the truest bastion of reaction. I had decided that I was most definitely a Conservative girl, but was determined not to grow into a 'Conservative Woman'. That is the kind who refers to herself as a 'lady', who defines her political platform as the polar opposite of 'political correctness gone mad' and whose key political motivation is to ensure the selection of a nice 'young' man to represent the constituency in Parliament.

If the older Tories often seemed to fit their stereotypes, I joined the party just as many of the younger variety were set on tearing up the rules and rewriting the template for a Young Conservative. But in the process they were creating a whole new set of stereotypes that would keep comedians in work for years to come. Chinless wonders were giving way to blue trots, public school wets to state school subversives. In my attempts to resuscitate my little branch I was to encounter a fair few of Maggie's mini militants and a world where the greatest commendation was to be pronounced 'sound'. With so few people to juggle, Wimbledon YCs could barely afford the indulgence of factionalism; it was pretty much a splinter group in its own right. The first objective then was to increase the membership, the second to provide something to do prior to adjourning to the pub. Helpfully the two were closely linked. My strategy was to arrange interesting meetings, advertise them locally and through word of mouth hopefully create a positive mass.

With advice from the Central Office fact sheet I found that there were plenty of party groups from all sections of that famous 'broad church' to plunder for speakers: Conservatives for Electoral Reform, Conservative Friends of Israel, Peace through Nato, The Freedom Association, Conservatives for Homosexual Equality, Aims of Industry, Conservatives for every shade of opinion on the European Economic Community. I certainly lived up to my title of chalk monitor, although given how efficient and motivated I was I surely deserved to be upgraded to head girl. I was a one-woman letter-writing machine, taking time out of my homework to pursue an MP with a particular interest, a cultural attaché, or a local councillor, or a journalist who might take the time to come and address us. I was surprised by how many people would agree to give up an evening for nothing but a receptive audience and a glass of something never properly chilled.

As our membership and our reputation grew I became increasingly aware of the wider YC world. My opposite number down the road in Putney suggested reconnaissance. Timothy Evans was a revelation, an earnest, gangly, bespectacled, sixteen-year-old, hardcore – 'taxation is theft', government-control anathema – libertarian. He had the bearing of a troubled intellectual combined with the manner of a theatrical hypnotist. His even-toned, studied delivery suggested an older, wiser operator but his wholehearted, almost visceral enthusiasm for unfettered capitalism had all the energy and exuberance of a young Turk. A childhood saturated by the power cuts, national self-destructiveness and the almost unremitting resignation endemic to the 1970s had provoked a reaction in Tim, as it had in me, but his solutions had a certain macho radicalism I could not yet muster. At an adult height of six-foot two but still displaying the unavoidable signs of adolescence Tim was one of Maggie's acne'd avengers. In comparison I was really just a dabbler, dipping my toe into the clear blue water in which others were already busy skinny-dipping. He was an entry point into a different world. The Wimbledon Conservative Association and the YCs I had inherited were a cosy bunch, more of a hangover from the 1950s party culture than the dynamic ideologists of the early 1980s. Putney on the other hand, being far more of a marginal seat, was a tougher more street-wise operation, a portal to the world of radical YC-hood. Intrigued, I organised a joint meeting for Wimbledon and Putney YCs. We had an excellent speaker, a well-respected specialist on Eastern Europe, and I felt as though I was finally involved in a political project. It was seductive.

It was a packed event. Well, that's to say that the Tower Lodge meeting room was packed. We actually did have to un-stack the rarely disturbed piles of metal chairs and break open some party-sized bags of crisps. I sat at the front of the room chairing the meeting facing an unfamiliar sight: a room full of interested, engaged faces staring back at me! I was ridiculously proud and beginning to feel as though I was actually part of some sort of worthwhile movement. The meeting was even covered in the local paper. It was an event – a proper political event! And because we were discussing the Soviet Union, a subject guaranteed to provoke a bonding rise of right wing bile (to which we could add

Bruce Kent, Red Robbo, Arthur Scargill and Ted Heath) this was beginning to feel like proper angry activism. That is as much anger as well-behaved, middle-class, tie-pin-wearing professionals and exam-tired teenagers could muster. In fact it was a very sedate little gathering but at the heart of it was our knowledge that such a meeting could not have been replicated in the countries we were discussing. However passive our opposition it felt at least that we were listening to and equipping ourselves to speak out in solidarity for the movements rising in Poland, Czechoslovakia, Georgia, Estonia and bravely, tentatively throughout much of what Reagan would soon aptly designate 'the evil empire'.

The blood red slash of the Solidarność logo had become part of the iconography of the bluest of blue young right. The Polish posters reproduced by the Federation of Conservative Students and distributed by CCO had taken pride of place in many halls of residence and on bedroom walls like my own. Even if they did not receive much of an audience, it was our strike against the unchallenged ubiquity of those plaster busts of Marx, CCCP T-shirts and repro Red Army coats that were synonymous with educated youth culture and romanticised a very unlovely reality. As I stared into the bedroom mirror to back-comb my long hair, apply rings of eyeliner and the all-important ghastly shade of metallic mauve lipstick (Miss Selfridge's top seller which really was called 'Iron Lady') there was the graphic image of Lech Walesa reflected from the wall behind me. It would have been a discordant scene for most of the left who sneered at our association with the Polish workers. 'How hypocritical,' they chorused, 'that Thatcherites want to smash trade unions at home and celebrate them abroad.' But to us it was totally consistent. The battle, even for us mere passive resisters, was about freedom. Our little stab at activism with meetings such as those at Tower Lodge were tame when compared with the sort of indignant fervour we associated with, and admired in, socialists but underneath our small-c conservatism there was fire. And there was reason to be angry, angry with so much of the left that still insisted on excusing and idealising their flawed ideology and their discredited tyrants. But to give them their due the left has always had the edge over us on the passion front and the ability to be really angry, but then again that can all seem like posturing given that history has been on the side of the quiet Right.

If long term complacency had left the Wimbledon Conservatives bereft of troops, the challenge facing the Labour Party in the Wimbledon of the early 1980s was still more considerable. We did have the occasional debate with the Young Socialists, but in the days of Michael Foot they were few and far between in SW19 and the prospect of a Labour revival, let alone an ultimate victory in Wimbledon, was . . . well, they must know how we feel now. But the Labour Party was only the official opposition. There was another, far more loathed, far more reviled and far more feared opposition whose aspirations did provoke an impassioned response in the right. The Campaign for Nuclear Disarmament had the effect of uniting our tribe far more effectively than any other common enemy, and of raising the ire even of my low key colleagues in Wimbledon.

Over in Putney the talk was not of 'colleagues', but of comrades. Compared with my flabby compatriots in SW19 the Putney YCs were an elite corps. They were hard core. They wanted diatribes and dialectics of their own. They were already subverting the language of the left to fight the battles of right, and in CND we had a cause that brought the frontline right to our own doorsteps. For us CND were apologists for the Soviet Union whose unilateralism put our freedoms at risk. But it was worse than that. In our lexicon of insults – they were a sop for the KGB, a conduit for communist expansionism and, later, an insidious social virus undermining the 'British family' with their smelly peace camps. At that time, in that atmosphere, there was no room for a proportionate response, CND provoked full-on reactionary reaction from across the spectrum of YC views.

Many years later I appeared on a BBC chat show with Bruce Kent and afterwards we shared a cab to our respective homes. He was terribly nice, charming, I must have seemed slightly demented as I stared at him closely, looking for signs from this pleasant, distinguished-looking, grey-haired Monsignor that would justify my teenage suspicion and contempt of twenty years earlier. Not surprisingly, there were no telltale revelations, no barely suppressed Russian accent, no KGB earpiece, not even a menu from the Gay Hussar. We had a pleasant conversation and thankfully I contained the desire to say 'We told you so', although later on the radio I heard him discussing his objections to a war against Saddam Hussein and I realised the old differences were not so far from the surface.

Twenty years previously there was no doubt about the depth of such disagreements. The two sides of the nuclear disarmament debate could not have been more implacably opposed, each believing the other was hastening the likelihood of a nuclear winter. In their terms we were reckless warmongers, in our terms they were reckless capitulators. Disagreements over the means were so fundamental that it was almost impossible to see that for many activists there was a shared end – peace. But such was the febrile atmosphere of the time, with international arms talks constantly in the news, demonstrations across Europe, development of new and more accurate missiles, the arrival of cruise and Trident on British soil, deployment of Soviet missiles and the ratcheting up of international rhetoric, that respectful debate was out of the question. Besides which, who wanted respectful debate? Being in the YCs was after all supposed to be fun.

This was all way too exciting for respectful debate, not least because the Labour Party had so decisively hitched its cart to the unilateral cause. Even without the benefit of hindsight the leadership of Michael Foot seemed at the time like a good enough reason for Conservatives to gloat, and the phenomena of the 'loony left' definitely sufficient reason to unleash the forces of the fairly loony right. One such genuine eccentric received masses of publicity for his unilateral attack on Moscow. While I was merely organising Wimbledon debates with the local branch of CND, Harry Phibbs, a London schoolboy, had flown to Moscow with a pile of pro-dissident and multilateralist leaflets. Not surprisingly, he was arrested and detained when he began to distribute the literature. It was a defining moment in the changing culture of the YCs, attracting a lot of attention to the newly radicalised youth of the right. I was definitely impressed, although left wondering, along with the Soviets, whether Phibbs was a brave freedom fighter or hopelessly misguided? After questioning him, the Russians concluded that he was the latter. Certainly Phibbs was a maverick, but his actions that day, and the far more mundane activities of other YCs in challenging the 'peace' movement, were far from empty gestures and not without more serious concerns for the other side.

The leaflets Phibbs distributed in Red Square would have come from the same source that kept the rest of us less-ambitious campaigners well stocked in anti-CND information and well informed of the issues. The Coalition for Peace through Security was set up in the early 1980s specifically to counter the activities of CND. It correctly identified the YCs as a source of willing and energetic activists. Its literature was slick and professional, but most importantly well distributed. We YCs all had our 'CND♥KGB' button badges and our 'Fifty tough questions for CND' leaflets. On the face of it the coalition could have been an offshoot of the Tory Party, but although it fostered close links to the party, particularly the youth sections, its roots were rather more exotic.

Although I did not know it at the time the coalition was part funded by the CIA, anxious to find ways to challenge the anti-Americanism of the peace movement. I must admit that it never occurred to me while trundling off to meetings after school that I had become, by default, a low-level agent for the CIA. Had I known it I would have felt far more confident in asking those fifty tough questions at debates like one I organised between YCs and the short-lived and very unconvincing TACT, Tories Against Cruise and Trident. There was a definite irony in our taunts of 'CND♥KGB'. CND activists might well have been able to counter with YCs♥CIA, though it doesn't have quite the same ring to it. Amid this heady world of high politics another, though rather less glamorous, abbreviation stirred the blood of any self-respecting Young Conservative. After KGB and CND came GLC. Put them all together and it was simply too much of a provocation to ignore.

Compared with Arthur Scargill, General Galtieri, Colonel Jaruzelski and President Andropov, Ken Livingstone had yet to be designated Thatcher's key target. But even before the most obvious extravagances of the GLC Ken's posturing was enough to fire up a red-blooded response from my colleagues. We did not need to prove a connection between Livingstone and the KGB because in his nuclear free zones we had as much evidence as we needed of, at the very least, a spiritual link between County Hall and the Kremlin.

In contrast, pioneering Thatcherite Wandsworth Council, neighbouring my home borough of Merton, was blue in tooth and claw. Apart from leading the way with council house sales, it was also upsetting the left with its decidedly politically incorrect approach to nuclear free zones. Not only was the council refusing to adopt such a policy for Wandsworth, it also made a feature of its commitment to welcoming the transport of nuclear waste through the borough. In exchange for the lowest rates in the country the locals were not much moved about the prospect of potentially radioactive canisters trundling past the Arndale Centre. Not surprisingly, CND were keen that they should be. News that they planned a major demo in Wandsworth was just the kind of thing the YCs thirsted for, bringing the much-discussed theatre of war to our local neighbourhood stage. CND planned to circle the Tory bastion that was (and still remains) Wandsworth Town Hall with protesters. Knowing that we'd never rouse sufficient numbers of apathetic Conservatives to match a large scale CND demo we had to think creatively.

What they could offer in people power we would counter with paint pot power. These are the moments when a childhood spent watching *Blue Peter* comes into its own. In the days before the Internet, where else would you learn how to knock up a home-made, highly effective, piece of agit-prop communicating a sophisticated political message, with just a few discarded household objects? It was simple. It was brilliant. It was a whacking great tarpaulin painted in three foot high letters, CND♥KGB. Tim and some of the Putney boys owed a lot to John Noakes in their stunt to attach their banner to the tops of the two street lights spanning the traffic islands outside the front of Wandsworth Town Hall. More than a degree of subterfuge, ingenuity and DIY were required to pull this off at three in the morning the night before the demo. In addition, diplomacy was called for to stave off the understandable interests of the local police. A passing patrol car of police officers stopped and chatted, but apparently they 'had not seen a thing'.

To give CND their due they did have their demonstration and it did surround the Town Hall. It was quite impressive. But awaiting them was, yes, only a mere handful of YCs drawn from surrounding branches, but also an enormous, street-wide banner which received just as much coverage in the local media as their demo. Looking back the whole episode might now seem rather comical but back then people on both sides did feel seriously enough about the issue to take sides and I must admit that in some ways I feel quite nostalgic about those lost certainties. A little bit of the Cold War was being played out on the streets of Wandsworth. In that microcosm of world events our tarpaulin proved an effective CND defence shield and Wandsworth remained a nuclear-friendly zone.

Our mutual interests clearly gave Tim and the Putney crowd the rather mistaken impression that Wimbledon and myself were gearing up to enter the turf wars that were breaking out all over London, with branches competing to replicate the bitterness of ever-emerging cabinet splits between wets and dries. I think the element of well-brought-up young woman in me made me resistant to the appeal of this internecine warfare, much of which seemed like a lot of willy waving, but real war, on the other hand, proved quite another matter. When confronted by the momentum of a genuine conflict the passionate patriot came to the fore.

The Falklands War erupted just as I was making a temporary exit from the YCs, distracted by the demands of impending exams. Of course it did far more for my YC recruitment campaign than I could have done, and vastly improved the government's standing in the opinion polls. 'Thank God we are doing something right,' I remember thinking, although the sinking of the *Belgrano* left me with very mixed feelings. I could see that the decision to fight and the ultimate victory were a tremendous boost to national morale, reaching into bits of our psyche that had remained dormant for decades. But paradoxically, although the war brought the government an immediate popularity boost it also brought to the surface some of our most vulgar instincts, the 'Gotcha' mentality, that have since blighted the record of Thatcherism and the Conservative Party. Making war not love, even in a worthy cause, is still a controversial notion among that thoughtful section of the English middle class, who although not fully fledged 'Hampstead lefties', are naturally liberal, reluctant to appear in any way remotely unreasonable, inflexible or unwilling to compromise. In despatching a task force into the middle of the Atlantic to protect a few islands which most of us had never heard of Thatcher convinced her admirers that she was magnificent and her detractors that she was malevolent. I was a student interested in history and this was certainly history in the making so it was gripping stuff, but sensing the distaste as well as the pride that it provoked, was the clearest insight I had yet of the extent that Tories are hated and of the visceral nature of that disapproval.

Of course the natural response in such circumstances is to defend your own tribe to the hilt, and I was happy to on that issue, but as I became more involved with the YCs I felt myself becoming increasingly ambivalent about many of my political colleagues. As much as I agreed with what they said, I could see all too clearly what it was that other people found so easy to dislike about Conservatives, particularly the young variety.

My post-exam return to active operations also brought promotion to Wimbledon Chairman – in YC terms the chalk monitor had indeed become the head girl. And at school I had graduated to the sixth form torn between a future at art school or university. Its curious how being a Conservative even at a private girls' school should have classified me as an eccentric (to me it seemed wholly consistent, if not an entry requirement) but that was certainly how my extra-curricular activities had cast me. I commandeered an unused noticeboard in the common room to highlight current affairs and political issues, but no one else was much interested. I think the teachers, who were mostly by-default Liberals, turned a blind eye to it assuming it was just a phase. My history teacher reassured me that, 'You're just experimenting with Conservatism. You'll grow out of it. You do get more broadminded as you get older.' I'm not quite sure how old she was.

Despite feeling really pleased that we had a female prime minister and that it was the Conservative Party that had supplied this role model, I was not sure I wanted to follow her to Westminster. I was inquisitive and interested in ideas but not really ambitious for a place in the political rat race, having pretty much decided at four-teen that I wasn't set for fashion design or acting but that I would become a journalist. Being chairman of Wimbledon YCs offered the potential of a small step on to the party career ladder if I wanted it, but though I was happy to do the job, it was really rather foisted on me. In a similar vein came the suggestion that I should stand for chairmanship of the local group, which covered around ten of the nearby branches, including Kingston and a large chunk of urban Surrey. Other than the odd joint escapade with Putney we Wombles hadn't had much to do with other branches while we had been concentrating on building up our own. Hence I was surprised and somewhat bemused to receive an earnest and rather secretive approach from the then GLYC chairman, by reputation a committed 'wet'.

Just as I was clearly a little naive in failing to recognise my programming by the CIA, I found it hard to see myself as a pawn in the factional battles of left and right, so I agreed to stand. Well, having been asked, who was I to deny the electors a choice? At the hustings, a room full of pitbulls in pin stripes, I quickly realised both that I had been set up and that I was totally out of my depth. The back room of Kingston Conservative Association was no more glamorous or populated than Wimbledon, but there was a harder edge, an uncomfortable tension in the air. The electorate was a mere handful of people, but I felt as I stood to make my case that some were definitely snarling at me. As I spoke I could see the disapproval rising; although what I had to say, a practical manifesto based on being a good organiser, was perhaps unexciting but hardly controversial. My opponent, an impassioned Ulsterman, knew the mood of the meeting. Whereas I had promised to get the leaflets out and raise the membership, he had committed us to causes somewhat beyond Surrey: backing Unita, Renamo, and cutting the size of the state.

He won, deservedly so, for the audience at that meeting was all of the same mind, and their chairman had to be nothing less than an agent in the struggle for world capitalism. With ever-bustling Kingston town shopping centre a mere stone's throw away the fate of capitalism did not seem in particular jeopardy, but I could see the point. This after all was the age of the conviction politician and these YCs wanted to capture some of that spirit and anger we couldn't help admiring in the Left. The new chairman was definitely and defiantly 'sound'.

'Sound' is one of the very few onomatopoeic political epithets. As I started to go to more of these meetings in the wider YC world I became aware of the strange, low noise that emanated like a distant growl at moments of particular excitement, built into a resonant tone and then often reverberated like a chorus around a room. It was somewhere between a football chant and a primate's mating call. It was always provoked by reference to the most trenchant of right-wing views; certain subjects were bound to call for a 'sound' rating – South Africa, Northern Ireland, the miners' strike. A speaker might say something about, for example, 'privatising the pits', and there it would be – the sound, 'Sound', at first a rumble, then a roar. 'Let's all transfer our bank accounts to Barclays.' 'Sound, Sound,' would come the response. 'Let's introduce internment.' 'Sound, Sound, Sound.' It was curious how boys whose voices had barely broken suddenly found themselves a deep bass or baritone when it came to singing this, their team song. I don't think I ever heard a girl, that is apart from Mrs T, either being described as sound or using the word herself. The mere sound of it didn't seem right coming from a girl, but then there weren't many girls in that world so the boys' club culture was self-perpetuating.

The sort of boys who most easily and readily used the 's' word were the Billy Bunter types, pudgy with stiff suits, short greasy hair, little round glasses. Perhaps I'm remembering more of them than there were, but for a while they seemed ubiquitous. There was something very off-putting about them, prematurely old, precociously pompous, smug and self-congratulatory. Along with the stiff suits I also noticed a growing contingent of shiny suits. Essex man had Essex kids and as YCs these seemed to have a lot in common with their fogeyish contemporaries. Together they were tough on a lot of things, tough on immigration, tough on unions, tough on defence, tough on crime and they certainly didn't give the impression of caring to be tough on the causes of any of them. The Monday Club, the bastion of reaction, a hangover from an imperial past, still had a profile in those days. Their speakers did the rounds of meetings. Their advertisements featured in YC magazines. I winced at their agenda. I was most definitely 'unsound' on their calls to encourage voluntary repatriation, restore capital punishment and forge closer links with the South African regime. I knew that what they stood for was in many ways the opposite of the ideas and influences that had brought me into the Conservative family. It would be easy to say that this small group was unrepresentative of majority opinion, which of course it was, but their visibility was higher and I suspect their views had a larger potential audience than I was comfortable with. Their sentiments were perhaps to be expected from a certain type of older member one hoped was dying out, but it did seem particularly unpalatable and almost deliberately perverse among the young.

Even if we were all political fellow travellers (and I was some-times sufficiently put off by this exaggerated young fogeyness to wonder if we really could be) we were certainly never going to be political bedfellows. Given my convictions, my boyfriend of the time (I had eventually seen the point of them), Charles, had to be (and was) a Conservative and the nearest I could get to Nigel Havers, blonde and a marathon runner. Looking back I can see it was an earnest relationship, with long discussions about politics and religion, but although Charlie was serious he wasn't prema-turely elderly like some YCs who seemed to relish their fustiness. Neither of us would have been deemed 'sound', although we cer-tainly were not 'wets' or 'communist scum' as the fading left of the party were usually referred to in these circles.

The thing about being 'sound' was that although it was a uni-versal and defining compliment of the right, its meaning was subjective. I associate it most with the old school Tories, those who wanted to recapture the golden days of the Empire, the tradition-alists, disciplinarians and the little Englanders. But although united in its hatred of the wets the right was hardly a homogenous group. The early 1980s were a time of smouldering revolution. The sort of thinking that had been harnessed by the Centre for Policy Studies and formed the basis for Thatcherism was at odds with much of the Tory tradition, resuscitating a different strand drawn from the 'sound' free market principles of Gladstonian liberalism. Of course this shift, particularly with its emphasis on empowering the individual through economic reform, was appropriately icon-oclastic to appeal to youth. It held all the bold, uncompromising rhetoric flourish of the left with a genuinely radical, socially reforming agenda. The Conservatives had always been known as the stupid party, the party of privilege and lack of imagination. The braying Monday Club tendency that automatically bleated 'sound' at the most reactionary of statements personified those elements of its complex make-up. To voters the new wave Conservatives had offered an alternative to discredited collectivism in practical solutions to deal with our economic malaise. To the party itself, particularly to young Tories and students, what we were seeing was the emergence of a philosophy, even an ideology and that was very exciting. It was giving us the opportunity to wrest back the domain of ideas and intellectualism that the left had easily monopolised, and to challenge some of the lazy thinking of our own.

Margaret Thatcher was clearly a hybrid combining elements, sometimes contradictory elements, of tradition and change but as Thatcherism was then still in the making, still to be defined, there was an understandable rush to get in on influencing the script. Certain elements of her agenda encouraged the old right but there was much of it that inspired the liberal and the libertarians to get in on the act. The touch fuse had been lit at St Andrew's University in the late 1970s. From there a generation of graduates who went on to be MPs and political advisers had developed a radical platform that extended the logic of reducing the role of the state in economics to reducing its influence on all aspects of people's lives. For students, more than for the YCs, there was a rallying cause in which all these elements crystallised. The National Union of Students was then an unaccountable closed shop that claimed to represent all students, spent money on promoting collectivist causes and opposing government policy and supported and promoted 'no platform' policies. It brought the frontline of British politics and the increasingly bitter conflicts over trade union reform and industrial relations right into the effete world of academia. It gave Tory students a unifying cause and a platform from which to develop a challenging agenda that applied beyond university campuses. The first place to seek influence was in the rest of their party, and particularly their fellow young conservatives.

So gradually this impassioned debate between the old guard and the new radicals, and various shades of opinion in between, enveloped the YCs also. And as it did so there was a subtle but perceptible change in the sound and mood of these meetings. The studenty libertarian types were casually dressed, almost delighting in a sort of slovenliness that mirrored the 'real' activists of the left and punctured the old school tie pretensions of their traditional colleagues, as well as sticking a couple of fingers up at the party authorities. Their 'soundness' was an ironic take on their authoritarian brothers as well as a direct lift from the textual intellectualism of the revolutionary left. What they wanted was a definitive script to counter the campus Marxists, a global template for freedom and constant capitalist revolution. So while it was common to hear traditionalists pepper their conversations with references to Burke, Disraeli and Churchill, these guys (and they were guys, definitely not chaps) quoted the driest of dry economists and philosophers, Hayek, Rothbard, von Mises, Nozick and the Friedmans. Their names seem to hold an almost erotic appeal. These were the new 'sound' thinkers and the word would ejaculate around the room with fervour when the market-driven, pared-down philosophy was reduced to testaments of faith that had never before been associated with the Tory Party, and with which most of the party still had no sympathy whatsoever. It was deliberately provocative. It was fun. It was the stuff of student politics, the sex, drugs and rock'n'roll of new right thinking and sometimes in the issues championed literally so: 'Legalise heroin', 'Sound, sound', 'Decriminalise prostitution', 'Sound, sound, sound', 'Privatise the BBC' – too many 'sounds' to list! You can imagine the scene. There I would be, high-heeled and lip-glossed, trying to take all of this in as some hopeful libertarian Lothario slunk over. 'Feeling Randy?' and then before you'd know it they'd slip a copy of *Atlas Shrugged* into your satchel.

I can still see them very clearly, the sheer glee at the cleverness of being able to overturn so many of the party's accepted nostrums and yet argue the case as a natural extension of Thatcher's agenda. In retrospect it was deliciously and provocatively uncompromising, a brilliant hijacking and abstraction of Conservative principles, foisting a leftish aesthetic and revolutionary dynamic on a cautious and establishment party. But of course I am saying all of this with the benefit of hindsight. At the time I found it bemusing, confusing and more than a little intimidating. No doubt this lot were preferable to the young old guard (the 'shits' as they were known by the 'libbies') but legalising drugs, hardcore porn and privatising the police were challenging ideas to get one's head around if you hadn't, as I then hadn't, adopted the whole philosophy. The nearest to a narcotic I had come was Pro Plus — the drug of choice to a generation of exam takers. I might have been a bit wacky by the very strait-laced standards of my school but I was no rebel. At first I had assumed that YCs would be at worst dull, boffin-like and geeky (not traits one rushes to associate oneself with during the image conscious teenage years) but the reality was that few seemed so tame and many seemed set on controversy and feuding for its own sake. The pustular machismo added to the sense of a culture that excluded, rather than included, me and I am sure I was not the only girl to feel that way. Down on the dance floor at the Essex Moat House there was more than the blur of alcohol to explain why we were all dancing different steps.

The general election campaign of 1983 began back in Wimbledon with the perfect antidote to an overdose of philosophical fervour — Sir Michael Havers's adoption speech to the local association. In a scene which would have been replicated across the country a couple of hundred loyal local members squeezed into a nondescript church hall to go through the motions of reselecting, that is rubber stamping, their MP as the candidate for the next election. Sir Michael was everything expected of him, safe, sober, patriotic, avuncular and good enough. Understandably affection and support for him had grown after he had, through circumstance, become a symbol of the government's uncompromising rhetoric against terrorism. Since Airey Neave had been murdered in the House of Commons car park in 1979, the IRA had continued with a string of outrages that had added to the sense that we needed a strong government. The sound of the blast that blew up the Havers' Wimbledon flat in late 1981 boomed across the common to our house a couple of miles away. No one was hurt but it changed the way the Havers had to live, with constant police protection, and it was another reminder of how our way of life can come under threat. So Sir Michael won a unanimous reselection from Wimbledon's seldom stirred activists on his address about the renewed strength of the British forces, 'our glorious victories in the Falklands', and the record strength of the police. There was, of course, another vile and subversive threat to society, which he assured us, even those of us still unaware of this new evil, the Tories would counter. 'We promise legislation to deal with the dangerous spread of obscene and violent video cassettes,' he announced with a flourish.

With that vital reassurance on 'video nasties' we YCs lined up with our 'Vote Conservative' placards flanking Sir Michael and Lady Havers for a local press photo opportunity. We all shuffled nervously, not knowing where to look, but the Havers were picture perfect, the only people in the shot who knew how to smile, look straight at the camera and wave with coordinated authority. My nervousness was born out of the knowledge that our placards would soon be replaced with canvassing forms, and I was not sure how I would fare going door to door on the council estates of our neighbouring seat. Wimbledon was still considered so safe that all bodies were being shifted down the road to provide mutual aid to marginal Mitcham. One of my schoolfriends had given me a poster to add to my collection of political iconography pasted across my bedroom walls. But I was fairly sure she had not understood its implications. The slogan 'Vote Conservative for wider streets' stretched out over a Rolls-Royce occupying the whole width of a narrow road lined with poor, terraced housing. Sarah's parents were definitely Tories and they had a Jaguar and a Bentley and lived on a very wide, private road. As a canvasser I knew my limitations. I knew I was a nicely spoken, private schoolgirl with many privileges and living a fairly sheltered life. If I had been living ten storeys up in a neglected estate on benefits I'm not sure I'd have wanted me and a chap in a tweed jacket ringing on the door explaining the benefits of monetarism, the sense of expenditure cuts and the advantages of cutting top rate tax. I did believe in all these things and passionately (A-level economics adding to my conviction), but I could see that being at the sharp end of these policies would hardly endear anyone to the cause.

As it happened the canvassing was fine. I didn't have to change people's minds but just to find out how they intended to vote. Responses were mainly good-natured, at worst indifferent. They should have been, could have been much worse, but for the issue on which Michael Havers had concentrated most of his opposition-attacking address, the 'longest suicide note in history'. Gerald Kaufman's summation of the Labour Party manifesto 1983 was vivid and accurate and at so many doors we called on the response suggested there were plenty of people who would happily add another cyanide pill to the stock building up at Labour Party HQ in Walworth Road. The positive effect of the 'Falklands factor' was amplified in its contrast to Labour's obscurantism, self-absorption and ideological inflexibility. In the days, before it was necessary for politicians to emote, people did not feel they had to like Margaret Thatcher but more importantly they respected her. In 1983 they thought she was strong. Labour on the other hand were weak, weak on defence, weak on law and order and weak on the unions. So I needn't have worried about the canvassing, it was almost certainly the best general election of my lifetime in which to go door to door wearing a blue rosette.

5

DICTATORS AND VIBRATORS

Wembley 1983

Wembley's twin towers had never seen anything quite like it. In the far distance the stage. One very small man. An unlikely orator. A pair of colossal plaster hands outstretched like a giant semaphore. An impressionable audience in rows as far as the eye can see, chanting and whooping, supplicant and malleable, their attention held in his ludicrous palms. A simple message.

'Let's Bomb Russia!'

Kenny Everett's shockingly tasteless suggestion was music to the ears of the thousands of YCs who had followed the order to go west, and ended up at what I think is the most surreal event I can remember in association with the Conservative Party. Lucky for us that Labour's 1992 Sheffield Rally has since passed into political demonology as *the* example of ghastly election excess, because it has helpfully distracted attention from our truly embarrassing spectacle of a decade previously. When Lynsey de Paul had represented

Britain at the Eurovision Song Contest singing 'Rock Bottom' many people assumed she was referring to the point she had reached in her own career. I don't think any of us were anticipating a further dive with her performance at Wembley that day. 'Tory, Tory, Tory' is hardly a promising title for a pop song. Agitpop it was not. They get Billy Bragg, the Style Council and the Specials. We got Lynsey de Paul and Tim Rice. Enough said. Thankfully she was preaching to the converted, although I think many of us were shifting with embarrassment in our seats. With the benefit of hindsight at least I can be grateful it was the days before our celebrity endorsements plumbed the depths with Jim Davidson.

Kenny Everett was, to be fair, as cool as we were ever going to get, and to the total horror of the party professionals who had deemed this thing a good idea he was delightfully vulgar. 'Michael Foot. Let's kick his stick away.' I'm sure it wasn't what CCO had wanted, but the party planners did not seem to realise how the revolution set in train by 1979 had also released some of our inhibitions about good taste. If the left were going to judge us as selfish, stupid and Philistine it was quite a relief occasionally to live up to their expectations – in place of their airy fairy pacifism we'd give them positive pugilism. That day Kenny Everett in his pseudo boxing gloves was our Dirty Harry: you want to have a go at us about spending cuts? About the Falklands? About council house sales? About the trickle-down philosophy? About top rate tax cuts? About job losses? About controlling the money supply? About our bird who's not for turning? Well, go ahead. Make our day!

The Wembley election rally was part pantomime, part politics and part parody and completely 1983. Twenty years ago UK politics were still tribal; there was right and wrong, there was left and right, there was yes and no, you were one of us or one of them. At home the recently formed SDP was making a mark but it was not yet a stain. Abroad we knew who our enemies were and where to find them. 'Let's Bomb Russia' was a uniquely 1983 joke. It was the last of our Cold War elections. By 1987 Margaret Thatcher was taking tea with Gorbachev in Moscow and the domestic agenda was foremost in most people's minds. By 1992 even the Wall had come down. But in 1983 Russia was still public enemy number one, still the external bogeyman who could rally the Tory troops against everything we opposed at home and abroad.

The occasional tension-releasing explosion of political incorrectness is perfectly understandable, particularly during an election, although it does risk confirming other people's deep-seated prejudices about those aspects of Conservatism they find so unpalatable. I realised sometime previously that the cost of calling oneself a Conservative was to bear its many negative associations, some more bearable than others: by default we are all racist, misogynist, uncaring, dim-witted, nationalistic, homophobic, selfish, materialistic, militaristic, jingoistic, meat-eating, double-barrelled, unsophisticated, fox-hunting, anti-intellectual, brutish, elitist, high church, no church, reactionary, iconoclastic, country dwelling, two-house owning, bulldog walking, white, English men. Given the extent to which, at first sight at least, many Conservatives appeared not only to personify but actually to relish some of these characteristics I took it for granted as I headed for university that my allegiances wouldn't necessarily be popular in the modish environment of a red-brick campus. Also, knowing of some previous Tories who had studied at York University I had a certain sympathy with the reasons why I was likely to be judged guilty by association. York University Conservatives had produced two well-known alumni, the ill-fated Harvey Proctor and the curious Christine Hamilton. Neither were the best ambassadors for the party or role models I aspired to be like, but that aside I was anyway proving a rather fair-weather friend to the party.

By then I knew I wanted eventually to go into journalism and had decided to become a campus hack rather than a campus politico. York is a small university with a self-contained modern campus that had, during my time there in the mid-1980s, an unexciting and unimaginative political scene. Of course there were a few noisy lefties in competing cells, The Revolutionary Communists and The Socialist Workers, Militant, the *Tribune* sellers, and the *Marxism Today* crowd. Union meetings were often bad-tempered, suggesting some kind of debate, but seldom really passionate or from what I recall, intelligent. The chant 'We hate Tories and we hate Tories, We hate Tories and we hate Tories, We are the Tory haters' was a common refrain, but although the cadence varied the subtlety of the argument never did. Any mention of student loans, the big experimental idea of the time, was guaranteed to set off another chorus, another 'sit in' (ten Trots in a bar). But unlike surrounding universities at Hull, Leeds, Bradford and Durham it was a very middle-class, relatively apolitical campus and the Conservative Association nearly moribund. I was told that it had been a libertarian trailblazer but by the time I arrived in 1985 to study history and politics it was relatively inactive. Given the beleaguered state of the Federation of Conservative Students, which by that time was seriously raising the ire of party managers with its rather dramatic campaigns, I felt no great need to repeat my revivalist efforts of the Wimbledon years.

A levels had forced an inevitable withdrawal from YC activism, but the increasing sniping and cliquishness within the organisation were hardly encouraging me to become any more involved. I had mixed feelings. On the one hand my politics were hardening: the previous year's Brighton bombing had been significant motivation. If not a philosophical driver it was certainly another confirmation that we still required strong leadership to defend freedoms under threat at home and abroad. I was still definitely a Conservative and had no compunction about that conviction, although I was keen not to sound too shrill about it. As I was getting older and more confident about my own views, I was more interested in those debates that were finding their most uninhibited, some would say extreme, expression within the youth sections of the Conservative Party. If we wanted to privatise industry and the utilities for example, why not the police or the armed forces? If we wanted to promote shopping on Sundays why not disestablish the Church? Were we meritocrats? If we were why not abolish the hereditary principle? Why not privatise the royal family?

It was right that if there were boundaries to push they should have been pushed by students and youth. And of course there were those great moments of two-fingered rebelliousness, like the 1983 rally, when it was just a sheer delight to revel in those things about us that so outraged the other side. But there my ambivalence kicked in. At times I felt those acceptable spasms of tribal bonding had spilt over into an almost pathological behaviour pattern among some of my Conservative contemporaries, those who took the logic of free trade into arguments for legalising heroin, euthanasia and child sex.

For some it seemed the desire to shock had become as much a motivating factor in their politics as had economics or foreign affairs. I had never associated myself with the wets or the traditional ruling class from which they emerged, hence I was a Thatcherite, yet I found myself looking at the bumptious boys of the Tory right and hoping I didn't come across like they did. There was another Tory who graduated from York (in fact the year I arrived) who came to personify this phenomenon with deadly effect. 'Tory Boy' was the socially inadequate, precocious prat created by comedian Harry Enfield (who did politics at York), in a brilliantly observed and painfully accurate satire of some of my contemporaries. I had known the real Tory Boys and they weren't a pretty sight. I was in no hurry to let them cramp my style no matter how much there was that we agreed on.

When I arrived in York in October 1985, it was a few months after the end of the miners' strike. Although the strike was over the drive north up the A1 from London to York revealed a landscape indelibly marked by its industrial past and scarred by recent history. Where the road reveals its most dramatic horizon there is the distant but unmistakable profile of a pit head. The black iron tower marks one of many communities that had been divided by picket lines, by police lines, along political lines and caught up in the ultimate and unavoidable fault line between tradition and modernity. Road signs pointed to places, like Cortonwood, that suddenly became real to me, not just a mythic backdrop to the dying embers of the Industrial Revolution. Sherwood Forest with its lush greenery seemed to suggest the softer, moderate approach of the Nottinghamshire mineworkers, the sparser, raw countryside of South Yorkshire apparently a clue to the militancy of Scargill's self-styled socialist republic. Somewhere between Bedfordshire and Yorkshire there was another line to cross, the infamous North–South divide, which had become the media's crude though telling catchphrase to encapsulate the best and the worst effects of Thatcherism.

A drama that had played out night after night on the television screens, but from which I had understandably felt distanced, seemed more vivid as I made this journey. I had been one of those armchair activists who had never doubted that the government's line was both right and completely unavoidable. Like all young Conservatives I found Scargill a very easy figure to demonise. He had, after all, assured us with all the conviction and accuracy of a practised propagandist, that Soviet placeman General Jaruzelski had been elected in Poland with over 97 per cent of the vote. To my mind, Scargill was no working-class hero but a loutish, manipulative Luddite whose cause could never have served the people he claimed to want to help. Despite my self-styled glib 'I shop therefore I am' philosophy I wasn't a capitalist just because it suited me. I was convinced that free markets are the best, if not perfect, mechanism, for enabling the most people access to the best livelihoods. That was why, it seemed especially clear to me, making my journey south to north, that the best and the most committed of the Thatcherites had made their political journey from left to right: Tebbit, Walters, Parkinson, Sherman, Griffiths, Joseph among others. They had been correctly motivated by social concern, only to realise that it was not possible to achieve the aims of the left without employing the means of the right. For all his posturing and overblown rhetoric it was Scargill who seemed to me to be the real class traitor, and Thatcher that had taken a radical agenda born from her own modest background to effect a real and ultimately liberating revolution. So I did feel fiery about it but that did not stop me wincing at the 'Dole not Coal' button badges that had done the rounds of the YCs before my departure for York. I should have been bolder but I thought we did ourselves a disservice by appearing to belittle the understandable worries of threatened communities.

At least they weren't quite as toe curling as the 'Hang Mandela' stickers or the 'We Sunk the Belgrano and We'll Sink the NUS' posters. Although I have to admit it was very funny that some Labour students ended up wearing the Federation of Conservative Students' 'Nicaragua Must be Free' badges, without realising they were inadvertently supporting the Reagan-backed Contras against their beloved Sandinistas. While it was fine to goad the daft Trotskyites and the ludicrous Leninists (not to mention the fast increasing Greens) I could well understand how Conservative students were reinforcing their less-flattering images in the eyes of a largely apolitical student community. Tories had been seen as Hooray Henrys and chinless wonders; now we were less stupid but somehow more nasty.

In a new and determined effort, the libertarian leadership of the Conservative students set an agenda that had little to do with student issues, or indeed loyally supporting the party, but aimed to prove themselves the outriders of a Reagan/Thatcher worldview. It was a very successful coup, because, although I doubt that their approach represented the views of the sleeping majority of campus Tories, a few very committed students had succeeded in politicising the organisation as never before. At a time when few Tory MPs would have had an informed opinion about the situation in Mozambique or Angola, the FCS were leafleting in support of the Mozambique National Resistance and Jonas Savimbi's Unita against their respective Marxist opponents. With talk of the odd member of the FCS taking off to the front line in Central America, toting a Kalashnikov with the Contras, the organisation had developed a hard and dangerous edge.

I felt queasy about some of these activities, although not as queasy as Central Office, which in 1986, halfway through my student career, closed down the FCS, eventually replacing it with a centrally controllable and more supine student body. For many of my more committed contemporaries, however, the campus crusades were the most exciting period of their political lives, for which they remain nostalgic even to this day. There was an element of pantomime in the excesses of the FCS but, importantly, the organisation challenged Labour students in a seriously political way. Not least on the creeping policy of 'No Platform', which sought to deny contentious speakers the right to address student groups, and the unrepresentative monopoly of the NUS. I was lucky at York. Political debate might have been a bit dull but at least it was seldom vicious. Elsewhere, Conservative students felt under siege, in some cases actually fearful of a violent or intimidating response from left-wing militants. Even where this was not the case there was the prevailing sense of disapproval from most of the rest of the student community and often from the academics as well. Even so, I have since thought that it would have been fun to have taken a more active role in the FCS; but I am sure that, just as I'd felt in the YCs, I wasn't the only woman slightly disconcerted by the unrelenting machismo of it all. My reservations were again confirmed to me some time later, even after I had graduated, when I found myself attending a FCS reunion. I had called round to visit a friend to find a group of former FCS 'cadres' reliving their student camaraderie in a 'Porn and Pinochet' evening.

Even Margaret Thatcher kept her admiration for General Pinochet reasonably quiet; she advised her economic guru Alan Walters to be discreet about the visits he made during the 1980s to observe the free market reforms and privatisation programmes in post-Allende Chile. For many Conservatives our preference for Pinochet's economic liberalism over the previous Marxist regime was muted by the evident brutality of the general's rule. This did not seem to be a straightforward case of the benefits of the right versus the disadvantages of the left. It was the left's hero-worshipping of Allende which contributed to some of the right's enthusiasm for Pinochet; yet the support for him as another test of 'soundness' was definitely a test too far for me.

This was a particular type of boys' bonding I had no problem leaving aside, and was extremely grateful that I did not have any of my non-political friends in tow when confronted by the sight of sweaty chaps barely able to contain their excitement at the prospect of an evening indulging their favourite fetishisms. Alongside videos of *Panorama* and *Newsnight* there was a stack of rather less salubrious material and a small audience of dribbling onlookers. Not wanting to intrude on this sacred ritual I left but I think that evening Pinochet did Chile and Debbie did Dallas. Dictators and vibrators – it didn't do it for me. But for a lot of Tory Boys the libertarian defence of pornography was as noble a cause as supporting the overthrow of Marxist regimes. For these guys masturbation wasn't just a solitary pleasure, it had a moral dimension. Purchasing porn was an active step in defending a free society, a vital strike for liberty! Plus it had an obvious added advantage; it was the kind of political campaigning to which anyone could turn their hand.

Back at the start of my life as a student, York was a Conservative seat. By the time I graduated it had swung to Labour. Proving that the north–south divide was a rather crude description of the state of the country, York was hardly a typical northern town. Chocolate and tourism had replaced railways as the industrial staples. Both had proved relatively recession proof and had helped to insulate the town from the worst effects of unemployment and the decline of manufacturing that were clouding the government's record. York had an air of affluence that partly explained victories for the Tories despite its northerly status. These though were increasingly marginal and finally eradicated by the general election of 1987. Conal Gregory, the outgoing Tory MP, never added much to the political discourse of this country other than doggedly raising the issue of the chocolate industry in the House of Commons. With Terry's and Rowntree's (later Nestlé) the biggest local employers, his job largely was to defend the interests of the Chocolate Orange and the Kit Kat, but despite canvassing for confectionery the people of York voted for Gregory to have a break.

For me the 1987 general election was the first great opportunity to practise my chosen profession. Having rejected political activism, I threw myself completely into the campus media. I had spent eighteen months playing at being a reporter, dashing around the campus with a notebook, toting our reconditioned 'Uher' (reel to reel tape recorder) around York, rushing between odd bits of freelance work on different local radio stations. But thus far the biggest stories had been student rows and flower shows. The university radio station broadcast eighteen hours a day, mostly music shows but we could do whatever we wanted with it. The election was a chance to raise our profile and make some programmes about the real world. We were ambitious; as far as the campus was concerned we were ready to take on Dimbleby and Snow and there was good reason to cover the campaigns. Labour Students was very good at encouraging its members to register to vote in York, rather than their home seats. In such a marginal seat the student vote could make the difference between a Tory and Labour victory, especially as the broad body of student opinion, or at least of politically motivated student opinion, was on the left.

That middle year, 1986–87, I lived off campus with friends who helped run the radio station. We shared a red-brick, terraced house on the outskirts of the town towards the racecourse. My house-mates comprised one Liberal and three Labour supporters, respectively a philosophy, a literature and two politics students. They liked me but they despised my politics, both because of the Tory Boys and because of the chief Tory girl. It was by then de rigueur to hate Mrs T, and as her hair had grown increasingly bouffant and her voice increasingly deep I could see that she had come to resemble too closely her less than flattering cartoons. But to preserve peace in the household politics were seldom discussed. Debates over whether Morrissey or Neil Tennant was the greatest living English lyricist, whether toast or pasta was the best late-night snack or whether AIDS really was a threat were all acceptable and passionately indulged but when it came to mounting any sort of defence of the Tories the house policy was strictly 'no platform'. It was hard enough to establish a cleaning rota without provoking any further domestic problems based on political differences. It wasn't so much that we agreed to disagree; we just didn't go there.

Apart from the by-then-famous antics of the FCS it was the strident tone of the government that as much as anything sealed their contempt for anything to do with Conservatism. The miners' strike, as I have said, hardened the positions of the established campus politicos (either for or against) but for most that was a memory obscured by all the other distractions of student life by the time they came to vote in 1987. The Westland crisis of the previous year had barely impinged on our consciousness, except that it had spelt trouble for the government and thus went down well in the post-union beer and burger sessions. Westland was about the business of government, who said what to whom, who was pulling whose strings, but we weren't really interested in that sort of technical issue. It wasn't banner raising. Even the delayed plans for student loans and cuts to university funding, although significant concerns, were not the emblematic, defining issues that really did for the Tories among the majority of the student fraternity. The things that really put me beyond the pale, that raised an empathetic smile from all quarters when the Trots struck up another chorus of 'We hate Tories and we hate Tories', were the bigger, cultural issues about race, sexuality and morality. And on these there was one conclusion: Tories were bigots.

If I had been a small minded reactionary I hope I would have had the courage to defend those misplaced convictions, but I had never thought I was and it both worried and angered me to see the unquestioning assumption that all Tories were. As I was growing up I had assumed that the politics I had been pursuing were liberal, reasonable, cosmopolitan and universal, but as practised I could see that it didn't always seem that way. Despite the liberalising thrust of the government's economic policies: the right to buy, wider share ownership, deregulation, tax cutting, all of which I enthusiastically supported, there was a strong whiff of reaction and authoritarianism rising from Number 10 even before Margaret Thatcher had invoked Victorian virtues. It was a difficult paradox: on the one hand the Thatcherism I cheered was a modernising movement aimed at empowering individuals; on the other, the logic of diminishing the power of the state meant emphasising the importance of other institutions, particularly the family, which for many suggested a philosophy that was hidebound by tradition. Some Conservatives found themselves on one side or other of this divide, hence the time it took to get Sunday trading through the House of Commons, but most straddled elements of both with Thatcher herself embodying the most contradictory elements. There were, of course, very strong strains of reaction and conservatism within the left (so many of the insults aimed at Margaret Thatcher were simply because she was a woman) but somehow they presented a convincing claim to have a monopoly on broad-mindedness.

That claim was made much easier set against the uncompromising style and resolution of the government, especially in the context of the most emotive political issue of the mid 1980s. Whatever the arguments against imposing sanctions on South Africa, Margaret Thatcher's determination not to meet the pressure to do so was easily and lazily interpreted as racism. In student terms it's hard to think of a more stirring issue. The Anti-Apartheid movement had really taken over from CND as the focus of activism for the non-partisan left and many people were simply motivated by a genuine sense of outrage. But I found the total dismissal of the government's stand too easy as there were legitimate reasons to argue that cutting South Africa off would actually impede the progress to change. It was too simplistic to accuse Thatcher of racism and certainly too simplistic to accuse the rest of us by association. However, to many the government's stridency was totally inappropriate and unsympathetic, and it implied if not

racism then a willingness to turn a blind eye to it or to play to the
racist gallery, which certainly does exist on the right. I wanted to
hear Conservatives make explicit condemnations of apartheid,
which was so obviously an affront to freedom, and yet in refusing
to give in to what they saw as a sort of moral blackmail they left all
of us wide open to charges of racism. The 'Hang Mandela' badges
of the FCS were the crudest example of that; most people would
just have heard Norman Tebbit's condemnation of him as a terrorist and doubted that the prime minister could be, as she
maintained, pressing for his release behind the scenes. It was an
issue of blacks and whites, which was never a black and white
issue but which, in the heat of the arguments certainly seemed that
way.

Racism, the fight against it, was just one of the good causes
which Ken Livingstone had most extravagantly adopted as the key
tasks of London government. The final dissolution of the GLC
came halfway through my university career in the summer of 1986.
It was the culmination of a longer and rather more mundane battle
against the worst excesses of what were dubbed 'loony left' councils. It had started with rate capping and transmogrified into what
seemed like a cultural battle between *Daily Mail* values and minor-
ity interest groups. There weren't a lot of *Daily Mail* readers on
campus. On this issue I had no qualms about backing Maggie. Her
tone and actions seemed totally justified and it was, to borrow a
phrase, our 'necessary stage'. Centralisation of power should not
have been the natural corollary of Thatcherism but here it seemed
necessary to safeguard the national finances, rescue local businesses and eventually develop a more accountable system of local
finance. The demise of the metropolitan authorities, particularly
the GLC, was hastened by their provocative excesses, but justified
anyway as a rationalisation of government. Cutting back on the
number of politicians is generally a good thing. But again this was
not a popular view, or at least not one that was going to get a fair
hearing in my household. In one fell swoop Thatch had confirmed
to her critics that she was a centralising, dogmatic harridan, and in

my house I was in danger of being permanently saddled with loo cleaning duties if I had seemed too enthusiastic about the changes.

Along with racism there was also the charge of homophobia for good measure. Ken's crusades in London were the most flamboyant examples of rainbow leftism. It wasn't the crude, unreconstructed corruption on which Neil Kinnock had rounded so effectively in his spine-tingling conference speech against Militant in 1985. It was a mish-mash of 1960s utopian progressivism, not unreasonable sentiments, but not exactly the stuff of government and certainly not of local government. The furore surrounding Clause 28 and its aim to outlaw the promotion of homosexuality in schools was still just the glint in a backbencher's eye (Dame Jill Knight who had introduced a Private Member's Bill proposed such a change) in the run up to the 1987 election. Nevertheless the battle lines were hardening. Clause 28 emerged as another symbol of Tory reaction that brought out the worst kind of twin set and pearl moralisers. There simply was not another issue so well guaranteed to bring out the worse in the Tory character. And for someone like me keen to argue that 'we weren't all like that' it was cringe-making.

Leaving aside whether there really was a substantive problem of public money being spent on inappropriate sex education, this was bound to be an own goal. Tories and sex never make a comfortable combination. I am sure that most of the country looked at the Cabinet and felt the same kind of queasy reaction at the thought of any of them having sex in the same way they did about their parents. And on top of that the idea that these people would wish to comment on how other people had sex was even worse. Throughout the 1980s we had seen the awkward fumblings toward some sort of neutral language with which to address the challenge of AIDS. Tories who were obviously conversant with the language of the boardroom were curiously embarrassed and inarticulate when it came to finding a language relating to the bedroom. It was some time before 'sleaze' arrived in full but we had already had the first and the worst of the Tory sex scandals with the resignation of

Lord Parkinson, on the face of it a story so gruesome that it did by itself taint the ability of the party to make grand public statements about other people's private morality.

For some, Clause 28 may simply have been an issue of wasted public money, but for others it created a legitimate platform from which to indulge in a bit of gay bashing. In turn that provoked the more outré protests from gay activists that probably confirmed the prejudices of the bigots they were trying to beat. What should have been a very marginal piece of legislation became a major cause célèbre, giving it a totemic significance it should never have had. For a whole generation of young voters it neatly encapsulated everything they disliked about Conservatives — we were judgmental, mean, prejudiced, divisive, unimaginative and old-fashioned. I did at times wonder if I could carry on with my, albeit by then, loose association with these people, but I believed that at the heart of it lay a liberalising philosophy which would ultimately undermine the bigots and I did not want to concede that all Tories were like that.

The campus radio election programmes were a success. We had fun careering around Yorkshire looking for any politicians who had the time to talk to student journalists. The Greens consequently received a disproportionate amount of coverage. For those of us who had gone up in 1985 it was the last big distraction before settling into the finals year. The things that made Tories so disliked on campus clearly had very little relevance to the outside world where the combination of 2p off income tax and strong leadership proved a winning one, securing a majority of over a hundred seats for the party. There was no doubt that Labour had polished up their act but despite the best of Peter Mandelson's efforts the result did not come up smelling of red roses. Even in London Tories actually picked up seats however unfashionable the government's moves there had been. Amongst anyone paying rates the 'London effect' had hammered Labour.

Despite the fact that the Tories' small majority in York had been lost to Labour and it was Labour that was widely considered (by the media) to have fought the better campaign, the result of the 1987 election rather reinforced the sense that the Conservatives were an awesome political machine, perhaps invincible. But York, exactly halfway between London and Edinburgh, should have been a good place to read the runes. The well-established Scottish antipathy towards the Tories had become increasingly evident in their poor election results north of the border. The party argued that that was nothing to do with its announced plans to pilot a new tax there, the community charge, but in the years between 1987 and the next general election that early rumble of Scottish discontent was to grow into a national roar the Conservatives could not ignore. In July 1988 I did not take much notice of the fact that legislation introducing the poll tax to England and Wales had been passed. The only thing on my mind was celebrating the end of finals and thinking through what I'd say at my forthcoming job interview for the BBC. If things went well I'd be on my way to a rock'n'roll lifestyle. Politics? I thought I'd done that. Now it was time to get the job, get a flat, get a life and admit the Tory Party had just been a phase. I thought I could afford to get lost in show business and turn my nose up at fellow Tories, but before long I would find that politics was really the only show in town.

6

TRANSITIONS AND TRANSMISSIONS

Broadcasting House, London 1988

'How would you win back the audience we've lost to Capital Radio?'

It was the clincher question in my third and final round of interviews for a job as a trainee producer with Radio 1. Resting on my answer was the prospect of a fairly swanky opening straight out of college. I was shifting nervously, feeling rather sweaty, considering my response. My interrogator was one of three facing me in a deliberately intimidating configuration beloved of the BBC. He went on, 'You know the type, the skilled working class around the outskirts of the M25, out every Friday night at the Epping Forest Country Club, drives a Cortina, furry dice in the back of the car, but it's always independent radio tuned in at the front. What are we going to do about it?'

'Play more Luther Vandross!'

It seemed the obvious answer. It was certainly true that Essex

Man liked soul music, of which London's independent station Capital Radio played a lot, while Radio 1 was wall-to-wall Phil Collins, Eric Clapton and the Travelling Wilburys. While I had been a temporarily displaced Londoner myself it had always been a blessed relief to hit Elstree at the bottom of the A1 on the drive home from York. Here was the chance to tune out of Radio 1 and the dirge of ageing hippy rockers and into loud, brash 'dancey' Capital. It was the sign that I was home, in radio terms back in the land of the living. Unsurprisingly I did not add that observation in my response just as I had not played up my YC past when outlining my suitability for the job. Whatever the reality it hardly spelt sex, drugs and rock'n'roll.

I had applied for the job during my final term at university almost as a joke but, without trying, I had apparently obtained the necessary qualifications; an encyclopaedic knowledge of pop music, I had run the campus radio station, I was articulate, ambitious and female — which had marked me out among the applicants. And so, to my great surprise, I was in.

So in September 1988 I nervously made my entry into the world of work. I had never imagined myself in a job like that, but I was going to make the most of it. I wasn't going to let a frivolous thing like politics distract me from the suddenly very serious world of pop music. Although in a curious way I felt there was a sort of connection between the two. After all, I was starting work just as Mrs T was making her Bruges speech, upsetting most of Europe but delighting Essex and I felt that my success at the interview had somehow come courtesy of Essex Man with whom I shared a taste both in soul music and Euroscepticism.

On joining Radio 1 I was struck by *déjà vu*. Just as in the Tory Party here I was again stuck in the middle, a fading establishment to the left of me and hungry young men to the right. The station was on the cusp of major changes but for the time being it was still the home of dinosaur DJs and the dreadful summer roadshow. The reasons I had been offered a job, that as a crisply spoken female graduate I was different from anyone else they had previously employed, were the reasons also that I found it difficult to fit in. It didn't come naturally to me to do the main business of the day in the pub. I didn't fancy decorating my office with signed pictures of naked nubile wannabes. And I couldn't bond by reliving my greatest broadcasting moment at the Reading Festival 1973. Probably because I was so obviously a fish out of water my new employers decided on a radical initiation programme.

Any vague pretensions of coolness they may have thought I had were to be expunged in my role as producer to Dave Lee Travis. I was a Tory and I produced the DLT show, how much further down the pecking order of metropolitan chic could I get? On hearing my mission impossible I was at first despondent, nursing a cup of coffee in a Smiley Miley mug in John Peel's office, reflecting on my decision to bypass journalism college. The late John Walters told me I should treat the DLT assignment like a defence lawyer taking on a guilty man: do the best I could to get him off. Given how the management guillotine was already primed to fall on the neck of the 'hairy cornflake' the partnership did go on to prolong DLT's time on Radio 1's death row. Indeed he outlived my life at the station because most inconveniently for the BBC he was very popular. Though hardly at the cutting edge, his show was strikingly successful despite all the efforts of his detractors to prove otherwise. We were certainly an odd couple, but against expectations it worked. I chose the records, he played them and lots of people listened. I even had an alter ego (albeit created by DLT) — 'Noodles', which offered a useful cloak of anonymity in the outside world.

Before long I was used to this new politics-free life. I was — well, Noodles was almost — a household name; well, a certain type of snooker-playing, beer-drinking household that is. I was established in London, living on my own, absorbed in the very beguiling social life aided by free concert tickets and frequent record company parties, and I was busy with new friends. Even putting work aside it seemed that for the first time in ages there was little reason to be concerned with politics. I thought I had better, or at least other, things to do.

After ten years of Mrs T her premiership was no longer a novelty, it had become a fact of life. In that ten years I had grown up and grown used to the gutsiness of her style, her determination to challenge the consensus, and increasingly her tendency to challenge her own cabinet. Yes she was domineering and matriarchal and sometimes on certain issues it grated as it had done off and on throughout my student years, but she seemed so combative and resilient that it was hard for me to imagine an alternative. Cracks had opened up in the economy but starting work in London, and in an industry that both seemed to be buzzing with energy and possibilities, had been a great feeling. The capital felt very glamorous, light years away from the charming but tired city of my childhood. I put that down to Thatcherism. The spirit of the big bang had spilt over into other areas, with the city boom years fuelling expectations in the capital, which had changed over that decade from a sedate, slightly fraying town to a property-developed, VW-driving, gold-plated, Japanese-restauranted, international, modernised playground. The promise of popular share ownership had not, and unfortunately would not, take off in quite the style it had in the States. But the difference that the early privatisations had made to general expectations had been tangible and exciting.

Although my precocious enthusiasm for the grocer's daughter had over the years grown more discreet, and more questioning, I remained unwilling to acknowledge the signs of bust that trailed the excitement of boom, let alone the portents of her downfall that accompanied her approaching ten year anniversary. It was hardly relevant to my job, we were years off the next general election and I had left university politics and the student union well behind. Also I thought I'd left behind the carping left and their clumsy chastisement for anyone related to the Conservative Party. I was well used to the sense of disapproval that revealing my true politics had often provoked but it was not until I had graduated that I was actually told that I was 'too nice to be a Tory'.

Lizzie was a fantastic hostess, blonde and extrovert, always throwing parties and always bringing together new sets of friends and neighbours. We were both recent graduates and neighbours in West London, the rather anonymous grid of converted houses and Victorian mansion flats called Barons Court; a haven of young professionals in a no-man's-land between Sloaney Fulham and cosmopolitan Kensington. She was in banking and I was in the music business and when not at work I was often on her sofa with a bottle of wine and a new circle of friends.

It was a very girly scene. Boyfriends came and went but we had found something more distracting and enduring – particularly with the right battery pack. Ann Summers parties were a speciality of the house. Very enterprising, I thought. Lizzie had a tremendous capacity for hard work and she has since set up a demanding business. Back then it was a party place, there was always something going on and when we all got together for drinking, eating or to review her latest catalogue Lizzie always found a couple of new additions for the group. She'd make all the introductions: 'Hi, this is Jane, she lives downstairs and is in PR. She does a lot of dressage, you know.' 'Have you met Jacqui? She's a friend of Debbie's and she's in fashion. Oh and, everyone, this is my neighbour Jo-Anne. You'll love her. She is really funny. I should point out that she is a Tory but she is very nice really.'

The odd thing was that it never occurred to me to counter, 'Lizzie's great, way too clever to be a socialist.' Worse still would have been if I had suggested, as seemed fairly obvious to me, that with all her natural instinct for business, she was probably more of natural Tory than I was. But she had me in a double bind. If I had lost my sense of humour it would hardly have helped my cause. And unlike my recent observations at university her teasing was not meant to offend. We were having fun – there was no reason to hasten an outbreak of hostilities across the dining table, particularly as I was determined to concentrate on other things anyway. So at that stage I was happy to be an Eames chair Tory to her armchair socialist, but it's amazing how the old instincts come rushing back when you are reminded of the fundamentals. This was my new world. I didn't even want to think about politics, yet as the rest of the world began to change it became impossible not to.

Berlin, Spring 1990

Standing that close to the stage as the electric guitars and the drums kick in and the lasers suddenly rip through the darkness must be a little like standing on a runway as a jet takes off overhead. It's the moment of release you wait for all evening, after queuing and sitting for ages. After chatter and the odd announcement over the PA suddenly a great wave of sound lifts off and echoes from the back of the stadium in recognition as the band are revealed in smoky explosions of pink and green light. Vibrations begin in your feet and work their way up and through your head; for a few moments all you can feel is the noise until your ears acclimatise and focus on a familiar riff, a tune or a voice which turns the noise into music. To the front of you black towers of amplification boom, behind you the crowd responds and somewhere around your ears the two merge in a seamless wave of sound that unites band and audience.

It was like that one sultry evening in 1990. Stadium rock isn't my favourite but there is no denying the sheer gutsy star quality of Tina Turner. There is also no mistaking the opening bars of 'Nutbush City Limits' and when they pierced the relative silence of the waiting crowd, and she strode out on to the stage with her hair flaming orange and purple in the lights, it was unadulterated spectacle; we had lift-off. The slick black sky was suddenly spotted with dancing beams of colour and everyone was singing along, the sound running around the outdoor auditorium and spilling out over the edges into the surrounding emerald forests.

Moments earlier, before Tina had appeared on stage, whirling the mic stand over her head and looking every inch an Amazonian rock goddess, I had been chatting to her quietly behind the scenes.

The 'Access All Areas' pass was just one of those perks you could almost take for granted as part of the job of being a Radio 1 producer. On that occasion I was accompanying a prizewinner who had won the chance to meet Tina on the continental leg of her 'Foreign Affair' tour. It was a great prize: three nights in Berlin in a good hotel, a tour guide supplied by the record company and, of course, the concert and Tina up close and personal. Regular access to celebrity was part of my job but often the 'stars' were less impressive versions of their own publicity. Not so in this case. In a remarkable transformation taking only a few minutes the polite, charming woman who signed autographs and did a short interview, became the mic toting, hip shaking, whirling demon who hit the stage running once we had been settled into the VIP enclosure.

Superficially, the youthful audiences at rock concerts look pretty much the same whether they are in London, California or Germany, but looking a little closer into the seas of ubiquitous denim the national characteristics are revealed. In this audience the hair was rather more shaggy, the jeans rather more stonewashed and the T-shirts generally more sleeveless than they would have been elsewhere. It was certainly a German audience but the crowd was not uniform. Alongside the mullet-sporting bank clerks there were pale-faced, aubergine-haired Goths in their message-daubed black singlets. There were Germans and Turks, Trabants and BMWs, East and West singing along together in English to decadent American rock'n'roll.

It was only a few months since the wall had come down and here at the Waldbuhne open air auditorium, on the former Western side, this concert seemed to me as much a celebration as any such event could ever be. It was the sort of gig that in London people would rightly take for granted, at the most consider an outing, a treat, but there it was a political statement – not a conscious one but nonetheless a testament to the recent release of constraint. Music is always rather crassly described as a universal language and here that hackneyed observation seemed fresh and vital, rather than a dull cliché. So recently many in that crowd had been denied a voice. That evening I thought their enthusiasm and energy were perhaps a sign of their continued defiance, and certainly a sign of their newly liberated sense of fun. And just for a moment while we were all singing along to 'Simply the Best', I saw something statuesque in the figure of the singer. As she held her microphone high above her head to amplify the sound of the crowd the red and orange lights bounced off its metal casing so that just for a moment it resembled a burning torch. With the drapes of her leather dress, her arm held high and outstretched, her microphone apparently alight she was every inch a moving statue of liberty.

Good though Tina was she was not the high point of the trip for me. I had leapt at the chance of taking charge of this particular jaunt because of the destination. The day after the concert we set off on the sort of sightseeing tour that we could not have taken the same time the previous year. Shaking hands with celebrities was cool, but this was the real privilege. Driving along past the Tiergarten, the fashionable boulevard of aristocratic old Berlin, we could actually approach the recent no man's land that had frozen the Brandenburg Gate since 1961. From there there was nothing to stop us wandering into the Unter den Linden, the avenue leading to the heart of former East Berlin. We meandered along bits of the wall still remaining and chipped off blocks of concrete stained with fluorescent orange and green. These pieces of graffiti were messages of protest turned now into saleable souvenirs. Enterprising hawkers rented out hammers and picks to make our scavenging into history more efficient. It was a curious sensation, rather voyeuristic, like being a tourist on a sightseeing trip around someone else's pain. But the history of this city during the course of the previous century as well as the proceeding few months had influenced all our lives and I was totally unapologetic about wanting to make my own rather pathetic, late contribution to ripping out a little piece of the Iron Curtain.

Six months before, in November 1989, I had been thoroughly wrapped up in my new routine. Just having to get out of bed at a reasonable time was still a challenge in itself. Having left politics behind me I found that the BBC had its own brand of politics and that was quite distracting enough to take ones' attention off the real world. Not so much that I didn't register the resignation of chancellor Nigel Lawson but quite enough to prevent me from poring over every detail of newspaper analysis that followed his sudden departure. Obviously it was seriously bad news for Maggie but ever since she had negotiated our rebate from the European Community I had been inclined to take her side over British relations with the continent. If Lawson's resignation was really a fit of personal pique at having to compete with Thatcher's personal adviser, Alan Walters, it seemed petty, although understandable. If it was that he had wanted to pursue, and indeed had discreetly pursued, a more 'Europe friendly' and specifically a more ERM-friendly economic policy I guessed that on that point most voters would sympathise with Thatcher. The stalking-horse challenge to her leadership that came from backbench MP Sir Anthony Meyer within a few weeks was also a sign of mounting problems, despite her easy victory. But I had a demanding job and places to go, people to meet, programmes to make, records to choose, bands to see. In the scramble and fierce competition for any job in the media I knew I had been given an enviable opportunity, even if I had imagined myself making current affairs programmes rather than organising snooker on the radio. Well, as I told myself, it was a first job! But while my focus had changed the rest of the world was exploding in a spasm of change that really made snooker on the radio seem like a load of balls.

Television pictures of the wall being breached in mid-November were totally amazing, arresting, a graphic tribute to a grass-roots revolution that even so recently, with the experiments of perestroika and glasnost and relaxation of the East German border, had still barely seemed possible. In comparison, the domestic news of Lawson's resignation did seem like a little local difficulty. Like all of Thatcher's children I had grown up with the wall as the single most potent example of everything we opposed and that had motivated my own early interest in politics, and shaped my particular convictions. Things were never going to be quite the same again either abroad, or as it has turned out, at home.

At home it was still no more comfortable being a Tory despite the recent vindication of the right and the bullish foreign affairs approach of Reagan and Thatcher. The culture of my workplace, the BBC, was lazily leftish, not the Bolshevik Broadcasting Corporation as histrionic ministers would protest, but it was nonetheless hard to ignore the prevailing antipathy to Thatcherism which was bolstered by the corporate belief in the holy grail of the licence fee. The government's ill-judged cuts to World Service funding (which came out of Foreign Office spending – not the licence fee) did not boost its standing among BBC top brass, adding legitimate complaints to those of the sceptical glitterati who considered all Tories to be Philistines. Working for the most commercially viable part of the BBC meant that it was not hard for me to see why Conservatives were beginning to question the validity of the licence fee. But until then my attachment to the BBC always had been sentimental, for obvious reasons, and when the World Service came under attack I felt a sense of personal betrayal by the government.

In the battle of John Tusa versus Mrs Thatcher I firmly backed the former even though I resented the generalised criticism the latter received throughout the BBC. Thatcher was becoming a rather confusing icon for me. I regarded her with an uncomfortable mixture of admiration and embarrassment. She was magnificent but annoying. I still loved her refusal to compromise, her willingness to handbag, but her shrillness and her special skill at sounding patronising made me wince. Though I disagreed with friends who thought her heartless, I did wonder whether, being such a strong woman herself, she just expected too much of other people. Perhaps she thought they were capable of helping themselves when they really were not? When she fashioned herself the nation's headmistress I saw why the BBC was mainly populated with people who instinctively recoiled from her. But it was not a left-wing conspiracy, and certainly not in Radio 1, but just a general cynicism born out of laziness and studied indifference. And even in the surreal celebrity dominated world of Radio 1, where all conversation was about the sugary world of show biz, there were plenty of signs that the government and the Tories were increasingly despised.

When sitting in my cupboard of an office listening to all the new records each week I never heard any right-wing protest songs! But there were frequent references to the madness of Maggie scattered in rave records and 'Balearic beats' just as much as anguished singer songwriters. From 'Wham Rap' to Simply Red's 'Money's Too Tight to Mention' through the Fine Young Cannibals' 'Blue' (is a colour so cruel) pop was full of just how horrible we were. Irritatingly for me they were generally very catchy records, I had to exert tremendous self control to stop myself singing along. Each day there was yet another pile of new releases to go through. Not a particularly tough job – but I had to do it. Most were discarded within thirty seconds of the opening bar but occasionally something grabbed your attention by the scruff of the neck.

'Choice' by the Blow Monkeys was a favourite. Right from the opening burst of brass it just hammered its way into your head. Within a few listens I knew the lyrics inside out and had to keep stopping myself from bursting into spontaneous choruses of words that attacked everything I believed in.

They were clearly indignant but so was I! In the West we had all been born with more choices than the people on the wrong side of the Berlin Wall, and our freedom, which they craved, was certainly substantial. It may not be perfect but it is not 'built on sand' as the lyrics suggested. But, despite being misguided, Dr Robert's song was in its way a brilliant attack on Thatcherism. It absolutely captured the anger she managed to provoke with considerably more flare than the 'Maggie, Maggie, Maggie, Out, Out, Out' protesters who were ever more visible on the streets. It spat venom over Clause 28, the profit motive and our perceived lack of compassion.

It was catchy, it was clever and it was another slice of protest like the *Spitting Image* puppets, the Ralph Steadman cartoons, Alan B'stard and the liberal 'luvvies' that dominated the culture of the 1980s, providing far more subversive and effective propaganda than any opposition party could have mustered. It was a decade throughout which protest had become a leitmotif just as much as shoulder pads, Rubik's cubes, the property owning democracy, 'rolling back the state', and the Filofax. And as the 1980s tipped over toward the 1990s we witnessed an epoch-making grass roots rebellion, the spontaneous uprising against tyranny on the continent. In Britain, by contrast, we had just witnessed the 'second summer of love', a spontaneous uprising against the music business establishment and all of adult, conventional values. 'Smiley' culture was the punk of the late 1980s. Cheap home-made music and cheap home-made drugs, synthesisers and chemicals, were a potent mixture that was yet to lose its original spontaneity when exploitative operators moved in to organise aircraft hangar-style acid house parties.

As a Radio 1 employee I was by definition an agent of the establishment this movement was set to challenge. Radio 1, in those days, was as far removed from grass-roots youth culture (John Peel exempted) as any of the corporation's more rarefied departments. So by the time rave records made it on to our playlist they were necessarily the most commercial distillations of the genre. Many had no lyrics. But even without words, their pared-down sounds and unpredictable rhythm patterns hit a note of defiance, the sounds of an alternative culture. Defiance that was to fuse with an ill-defined, larger movement of anti-roads protesters, new age travellers, animal rights activists and politicised party people.

But long before the infamous Criminal Justice Act was even mooted or became the focus for youth's growing hatred of the Tory government and ravers started fighting for their right to party, I was already having it tough just fighting for the right at the Barons Court dinner parties. We weren't 'smiley' people – far too square for that – but even in my little enclave of middle-class convention the Tories' natural constituency was finding its critical voice. I had the impression that while a lot of people had professed squeamishness about the Falklands, the miners' strike and the 'No, no no' to Brussels they had nevertheless privately considered that Maggie had been right. But as the 1980s went on the gloves had come off.

If we had stuck to discussing the sex toy catalogues things would certainly have been a lot less controversial. When the conversation veered to other things I really did have to conjure up the skills of a defence lawyer to emerge in one piece. Delia's fish pie and Chardonnay became a little indigestible when I was doubly in the dock – having to defend Radio 1's music policy, and having to defend Maggie. Sometimes I felt as though they held me personally responsible for a whole gamut of misdemeanours – ranging from too little Randy Newman on the radio to too little mention of 'society' on the lips of Tory politicians.

It seemed that Maggie's recent quote to a women's magazine had acted as a catalyst, finally allowing even the stockbrokers, bankers and entrepreneurs of our dinner party set the licence to turn on the Tories. These natural Conservative voters did not like to think that their own money-making activities meant they were devoid of a social conscience. They had grown increasingly disenchanted, and now Mrs T and her mischievously misreported line about there being 'no such thing as society' had robbed them of any restraint when it came to putting the boot in.

'I know we probably had to cut taxes and it was right to have a go at the unions and I guess we did the right thing in the Falklands and she is right to stand up for us in Europe but where's your compassion? I might have been quite happy to vote Tory when you were all dumb and patriotic, but not now you are so mean and competitive.'

'Hmm,' I considered the congealed fish remains on my plate along with the irony of being castigated in such terms by a fund manager. 'Well, at the risk of being cut out of the tiramisu, I have to say I think Maggie was absolutely right when she said there is no such thing as socie—'

A barely stifled screech emanated from the end of the table, 'It's worse than I thought – you're not just a Tory – you're one of the new ones!'

'She's been totally misunderstood,' I came back. 'You should look at what she really said – at the context.' I dropped my voice in an effort to do my best Maggie impersonation, 'There's no such thing as society, there are individual men and women, there are families. And no government can do anything except through people and people must look after themselves first. It's our duty to look after ourselves and then to look after our neighbour.'

'Bravo, great news, as you're our neighbour you can do the washing up!' said Lizzie.

Apart from a row about what to put on the stereo, peace, or at least agreement to disagree, had broken out again by the time the After-Eights came out. But something approaching war, a last-ditch attempt at class war, had broken out the afternoon Dave Lee Travis and I returned to Broadcasting House after one of a series of programmes we had broadcast from pubs around the country. It was spring 1990 when we decided to take the show on the road. This, I thought, showed great conscientiousness on my part. I was giving up Friday nights to journey to various parts of the provinces, spend Saturday in a pub and even worse having to forgo my own clothes in favour of a Radio 1 sweatshirt.

That particular day, Saturday 31 March, had not been a humdinger. Friday night had been spent in a lumpy single bed some-where outside Ipswich. Saturday morning started early to oversee the technical transformation of the Dog and Duck from a friendly local boozer into a state of the art radio studio. Breakfast was a half pint of pale ale and a pickled egg. This was definitely Noodles ter-ritory; Jo-Anne had been left at home in W14. The programme was set to revolve around a pub quiz which would run in heats through-out the three hours on air, leading to a final just before lunch. We were due on air at 10 a.m. By 9.56 we had everything in place: estants, score sheets, pencils, audience, DJ, CDs, satellite dish, satellite link. By 10.01 we still had everything in place except the satellite link. Something had gone wrong. We were not on air. Each minute we weren't on air we were wasting thousands of pounds of licence feepayers' money. As the producer all eyes were on me. I hadn't imagined that things could get any worse than the pickled egg, but in those minutes of panic I'd gladly have eaten the whole jar if it got us back on air. In the end it took forty minutes of painstaking technical probing and prodding to get the show back on the road. In the meantime a DJ back at base had been filling in, but had we had to wait any longer I felt I was in danger of being filled in by a group of frustrated pub quiz players missing their moments of glory and an anxious DLT denied his audience.

By the time our train drew into London I was desperate to get home. First stop had to be Broadcasting House to return record boxes and finish planning the next day's show. I fell into the taxi with DLT and anticipated a straightforward end to what had been a fairly surreal day. That was wishful thinking. Cocooned as we had been in our own little disaster we had completely failed to catch up with the day's news. So it seemed had our taxi driver who led us straight into the path of riot, fortunately by that late stage of the afternoon a receding riot. The detritus of the anti-Poll Tax protesters was strewn through central London, broken windows, smashed up cars, discarded scaffolding poles. Alarms were ringing eerily and sirens sounding almost continually. There were still some smaller scale disturbances going on and great vanloads of police as well as mounted officers still patrolling. It was a shocking return home and a particularly shocking re-entry into the real world after the absorbing distractions of our provincial sojourn.

The community charge, poll tax, was due to come into effect the following Monday. I had been following its progress but only scantily. Local authority finance has never been the sexiest political issue and set against the many seductive attractions (pickled eggs apart) I had on offer it hadn't been much of an attention grabber. It had seemed like a very sensible idea to me, given the widespread contempt for the old rating system. It clearly should have had the political advantage of showing up high spending councils as well as the principled aim of promoting accountability for the community charge payers.

But the one-size-fits-all approach made for easy, though misleading, criticism. Since its initial introduction in Scotland it had been the provocation for a well-orchestrated campaign of opposition. But the government was used to opposition, Maggie apparently thrived on it. The real problem the tax posed for the Conservatives was not the 'usual suspect' militants who were exhorting people not to pay. It was the fear among its own supporters that their bills would be too high, exacerbated by the decision not to phase in the tax, and the Tory MPs who saw themselves losing support as a result. If anything the violent fringe that ripped up central London was a temporary distraction from the real politics of a day that had brought at least 70,000 peaceful protesters to London. I doubt that all Tory MPs would have had the stomach for the tax anyway, especially the controversial attempt to levy a flat fee on everyone. They might have had to explain that in reality most local authority spending was actually financed out of central funds, drawn from progressive taxation, but that would have begged questions about how things had become that centralised. Of all the protests and riots and terrorist attacks that had become a sporadic feature of the 1980s none had seemed so ominous for Mrs T. Where was St Francis of Assisi eleven years into her dominion?

During my cosily introspective existence I had been slow to compute the government's increasing problems. But even with cursory attention to the news it was by then impossible to avoid the fact that the cabinet was deeply troubled and that Mrs T and her handbag were looking rather beleaguered. Maggie's first term had been marked by the 'us and them' divisions of dries and wets, the second by the 'us and them' divisions of east and west and, critics had argued, by the 'us and them' divisions of north and south. During the third, the divisions had seemed to crystallise around attitudes to Europe. But despite the obvious problems, ministerial resignations, terrible by-election results, stalking horses and poll tax riots I still rather assumed Mrs Thatcher was unassailable. I could see how she got on people's nerves, how she often deserved her caricatures. Yet she was so obviously head and shoulders above her nearest rivals in terms of her sheer chutzpah, and a giant compared to miscast Mr Kinnock, that the mere thought of her departing the scene was tantamount to the scene departing altogether. So although there were signs that her ship was in danger of going down, I assumed the band would just keep playing.

London, Autumn 1990

As far as I was concerned the 1980s had been dominated by one particular blonde. Pushy, forthright, opinionated, a woman of conviction who defied convention and yet exhorted tradition when it suited her. An international figure. A self-made icon whose global reach spoke for universal values of enterprise and hard work. She had started off eager yet inexperienced, searching for the right way to express herself. She had had the image makeover and the voice training, walked on the international stage, inspired venom and adulation. When an invitation arrived at Radio 1 for a party in her honour I was thrilled.

The small dance floor was packed. The club was dark, hot and intimate. The bass pumped a thumping re-mix and the room went crazy. Around the edges of the dance floor a collection of fashionistas, models, music business executives and DJs were hanging in booths lined with red velvet. It was a chic crowd. There was more leather on the people than on the upholstery. Unfeasibly good-looking staff served up unfeasibly good-looking cocktails, strictly no umbrellas, absolutely no glacé cherries. The door policy was rigorous; no invitation, no entry. It was one of the summer's hottest tickets.

In one corner of the room was an immaculate, petite blonde woman causing a commotion. Though everyone considered themselves too cool to stare no one could resist the odd glance in her direction. When she got up to dance few stayed sitting, I certainly didn't. The chance to be on the same dance floor as Madonna was simply too great to pass over. The after show party at the now departed Club Valbonne, tucked behind Liberty's department store, was celebrating Madonna's 1990 'Blonde Ambition' tour. It was a pity Maggie had not taken any fashion tips from Madonna. Perhaps one of the famous conical bras might have acted as a breastplate appropriate for the battle that was shortly to put an end to her own Blonde Ambition tour.

I loved Madonna along with that other ambitious blonde who defined the 1980s. And however deep-seated my admiration for the other 'material girl', at that stage I'd still have taken an evening out with Madge over tea with Mrs T any time. So I was really surprised at how upset I felt at the events that followed shortly afterwards in November, suddenly the merest chance of tea with Mrs T would have seemed so much greater a thrill than rubbing shoulders with any pop celebrity, even a superstar like Madonna. They were both icons of their age – albeit in very different fields, but one had redefined it, the other benefited from those redefinitions.

The day that Mrs Thatcher resigned I was at first absolutely stunned, then soon absolutely furious. Earlier that week I found myself, despite my accruing reservations about her, cheering when she had told television cameras in Paris that she would fight on, fight to win. Michael Heseltine's challenge surviving to the second round was a shock. I had not realised that things had become so bad for her within the Tory Party, and yet all my experience at work, and with friends, suggested that she had indeed become the electoral liability her colleagues feared. I had let the sentimental part of my admiration for her colour my perception of her likely fate and indeed of her electability. I thought that people had loved to hate her, rather than realising they just hated her. Instinctively a Eurosceptic I believed that most people, in politics and beyond, would have taken her side against Geoffrey Howe, no matter how dramatic and damaging his resignation and Commons' statement of 13 November had been. As Maggie's first chancellor, Howe, with his radical tax-cutting agenda, had been right up there in the front line of Thatcherite reform. But it was this early agreement that made their eventual falling out, over Europe, more potent, perhaps even the killer blow. As the worsening rumours of her split from cabinet Euro enthusiasts rumbled on for over a year she had seemed a besieged and an uncharacteristically weakened figure, only reluctantly agreeing to ERM entry.

In response her combativeness was admirable. Looking on as a Westminster outsider I thought she seemed again at her most spirited, in contrast to all those dull, grey men and their pathetic, career saving concerns, their calculation and lack of appreciation. I felt indignant, recalling the reasons I had joined the party in my youth and specifically the way in which she had personified those reasons. This cheap overthrow was Westminster and the Tory Party at its worst, behaviour it has been all too prone to repeat. Bumptious MPs who had never had anything substantial to say were suddenly important for their opinion, their 'insight'. As we discovered, cabinet minister after cabinet minister assured her of their personal support but not of the likelihood of her winning the second round of the contest. Could she have fought on and won? Possibly not, but in adopting that line her closest colleagues had surely guaranteed that she would not win. They were the self-fulfilling prophets of doom. They had offered her no option. It was a spineless, bloodless coup; hardly a fitting end for a figure of such verve and flourish.

Watching parliamentary coverage was not quite the done thing in the corridors of Radio 1. If we wanted to give the impression of working hard we left the office doors open, stuck our feet up on the desks, cranked the stereos up and let the music spill out into a generalised cacophony. When a large part of your job is listening to records, amazingly, that does constitute work. On that Thursday afternoon, 22 November 1990, it would have been obvious that I was shirking my heavy responsibilities. I had closed the office door and had anyone been able to see in they would have found me glued to the BBC's live broadcast of the 'No Confidence' debate that featured Maggie's last stand. Cameras in the Commons were a recent innovation, a development Thatcher had not welcomed, but it seemed right that they were there to broadcast this extraordinary drama.

Neil Kinnock relished her downfall with such obvious glee that he temporarily managed to unite the Tories, otherwise split deeply and bitterly by these recent events. Putting aside the partisan indulgences, some of his criticisms of economic mismanagement were fair, the Lawson boom had taken the shine off hard-fought-for improvements, but to offer no reflection on the profound nature of change at home and abroad seemed particularly unstatesmanlike. It wasn't that the things he chose to concentrate on were not important, or that they did not affect the standing of the government, more that they were micro concerns at a macro moment. Couldn't they see what she had done, what she had achieved? It was perhaps too soon to realise then that Labour, finally sensing the possibility of success, would not be able achieve it until they did see – and acknowledge – what she had done.

My feet were up on the desk and I was staring out over a view of the BBC air-conditioning system as Maggie rose to defend her record. Although it was a particularly bravura performance I had to keep turning up the sound to avoid her being drowned out by the bursts of gothic rock and the spurts of Stock, Aitken and Waterman that were emanating from surrounding offices. She did, of course, run through her own hit parade of privatisation, union reform, extending home and share ownership, public service reform, economic reconstruction. She deflected the government's record, even some of its more recent mistakes, and added withering disdain for her Labour critics. Under such circumstances it was difficult not to admire her indefatigable spirit, although I could hear strains of the 'Maggie knows best' tendency to patronise that so inflamed her detractors and had also made me cringe.

It was gripping, but I wasn't really sitting on the edge of my seat until she moved to the macro issues. Neil Kinnock had had some valid criticisms on inflation and unemployment but when Maggie launched into her arguments on defence and the Cold War his credibility collapsed. Pointing out that he was still a member of CND, that the Labour Party had opposed the government's nuclear defence policy, went straight to my political erogenous zone. Suddenly I came over all Tory and I was by now spitting with fury at her fate. She had led one of those free nations that had been prepared to stand up to Soviet aggression and in so doing contributed to the fall of terrible oppressive regimes. Perhaps my response to her speech had become overly emotional, too personal, but hey, the thin lady was singing and I was feeling suddenly guilty for having been little more than a fair-weather friend. When she turned to the conflict looming in the Gulf, telling the House that in sending troops to Kuwait she had been struck with a sense of Britain's destiny, by centuries of history ensuring that Britain would take up arms when evil has to be overcome, I was also overcome. What she was saying went to the heart of why I had pledged my support for her in my teenage diaries, although back then I would not have been able to my express my instincts in those terms. I sat in the office surrounded by piles of CDs and paperwork feeling totally depressed and absolutely in the wrong place. Listening to the roars of approval she received from her own benches belied the fact that this was her swansong as leader. At that moment I felt intensely aware of a curious contradiction I have felt many times since. I had never felt more of a Conservative and yet I had never felt greater disdain for the Conservative Party. Perhaps it had secured a continuation in government at the expense of Mrs Thatcher's leadership; but in deposing her, rather than letting the public do it, what other problems had it stored up for itself? I knew that no single person was indispensable but it felt at that moment as though politics and the party might never quite recover.

That evening, although totally distracted, I worked late planning some programmes, organising competitions and sorting out features. I had quickly tuned back to the regulation soundtrack Radio 1 and opened the door so that colleagues could see I was once again hard at it, at the coal face of music radio production. But my heart really was not in it. Choosing between a Kylie record or a Sonja record, George Michael or Erasure seemed particularly ephemeral. On the way home I grabbed a copy of the *Evening Standard* as I pressed ahead into the late night shopping scrum at the top of the steps down to Oxford Circus tube. The headline summed it up well, 'It's a funny old world – says tearful premier'.

Funny indeed, I thought, as I stood squashed on the airless tube contemplating the previous year and its historic changes. Ronald Reagan had gone, Nelson Mandela had been freed, the Berlin Wall had fallen. Now Mrs Thatcher was also gone and yet there were certain things that remained unchanged: despite all efforts to the contrary come Saturday Dave Lee Travis would still be playing snooker on the radio.

7

From REM to ERM

Conservative Central Office, Autumn 1991

'We have a problem with the skilled working class, the C2s. You know the type, hard-working, family men. Drive a souped-up Escort, out on a Friday night at the Epping Forest country club, polish the car on a Sunday afternoon. New build house, two kids, another on the way. Loved Maggie in her heyday. Clobbered now by inflation, negative equity. They are angry with us. What should we do to win them back?'

It was the clincher question in my final interview to join the press operation at Conservative Central Office.

I was tempted to say, 'Tax breaks on Luther Vandross CDs', but I was not sure they would get the joke. I had thought the transition from working in show business to working in politics might be a tough one, but on the evidence of this interview I was more qualified for a professional role in the Conservative Party than I might have expected. Just like Radio 1 the Tories were chasing that fickle

Essex man. Poor sod. Fancy being wooed simultaneously by John Major and Simon Bates? A heady combination of the Citizens' Charter and 'Our Tune'. Some double whammy.

The unseemly defenestration of Margaret Thatcher the previous year had left me shocked and surprised; both at what had happened and the degree to which it had bothered me. I thought my active involvement with the party was over and politics were no longer a defining interest. But as I looked at all those tumultuous events at home and abroad it all seemed a lot more exciting than the rock'n'roll lifestyle I was supposed to be leading. In the days after Maggie's departure I found myself far more interested in the race between three middle-aged white men to reach pole position in the Tory Party than the race between competing pop stars on the Top 40 show I was producing. My boss seemed fairly surprised when I went to an editorial meeting to select some new jingles and all I could talk about was the leadership battle.

'What do you think, Jo-Anne?' he asked about the jingles. 'Do you prefer the traditional, solid rock feel? Or what about the "in-yer-face" punchy one?'

'Oh, God no, I couldn't possibly go for Hurd or Heseltine. It's got to be Major.'

Like the majority of Thatcher supporters I preferred the MOR one, thinking he was the 'right' one. It was hardly a positive vote of confidence for John Major that so many of his electorate (the Tory MPs) preferred his candidacy only as an alternative to either of the others. In my view there was no alternative. That oft-quoted cliché about the Tory Party being a broad church was true, but not always a recommendation. I was more than happy to float off the two wings seemingly represented by Messrs Hurd and Heseltine. Noblesse oblige had had its day just as much as corporatism. Port and Stilton, beer and sandwiches were equally unappetising. Given that the tapas option was not yet on offer I found myself settling for the egg'n'chips choice.

So the only real contender was Major whose own journey

seemed the perfect model for contemporary Conservatism; self-made, urban and inclusive. Although he was the third Tory leader to have risen from a relatively lowly background, Major somehow personified his own vision of meritocracy even more so than Thatcher or Heath. I approved of that, both for its own value, and because he seemed an image-challenging figurehead for a party that many still associated with unearned privilege.

There was a lot to like about this man and I was happy to put my trust in him, although at heart I knew he could not have inspired my teenage adoration. And the clues to his eventual fate were evident right from his first pronouncement as prime minister. A classless society may have seemed like a radical aim for a Conservative leader, rightly anxious to rid his party of its unhelpful associations with class and old money, but it was still meaningless utopianism. A property owning democracy meant something specific and tangible but a classless society, a stakeholder society, the third way – none of us knew what they actually meant and more often than not these ill-defined panaceas have come back to haunt their authors.

Major's journey was, of course, later realised on film and packaged for an election broadcast in which he was shown surveying south London from the back of a chauffeur-driven car. One evening in 1991 I also found myself in the back of a chauffeur-driven car, a limousine no less, faced with the reality of a fantasy that would have gripped most of my male contemporaries. In another of those bizarre everyday Radio 1 events I was being driven around central London with Debbie Harry. She was launching a comeback. I had played her record quite a lot on the radio and so, by way of a thank you (not a bribe of course), the record company invited me to have dinner with her. There we were on the cream leather seats whizzing from the Palladium, where she had just performed, to some exclusive restaurant. I kept telling myself that I was sitting with a pop legend. Before Madonna there had been Blondie, the acceptable face of New York Punk, and from 'Denis' onwards I had bought lots of her records. Perhaps if she had been the subject of one of my teenage crushes I might have been more inspired by our drive through the capital, but I am sure she was as bemused by the whole thing as I was. They should have sent a male producer.

I am very seldom lost for words but try as I might I just couldn't think of anything to talk to her about. I am sure she had some stunning stories but why would she want to tell me? This was the stuff of glossy magazines, backseat champagne chit chat with Blondie, but as I remembered back through the years to leaping around the bedroom to 'Atomic' I also recalled the vivid image of my homework books strewn across the desk, the clothes strewn across the floor, the posters of Maggie on the wall. And there it hit me. I'd had enough of all this hedonism: it was time to get back to basics.

And so I found myself in a series of interviews to work at Central Office. I was an unusual recruit for them: neither a seasoned hack looking for an alternative to early retirement nor a fresh-faced Oxbridge graduate looking for a fast track on to the political ladder. My experience of popular broadcasting struck a chord with Shaun Woodward, the recently appointed director of communications, who had been poached from the BBC's *That's Life* programme by the party chairman, Chris Patten. Shaun, although only in his early thirties, was already a grand figure, his office, the best in Central Office, was paper free and immaculate. Designer desk accessories and white lilies (delivered fresh every day) sat on the heavy, highly polished furniture. It was a far cry from the coffee stains, the pin-ups and the peeling veneer of Radio 1. I felt out of depth, but nevertheless strangely at home. We discussed the Euro – or rather the Ecu. Ten years ago the chocolate money of Europe was even more chocolate boxy – did we want the hard or the soft centre? Had we been right to negotiate an opt-out from the single currency? Yes, absolutely yes in my opinion. Shaun clearly did not want to rule us out. I did not want to rule us in. Had we been right to negotiate an opt-out from the Social Charter? In my opinion, yes. But my views were hardly the point, as long as he could be satisfied that I was Conservative there could be a communications role for me. Later, when as an MP Shaun defected to New Labour, I wondered if he had been required to meet the same qualifying criteria.

I joined the press office in October 1991 just after that year's party conference. Several things struck me immediately, and were confirmed, throughout my time in the nerve centre of the Conservative Party. First it was surprisingly youthful: researchers particularly were very young. I had expected to walk into the much-vaunted Conservative research department and feel intimidated by an atmosphere of scholarly concentration and deep thinking. But the influential post-war founding years of the CRD, when it had modelled itself as the intellectual heart of the party, had passed under Thatcher, as she had preferred to consult independent think-tanks. The operation had been downgraded to a different, though important, role of providing back-up research and information. Rather than bookish intensity the atmosphere was more that of a relaxed junior common room. Closely packed offices separated by pastel wall dividers held keen, earnest, graduates aided here and there by smiling, Sloaney assistants. With all the resources of government at its disposal the party had grown to rely less on its HQ. I was surprised at the ages of the researchers but soon realised that with no money to offer high salaries these jobs could only be seen as apprenticeships to political careers in parliament, lobbying or Number 10. Special advisers, whose job sounded so grand and important, were, surprisingly, often younger than me. I was sure they were bright but I wondered where they could find the wisdom and the confidence to advise cabinet ministers.

Most observers believed the much quoted cliché that the Conservative Party was an election-winning, 'Rolls-Royce' operation. I had never worked in Westminster before and I had nothing with which to compare it but I quickly saw that view was illusory. The reputation of the Tory machine had become inextricably linked with the party's record at winning elections, and particularly its recent glory days during the 1980s. But by this time it no longer deserved this unchallenged reputation. I suspected that much of the recent winning formula had little to do with the operation at 32 Smith Square.

The professionalism of Margaret Thatcher's image, presentation and ground-breaking use of advertising were well documented but had not been the responsibility of the party machine. Her particular strength of purpose, personality and direction had attracted a coterie of talented and committed individuals, speechwriters, public relations experts and advertising gurus, from which the party benefited; however, it couldn't be assumed that these services would always be on offer. The strains were already obvious by 1987 when Central Office and the leader had clashed over strategy throughout the election campaign. Conversely, Labour's campaign, although defeated, was considered the most professionally executed. This defeat ratcheted up the determination of a handful of committed and longsighted people to apply lessons, in part observed from Thatcher's success, to redesign and modernise the Labour Party. By 1992, New Labour, still some way off being christened, was already several years in gestation, while, in contrast, the apparatus of the Tory Party had been failing to keep ahead of the game.

The press office I joined was small but dedicated and long serving. My colleagues knew the party and all its foibles well but they were thin on the ground. Here and there throughout the building there were more experienced people (that is older, some very much older) who occasionally seemed to crawl out of previously undiscovered offices clutching pieces of never-before-seen opinion poll research or vital correspondence. Some were seasoned professionals, others did not inspire confidence and rather gave the impression that the institution had absorbed too much of the amateur spirit of the voluntary side of the party.

The geography of the building, with its rabbit warrens and inaccessible corners, militated against a team spirit even though the threat of Labour should have been the uniting factor. It was not, however, an ideological place; people were not divided by constant intense discussions over policy. I found that rather disappointing. I found instead that if anything the atmosphere was curiously apolitical, with definite nods to the civil service, particularly in the press office, where, after all, we were employed to communicate the party line, not our own.

But even without political differences Central Office was disappointingly stratified. Key departments, campaigning, press, research, presentation were on different floors and seemed little worlds of their own. There was insufficient communication between floors and an unstated sense that each was working to its own agenda. The building was also stratified vertically with a separate wing for the chairman's office and staff. Here the atmosphere was friendly but understandably rather more formal, a smattering of OBEs populated the offices and it seemed the perfect posting for the type of secretary who had attended a finishing school rather than finishing school. Throughout the building petty rivalries and personal antagonisms were on the rise in the run-up to the election. Departmental directors, on their different floors, gave every impression of being mutually suspicious of each other.

I was the apprentice, new kid on the block, unsure of my role but not quite as unsure of what it should be as my new employers. At first this was rather unsettling but I soon found I could mould it into whatever was required. The first big task was to help coordinate a regional press operation. This took hours of telephone calls to media all over the country. What would they require from us during a forthcoming election? How could we help them with their programmes? It was probably worthwhile but I could never quite see why this would not have been better coordinated through the network of regional offices. There was a sense that we were making things up as we went along, amplified by the lack of communication from our seniors.

It appeared that Shaun had the good sense to realise that management was not his greatest skill. When I joined the team he had already made himself unpopular with the established staff. His

self-styled baronialism did not endear him to many of his colleagues, who did not feel quite so 'to the manor born', or in his
case 'to the manor married'. As long as he did a good job I was
less bothered by his imperious manner than others but he clearly
realised it was an issue so he seconded a PR specialist to act as
his representative on earth. His appointee was a charming and
experienced communications professional who had acted at the
highest level in a top city PR company with close contacts with the
Tory Party. Unfortunately, she had never had any contact with
the Tory Party. Her appointment and her desk in a glass bubble
at the opposite end of the large open plan press office only seemed
to further confuse the chain of command.

As my brief took shape I became responsible for 'regional media
relations'. As the region closest to me was London I was soon
monopolised by the needs of the capital. This was a mixed blessing;
it took me away from making telephone calls to Mercia Sound and
the *Aberdeen Argus*, and put me out in the field. Being a political
operative in the field had romantic, dashing connotations. Needless
to say the reality was far more prosaic. The closest I actually came
to a field was standing in a pile of dogshit on a green verge over-
looking Alexandra Palace, my camera lens trained on the broken
windows and signs of neglect. The east London folly, managed by
Haringey Council, was being investigated as a possible example of
Labour waste and inefficiency. The idea was that we should exploit
what was left of Labour's 'London effect' (and find examples of it
outside London) that had helped the Conservatives so much in
1987, and might still have legs in the run up to an election five years
later. In the months before an official election campaign (much
expected and predicted but still to be announced) the Conservatives
would highlight the sheer ineptitude of Labour in local government
as a way of warning voters off allowing them any more power.

Efforts to get 'Labour's Dirty Dozen', as the campaign was to be
called, up and running had me dashing between high rise towers
and ivory towers. One moment I was trailing around the most
neglected estates of Hackney, Lambeth and Islington, councils

which had years of community charge and council tax arrears, where Labour was locally incompetent and seemed to benefit from furthering a culture of non-payment and its associated climate of dependency. Next there were the meetings in shiny ministerial offices with plates of gold-wrapped biscuits and pots of coffee.

The quest to find visual proof of Labour's misrule proved more difficult than we had imagined. Certainly there were no shortages of blocked drains, leaking pipes, vandalised walkways and burnt out flats that characterised so many of these desolate estates. It was not difficult to find examples of bad management and decay but more difficult for photographs to tell the whole story. The pictures looked grotty, the reality was often worse, convincing me, if I needed any convincing, that socialism – even here in its municipal form – was ill-equipped to help those who most naturally rely on it. Dramatic pictures, however, were fraught with dangers for a political campaign. Could a poster of damp walls prove Lambeth's negligence? Or would they counter with tales of government underfunding?

Throughout this period I kept my Dirty Dozen survival kit underneath the desk in the office. After the jeans and T-shirt philosophy of Radio 1 I was enjoying a job which required high heels and smart suits but these were hardly suitable for my new and somewhat ill-cast role as seeker of squalor. The rest of the press office knew when I'd had a call to rush off to Tower Hamlets or Newham as I'd slip off the slingbacks and slip on Wellington boots. With a long raincoat, a notebook, camera and pair of rubber gloves I was equipped for the search, even if it was proving rather frustrating.

At the heart of the projected Dirty Dozen campaign was a desire to contrast low tax, efficient Tory authorities with profligate, spiritually corrupt Labour ones. The genesis of the Major government had been the required death of the Poll Tax and the promise to replace it with something deemed fairer. So this was a potentially important campaign, another vehicle for selling the new Council Tax as well as for knocking Labour. Fresh back from the pavement politics of grot spotting, I'd throw off the mac, whisk off the wellies, quickly reinstate the shoulder pads and stilettos to join the rest of the team over at the Department of the Environment. Most were lowly operatives like myself, Andrew the earnest researcher, Steve the go-getting advertising coordinator, John the long serving regional coordinator and David the lantern-jawed head of the CCO local government department. The minister's office was fifteen storeys up in the (now demolished) 1960s nightmare government offices of Marsham Street. The view from floor to ceiling windows revealed a panorama of south London that looked from a distance far more impressive than revealed by the closer inspections I had been making. The view close at hand was most definitely improved by the addition to our party of the local government minister, Michael Portillo.

I had not had to work at Central Office very long to pick up on the star status of Michael Portillo. He was young and handsome, charming and exotic, loyal and efficient. He was a philosophical pin-up in the Conservative research department, an institution from which he had graduated, also he alone had emerged from the end of the Thatcher era with his reputation enhanced. Unlike all her other supporters, Michael Portillo had urged Thatcher to stay on. This together with his obvious personal attributes, his academic reputation, his impressive career rise and his perceived right wing credentials had his name mentioned with reverence throughout party circles. He already had a young and devoted following of male researchers eager to emulate his success and no doubt rather in love with him as well. It was not difficult to see why. Portillo, unlike most politicians, has real presence and an undeniable sexual charisma. He was easily the most glamorous thing I had encountered in my few weeks close to the centre of power.

And power was the point. Portillo gave the impression that he knew what to do with it, what it was for. That was impressive and reassuring given that my experience of politics was thus far proving underwhelming. A Christmas drinks party at CCO had brought the prime minister out to shake hands with the staff. We had been told that John Major was more impressive in the flesh, a comment which rather damned with faint praise. And in the flesh he was certainly taller than expected, a more imposing figure, with a certain avuncular charm, an ease of manner I had not quite expected. And as befitting a former whip, Major did have the air of a power broker about him, though more a broker than a generator. He could work a room but it did not light up in quite the way that it did for Portillo or Heseltine. So it was not difficult to become a Portillista.

He sat coolly taking stock of our progress on the Dirty Dozen campaign. He was far too well dressed not to have continental blood, yet his Jermyn Street tailor-made suit (as it appeared) coupled with a Hermes tie mirrored the complexity and the paradox of his patriotism – a particular enthusiasm for Britain informed by his personal proximity to different political cultures. Our progress on the campaign he would head was not going well. Although there were at least a dozen councils that would have met the 'dirty' criteria there were proving to be too many practical problems in making the case against them. Perhaps we could change the focus away from the specific councils to the generality? The advertising guy was charged with mocking up some posters and we arranged to meet again in a week's time. Portillo had been calm and authoritative. He knew what he wanted and what he expected from us. In my short run of experience these already seemed unusual talents.

Memories of the following meeting differ in detail but that it was uncomfortable is not disputed. As I remember, the mocked-up posters came back from the agency with a strapline that read something like 'Labour councils tax you more, Conservative councils serve you better'. None of us, particularly the unfortunate ad guy, were left in any doubt that Michael Portillo was disappointed and angry. We were failing to get this campaign up and running and now the advertising was also flawed. His objection was that the words 'councils tax' brought to mind the new Council Tax, which he was charged with selling. In the context on the proposed advert the associations were negative. But the anecdote is less about the

details and more about the authority of Portillo. He was clearly
frustrated and he had a right to be; this whole operation had an
amateur air about it. What did it say about the massed strength of
the Conservative Party operation that we could not manage to put
together a campaign based on the already widely acknowledged
belief that Labour had many problems in local government? What
were our councillors doing? Why couldn't the Central Office local
government department coordinate something? Why were ads
coming back with mistakes in them? Portillo was furious and
bemused. He was right to be. The campaign never got off the
ground.

With my efforts to literally dig up dirt on Labour aborted, I
returned from the field to concentrate on the office activities of
our 'near-term' campaign. Central Office may not have been the
powerhouse I had expected but a lot of people were talking a good
talk. The near-term campaign, a concept borrowed from the US,
was to be a period of concerted opinion-influencing in the run up
to the formal election campaign. From the time I arrived in
October 1991 political news coverage was dominated by the 'will
he, won't he' chorus of reporters wondering when John Major
would call an election. The recovery from recession, a government
made recession that had hit our favoured C2 man particularly
badly, was proving slow in coming so the decision to wait until the
last possible moment for an election was hardly surprising. In late
December Shaun took the press office and various key research
department people away for a weekend 'think in'. This was part of
our induction to the near term campaign, a sophisticated and ambitious project. Given all the conference facilities in Central Office,
the weekend in Cambridge seemed rather extravagant, but Shaun
was keen that we should stay at the hotel his parents had enjoyed
during visits to see him when he was a Cambridge student. A
touching thought, but I doubt that our weekend would have been
held in Hull or Birmingham had his starred academic career taken
a different course.

We had various presentations about the activities of the coming weeks and learned about the daily 'grid' which would run our lives once the election had been called. The grid was a daily count-down, each day designed to highlight a specific agenda setting theme, which was designed to counteract 'events' so that we could dominate the news with subjects of our choice. That was the plan. It was a well-thought-out and thorough plan, yet, as events were to prove, it was not always within our power to stick to it. But in the weeks and months before the formal election campaign the 'near term' assault scored some vital successes.

From January we were working on an election footing, leave was suspended and there was permanent cover in the press office. Poster unveilings and press conferences were regular events; two of these early in the year set the tone for the election itself and may well have secured the eventual result. The Tax Bombshell and the Double Whammy were crude, unapologetic, effective negative campaigning (although they were not personal). Party statisticians had calculated the cost per household of Labour's spending pledges, around a thousand pounds each year, and that was the tax bombshell. The Double Whammy referred to the higher tax and higher prices predicted under an inflationary Labour government. Each message was conveyed in dark, brooding graphics, the bomb-shell and the double ball and chain uncompromisingly threatening images. But although the messages were strikingly obvious it still fell to the party's high-church chairman, Chris Patten, to explain the concepts to the press. The expression 'double whammy' did sound particularly amusing as he gave it a characteristically erudite deconstruction. It was rather like hearing a bookish uncle reassur-ing himself that on mastering a street wise new phrase he was still able to 'get down with the kidz'. Chrissy P in da house!

Chris Patten was a popular chairman within Central Office. He was quite hands-on when he was able to be, popping in and out of different departments to check on progress. But despite his close-ness to the prime minister his appointment was flawed and we were all soon aware of that. With a marginal seat in Bath his

priorities were torn. As chairman of the party his was a particularly valuable scalp for his local opponents, the Liberal Democrats.
The vulnerability of his seat meant inevitably that he had to spend
more time in the West Country than was ideal, and that his press
officer, one of my most experienced colleagues, was also absent
from Central Office through most of the near term and actual
election campaign. In fact by some bizarre twist of fate I became
the longest-serving (all of six months) press officer left in Smith
Square when the election date was eventually called for 9 April.
The head of press remained, but was mainly in the House of
Commons lobby, others of my more experienced colleagues were
dispatched on John Major's tour bus and on the rounds with
Norma Major. A whole army of volunteer worker ants had been
drafted in. The press and broadcasting operations were split across
two separate offices, creating yet another division in an already
unexpectedly divided building.

Elsewhere in the building tensions were seldom far from the
surface and rumours abounded about arguments between departmental directors, between the advertising company and Central
Office, the communications director and the chairman, between
John Major's staff and the campaign managers at Smith Square.
From week to week it seemed that a different person was calling
the shots. When the much debated and discussed manifestos
returned from the printers for the start of the campaign one director was accused of having made unilateral changes in policy at the
printers. Then reputedly there were the thousands of Gujarat manifestos, part of an effort at multiculturalism that had to be quietly
pulped because they were printed upside down. Later Lord
Wakeham arrived, apparently dispatched by John Major, as the
latest emissary to coordinate the campaign and preside over
the conflicting parties. Rumours abounded in the press and in the
building about the splits in the campaign team management and
as the weeks went on, about the changes in emphasis away from
Shaun's stage-managed approach to John Major's soapbox. I cannot
claim to have been a pivotal individual, or to have been a party to

high level decisions, where perhaps things were more organised than they appeared to us, but there was no doubt that for most ordinary members of staff working on the campaign there were two over-riding feelings. First, that we were not quite sure who was in charge, press queries came in by the minute and our information always seemed out of date or insufficient. Second, throughout almost all of the campaign few of us believed that we would win the election.

As the near term campaign had indicated, the Conservatives wanted to keep attention focused on tax and spend, defence and law and order: accepted Tory strongpoints. Conversely, and sensibly, Labour wanted to draw attention to health, education and the public services, their supposed winning cards. It was proving a campaign for memorable 'soundbites'; Norman Lamont had been dubbed 'VAT Man' by John Smith who in turn had been accused of pursuing a 'prawn cocktail offensive' by Michael Heseltine. Vivid phrases caught the imagination but the first real 'story' (though it was hardly substantial) that knocked the carefully scripted sound-bites and daily themes of the grid off the agenda was the tale of Jennifer's Ear.

Labour's beautifully shot election broadcast sought to highlight the human cost of a failing, Tory run NHS. Proof that its PR machine was not as well oiled as we had thought came with the revelation that the real family of the girl whose ear operation had been constantly postponed was divided in its political loyalties. That was bad news for Labour. But who had leaked this informa-tion to the press, infringing the privacy of a real family? That was bad news for us. William Waldegrave, the cerebral health secre-tary, looked like a hounded rabbit at the press conference we had called to try to turn up the heat on Labour. Afterwards in the cor-ridor leading from the formal conference set, Waldegrave was pursued and cornered by a pack of hacks that wanted answers. His expression and awkwardness betrayed the unease many quiet intellectuals feel about the combative nature of politics, and for me became a vivid motif of our situation: we were all lacking confidence and feeling cornered.

Polls, except for a few exceptions, were generally bad – although of course we were all briefed not to comment on them. The short-term effects of the spring's foolishly generous budget had not yet had time to sink in with the voters. And the Labour cry that it was time for a change had a prosaically persuasive ring to it. But the idea we might not, indeed probably would not, win was never explicitly discussed. Central Office was working with a sort of Dunkirk spirit, but even that degree of fixed-smile resolution was testament to our lack of confidence. After all the Conservatives were the incumbents and there was far more in our mixed record of government to be proud of than not, but for most of the campaign it did not feel as if we were completely convinced of that.

Despite the many criticisms that Shaun Woodward attracted he deserved credit for his vital understanding of the needs of television. For this campaign the party mainly dispensed with the big stadium events, like the Wembley rally I had cringed through in my teens, and replaced them with more intimate, shirt-sleeved soirées with John Major. These played to his strengths and did make good, positive television pictures. But there were still murmurs of disapproval from the old timers at Central Office. Despite the fact that these pictures sold John Major to the public, the TV events apparently neglected the party workers who were due their morale boosting rallies. This was typical of the dilemmas the party was bound to face if it was to modernise in the following years. Labour was also to struggle with balancing the rights of its members with the need to address the wider, voting public. Unlike Labour, the Conservative Party I worked for maintained the curiously organic structure I had first encountered in Wimbledon, with no unifying structure and no central command.

In many ways this was a commendably democratic and devolved organisation. The voluntary party was independent, with local associations like the one I joined at fifteen fiercely guarding their autonomy. The MPs (and other elected representatives) also organised themselves through the parliamentary 1922 committee. The third arm of the operation was the professional party and just as I had suspected during my time as an activist, all these elements revolved in a cycle of mutual suspicion and disrespect. The real weaknesses of this system were yet to reveal themselves, but would do so in damaging ways throughout John Major's second term.

John Major's TV question and answer sessions had mixed reviews but contrasted him well against Labour's weakest link, Neil Kinnock. No one deserved the vitriolic attacks that the press heaped on Mr Kinnock, culminating of course in the *Sun*'s eve of polling call on us all to leave the country were he to be elected. But even the crudest exaggeration has a basis in fact, and Kinnock, despite his considerable ability as a speechmaker, never commanded authority. He was bettered both by John Smith and by John Major, hardly a desirable position for the leader of the opposition, and mercilessly harried by Michael Heseltine. In performance Heseltine was devastating, easily the party's strongest orator. In private he was also easily the least approachable figure I encountered at CCO. For a figure whose political persona was so red-blooded and impassioned he came across as surprisingly cool, or more accurately cold. The charm and wit which emerged at the flick of a well-used switch, or at the behest of the *Today* programme, was otherwise not in evidence. Accompanying him on a press conference I was intimidated. There was no small talk, indeed a frosty reception, not that it mattered because when the curtain went up he issued a toss of that famous hair and was off, belittling the opposition as no one else in the party could. Even if he was too important to acknowledge lowly press officers there was no one better able to boost party morale than Heseltine, despite his role in the events of November 1990.

Even without Heseltine's attacks, Kinnock himself was perfectly capable of boosting our otherwise low morale merely by appearing on the television and giving us plenty of opportunities to reassure ourselves that he was not a credible leader. Much of our response to him was fired by that gut tribalism necessary to strengthen our resolve. But, putting that aside, our morale was significantly revived in the final days of the campaign when the Labour

leader made his most self-defeating gaffes. On one of the gloomiest evenings, towards the end of the last full week of the campaign,
Labour was leading in a number of polls. There was an atmosphere
of quiet resignation among the staff at Smith Square when the first
editions came through. On the phones we parroted the same lines
of defence to enquiring journalists – that we didn't comment on
polls, but our despondent tone may have told them a different
story. It wasn't so much that we expected to lose but that we
would not be too surprised if we did. These polls only seemed to
be reflecting what had become, through months of repetition in the
media, an accepted fact rather than just a possibility. Perhaps if
Walworth Road and the Labour high command had taken a similarly downbeat approach things may yet have been different, but
the following night's Sheffield Rally was a definite turning point for
our mood.

In retrospect, the event has developed a dramatic significance
but on the evening itself, a week before the election, it was just
another item on the late evening news. As I watched the BBC
report in the media monitoring unit next to our press office, I did
something I hadn't done a lot of during the previous three weeks –
laughed. Poor Neil Kinnock, how he must have cursed that
moment, the sheer indignity of it, the toe-curlingly embarrassing
spectacle of politicians trying to be pop stars. Personally, I had
hated John Major's soapbox initiative. It was way too downmarket
for a prime minister, one minute international statesman the next
a 'roll up, roll up, get your nice tax-cutting policies here' market
stall trader, but I also saw that it could have a fresh, spontaneous
appeal. At that moment the sheer vulgarity of Labour's premature
triumphalism ('In nine days' time there will be a Labour government') made Major's low key populism seem so much more
appealing. The rally may well have been a brilliant morale boost for
those Labour party workers attending, and should have hardly constituted a deal breaker, but the television pictures and subsequent
coverage just seemed to capture and emphasise the nagging doubts
that many people still had about putting Labour into office.

Kinnock's curiously incoherent chorus of 'Well, all right, well, all right' sounded, in the mid-Atlantic drawl into which he had oddly slipped, more like 'We're all ri', we're all ri''. It instantly provoked an 'oh no, you're not' pantomime reaction from my colleagues huddled in the cramped and sweaty office.

Our change of mood was subtle but perceptible. It was enough to see us into the last week of the campaign feeling more optimistic. Neil's next faux pas, an ill-thought-out answer about PR on live television, also dented his credibility and bolstered Major's last-ditch attempt to swing the vote in our favour. The general election on 9 April 1992 was my fourth since childhood; the whole process still fascinated me. Coming at the end of a tense, hectic but curiously uneventful few weeks the day had an air of anticlimax I had not anticipated. There was every possibility that the party I had supported constantly, but with different degrees of enthusiasm, would soon be the losers.

As a political romantic I had responded to the vision thing. Major's rejection of it, at his first party conference as leader, in favour of a not so explicit managerialism had disappointed me, but the effect of working on this campaign had been to dispel any niggling doubts and transform me into a vehement, impassioned, bluer-than-blue party supporter. Though I had worries about the party's effectiveness these were technical concerns and I was more worried by the prospect of a Labour government. It was unthinkable, an unbearable possibility for me. So I felt more than nervous when turning up at a subdued Central Office for the nightshift that would take us through to we were not quite sure what; many were predicting a hung parliament. Although we did not know it, the campaign managers were quietly confident. Sensibly, Shaun insisted that the tone of the night's proceedings should be restrained and sober. Refreshments were set out for reporters who had chosen to cover the events from inside the Tory camp but this was not to be presented as a celebration party. Throughout the building, all the bright young things, the 'brat pack' as the press had labelled them, were gathered around television sets or chatting nervously on landings and in corridors. The phones were quiet; there was nothing to do, no more facts that needed checking, no itineraries to collate, or faxes to send, or briefs to write. There were a few 'lines to take' being prepared and practised to cover a variety of possible results but really we were all in limbo.

It was a reassuringly short-lived limbo. The exit polls with which David Dimbleby greeted us at the start of the night's coverage were gloomy, predicting a small Labour lead, but as results started to come in it did not take long for our nervousness to dissipate. Perhaps we had offered tax breaks on Luther Vandross CDs? Perhaps the soul crooner had played a secret support gig for us at the Epping Forest Country Club? The clues to the night's results came in an early result from Essex. David Amess, the most identifiably Essex Man of our MPs, had held Basildon. In the jargon, it was one of our key marginals but the symbolism was far more important than the psephology. If we had held C2 man, as it seemed we had, we had probably held the whole thing.

'Have you heard about Basildon?' The question reverberated around the building as we all rushed to reassure the few people who might have missed the result coming through. At that moment skinny David Amess acquired the status of a mythic superhero, but as the night went on, with results coming through very quickly, it was another unlikely hero who emerged to confound the predictions of the media and the expectations of friends.

John Major arrived at Central Office in the early hours to a genuinely warm and celebratory welcome. Some of the staff were hanging out of the sash windows waving flags, others crowded into the hallway and lined the stairwell, cheering Major to a chorus led by Chris Patten – himself no longer an MP having fallen to the Liberal Democrats in Bath. We were all clapping and hugging each other and sobriety had given way to champagne revelry. For a moment it felt disloyal to have ever doubted we would make it. And perhaps they had been right to get rid of Maggie? She might not have been able to win us this unprecedented fourth general election victory, which seemed to vindicate John Major's

leadership. Of course at a moment like that victory is the only consideration. It is only with the hindsight that comes long after the
champagne has gone flat that one wonders if victory at any cost is
really a cause for celebration. But I did not need any convincing
then – just sleep! So after our modest party (there really hadn't
been any preparations for one), and finishing off in the press
office, I wandered out into the crisp early morning of Smith Square
where ladders and platforms left by camera crews were clues to the
drama of the previous few hours. Apart from the detritus of the
media the square was deserted except for a woman who had
emerged from a nearby office clutching a mop and bucket.

I was tired but in a good mood and smiled at her.

'I can't bloody believe it,' she said. 'Another four years of those
bloody Tories.'

How quickly my bubble was burst. It had taken only minutes for
my mood to go from defiance to defensiveness. It did not seem as
though there was going to be much of a honeymoon after this
election.

If it had been a Rolls-Royce machine that had powered the
Conservatives to this unprecedented fourth victory, the clear out
at Central Office after the election left it seeming more like a Mini
Metro. The army of volunteers and temporary staff who had
swelled our ranks left within a few days. The election had cost a
fortune, now it was time to rein in the purse strings. The PA
machine in the press office went back. Everything was pared down.
Permanent staff started to take long lunches with lobbyists so that
they could jump before being pushed. The fax machine still
whirred in Shaun Woodward's office but in place of campaign
material it spewed out exotic gazebo plans for his landscaped
gardens in Oxfordshire.

The election-winning afterglow, which for me, had been punctured after about ten minutes in the early hours of 10 April, did
not last a great deal longer for the party at large. I was on a plane
somewhere over South East Asia trying to get as far away from

Westminster as possible for a post-election holiday, when my attention was grabbed by headlines on the British newspapers being distributed by the BA cabin crew. Who would have thought it? David Mellor a sex symbol! As a promising Treasury minister Mellor had been one of our brightest communicators, used a lot for media appearances in the run up and during the election, hence his consequent promotion to the cabinet. Clearly he had been communicating quite effectively behind the scenes as well, though not with as positive effect for the image of the party. I was greatly relieved to be thousands of miles from my pager and mobile phone and heading towards my holiday. The coverage was so lurid, almost cartoonish, that it was hard to see then how seriously this story would translate into a theme that would irreparably damage the government and play to all the worst preconceptions about Conservatives. Only a few short weeks after Major's victory, sleaze was a theme set to become a running sore.

By the time I came back from my holiday there was another running sore about to go septic – or should I say sceptic? Throughout August, tensions rumbled on ominously about the Exchange Rate Mechanism. Ironically, entry into this distinctly un-Thatcherite scheme was agreed in the last weeks of Maggie's leadership. As she herself had so famously told us in the 1980s, 'You can't buck the market.' Even so, joining the ERM was a market-bucking scheme, and the prospects for the pound's fate were made worse by the high rate at which the UK had entered.

Golders Green, September 1992

The Secretary of State for Social Security and the Chief Secretary to the Treasury were mixing cocktails in North London. There was a party going on in a twee residential street in Hampstead Garden Suburb. It was a meeting of like-minded right wingers and general friends. It was a belated celebration of the election victory, a joint birthday do, a barbecue and a fancy dress event. I was Michael Portillo.

Andrew, my boyfriend, with whom romance had developed as we struggled to get the Dirty Dozen campaign up and running, was Peter Lilley. I had greased my hair into a quiff and perfected a Portillo-like pout. Andrew, fair-haired and neat, was more obviously suited to the Lilley role. We were wearing pin-striped suits, old school ties, Union Jack handkerchiefs and an array of right wing button badges. 'Could you pass the vodka, Secretary of State?' I asked as we were attending to the drinks. 'Oh, but of course, Secretary of State', was the reply, 'and have the Blue Curaçao' — essential for the clear blue water cocktail we were mixing up. We were busy getting into character like this when I felt the first of what would be many demands on my attention throughout the evening. My pager reminded me that I was the duty press officer for the evening. On a normal scandal-free weekend I might have had a couple of calls, and it was highly unlikely that a Saturday evening would be disturbed, but this was not set to be a normal weekend.

With the party carrying on downstairs I had to spend the evening elsewhere on the telephone, papers strewn across the floor, contacts books lying open as I tried to help with enquiry after enquiry on the economy. Strictly speaking it was a matter for the Treasury to deal with, but the wobbling economy had implications for the reputation of the party as well as for the government, hence the calls to me. A couple of days earlier the prime minister had said that leaving the ERM would be a betrayal of Britain's future. The journalistic frenzy that weekend was sparked by the state of the markets and was portent of the betrayal to come. The following Wednesday, the 16th, was a political calamity that should have happened to a Labour government, and indeed would have happened to a Labour government if Thatcher had been deposed by the general public and not by her own colleagues. Labour and the Liberal Democrats had been far more enthusiastic about entering the ERM than the government. Falling out of it on Black or White Wednesday (depending on your view) precipitated an economic recovery, the considerable benefits of which were never able to outweigh the damage done to the Conservatives' reputation for

economic competence. The departure from the ERM also provided more ammunition for Eurosceptics whose passion, some
would say obsession, would drive them on to clash with Major's
pragmatism in the following five years. Sleaze, Europe, weakness
and incompetence: all the ingredients that would add up to a disastrous recipe for us Conservatives.

To that mix there was added another criticism – arrogance,
which added its own special spice. Despite my cheeky impersonation of Michael Portillo at the party, he remained a bit of a hero to
me, someone I hoped would emerge to articulate the next phase
of a radical, but not reactionary, Thatcherism. It would continue
liberalising the economy by breaking down monopolies in the
private as well as the public sector, would inject private sector
expertise into reforming health, education and social security, would
be sceptical about economic and monetary union but would not be
a home for po-faced little Englanders. It would be socially liberal but
economically sound (by then I felt sufficiently tribal to use the word
myself) and would stress the practical advantages of its agenda
rather than moralising or casting judgement. With his obvious
sophistication and his cosmopolitan background, I thought Portillo
was simply more interesting than most politicians and in a way
personified the complex influences that had contributed to my own
set of views. But putting the politics aside he was just plain glamorous.

One Sunday afternoon the remainder of the Conservative
Students held a conference in Church House at which Portillo
(their 'must have' guest) was the main speaker. Again I was the
press officer on duty watching with some amusement the familiar
types who had turned out in their blazers and cords for a bracing
afternoon of right-wing backslapping. The imminent arrival of
their torch-bearer was clearly a cause of some excitement and
when he walked into the room with his air of confident insouciance
he was instantly surrounded by a group of earnest, misty-eyed dis-
ciples, some of whom just stared in wonderment at the man they
had chosen as the saviour of their cause. This is all too cult-like, I
thought to myself. Being a sober, dispassionate observer, there in

my professional capacity to deal with any journalists attending, I found this unfettered adoration a bit distasteful. But then Michael spotted me from across the room and the crowd parted to let him through. 'Hello, Jo-Anne, how have you been?' It was several months since I had met him as a very junior member of the Dirty Dozen team and yet, like a true pro, he had remembered my name. In an instant I was transformed, just as pathetically droolly as the rest of them. I muttered some sort of half-intelligible response, which he smiled at appreciatively, treating my nervous rambling like a rare pearl of wisdom. 'Let me know if there is anything I can do,' he said, 'I'm available for interviews all afternoon and you can always call me at home.'

In my time at CCO Portillo's courtesy on such matters was equalled only by Michael Howard, who despite his then seemingly unfriendly public persona, was easily the most helpful minister and the one I always felt least bothered about contacting at weekends. It was frustrating that the brightest and most articulate of the right wing somehow managed to present themselves to the public as agents of darkness, as arrogant and uncaring. It's a lasting impression that some, and particularly now Howard, have found they have to address if they are ever to win back public acceptance.

Fortunately Andrew was very understanding about having to share my affections with Michael Portillo; in retrospect, I suppose I was lucky to find a sufficiently heterosexual member of the Conservative Research Department whose feelings for me would not be diluted with a similar crush on our shared hero. But our relationship suffered a downturn when, having ventured into the world of political lobbying, he replaced me with a corporate client on the table he had booked for a formal dinner with Margaret Thatcher. Fuming at this slight, I ended up occupying the very end chair on a very long top table and had to crane my neck in order to catch a glimpse of the Lady during her speech. Discomfort aside it was a great privilege to see my number-one heroine speaking in the flesh and I was not disappointed. She was unexpectedly relaxed and funny. In an effort to make up for what became known to us as the

'Thatcher Debacle' Andrew arranged tickets for the next best thing, the Conservative Way Forward annual dinner with Michael Portillo. It was more than adequate recompense. But something was not right about the evening. Our expectations of Portillo were almost certainly too high.

Could he really articulate a vision that was both dynamic and modern without seeming disloyal to a leader that the audience, myself included, might privately doubt but would publicly defend in the way that Tories do? I was sitting with a group of Wandsworth councillors, the driest of free market Conservatives, who didn't need the trappings of traditional sentiment to justify their effective South London regimen, but many of the onlookers were more conventional Tories. For our table the speech was a disappointment. It was adequate but it didn't press the right buttons. Our hero seemed to choose the easier course, adopting a cautious, reassuring tone. I couldn't bring myself to clap when he questioned the wisdom of televising parliament. For me the innovation that opened up the Commons to the scrutiny of us commoners was a great thing, and chimed with that early pioneering spirit of Thatcherism that wanted to open up and democratise institutions. It was just an observation on Portillo's performance yet one that for me, flashed a warning sign.

Later, after I had left Central Office and returned to the media, I often remembered that evening, as Portillo set himself on a curiously self-defeating path, which too often had him sounding as though he was arrogant and narrow-minded. It was the lesson of the downfall of Thatcher that her most loyal followers seemed not to have learned. From accidentally taped comments about foreigners buying their degrees, to the ghastly speech about the SAS, and the unintelligent demonisation of Brussels, Portillo sold short his real instincts and his very great promise.

It was a problem that beset a certain type of clever right winger. Conservatism is sometimes a kind of political 'tough love'; the admission that government can only do so much and often make things worse is a hard message when people are beset by the countless problems of life. It can offer solutions but not necessarily immediate ones. This can make policies hard to sell and is particularly a problem for those on the free market right whose convictions are benign but often sound hard-hearted. How best then to make these difficult-sounding policies seem more attractive? Too often it appeared they were prepared to pander to a cheap sort of populism as a packaging for the tougher ideas. Until John Redwood's emergence as a leadership candidate, the low key, softly spoken minister was seen as a dry intellectual not as a tub-thumping firebrand. Then suddenly, the brain who had headed Thatcher's policy unit was desperately trying to prove his 'touchy feely' credentials by assuring us he would save cottage hospitals. Michael Howard, a talented and nuanced politician who could have offered the intellectual backbone to the Major government, instead distilled his whole agenda into two words, 'prison works'. Up to a point it does of course, but offering soundbite panaceas is not serious politics and particularly disappointing from a serious politician. As leader, Howard must continue to show that he has developed a more engaging and three dimensional personality.

For concerned supporters like me these lapses into cheap sloganeering were disappointing, stoking up ammunition for friends or colleagues who would tease or even scold me about being associated with 'that lot', but more importantly they reflected a deeper malaise, a party that had lost its sense of direction. John Major was only a part of that problem but as leader he was more than just a symptom. He had styled himself the personification of non-conviction politics but he hardly had the charisma to make up for it. His decency, much remarked upon, was attractive in so far as we knew about it, but he just didn't have 'it', the wow factor, to spawn a political philosophy in his own name – Majorism meant little more than inconsistent compromise. This sense of drift worsened throughout the very long five years to 1997, exacerbated by the constant internal wrangling, but the indications of it were obvious in the first months after the election and throughout the eighteen months I remained working for the party.

*

As well as the drama of the ERM crisis in the autumn that followed the General Election, Central Office was also preoccupied with a necessary economy drive. A new chief executive was brought in from business to identify where savings could be made. The press office had slimmed down in the weeks after the election and there were no more real cuts to be made, but we were always looking for ways to economise. On occasions these economies seemed a sad reflection on the state of the Party and emphasised the surprising amateurism that infected the machine.

Our new Director of Communications Tim Collins, now a frontbench spokesman in Howard's team, was an experienced political insider but had not worked in the media. After working on the Major campaign bus during the election he was well known and well liked by journalists, although relatively inexperienced for such a pivotal role. His appointment and our reduced capacity were largely a reflection of where we were in the electoral cycle; also, with the party in government many press enquiries would go straight to the civil service. An opposition party inevitably needs a bigger operation, but the contrast between our set-up and the increasing professionalism and ruthlessness of Labour was too great, suggesting that the Conservatives would later struggle to match Labour's effectiveness. Given the resources we had we did the best job we could and the staff, though few, were dedicated and capable. In opposition, Labour were teaching themselves the importance of being proactive and setting agendas, things always more difficult to do when dealing with the complications of government. But even if these had been part of our remit, the complex structure of the party would have made it difficult to impose that sort of presentational discipline. Individual constituency parties and individual MPs could say what they liked with near impunity. We often had to answer press enquiries about errant candidates or councillors who had taken it upon themselves to set up their own campaign group on something (the self-titled 'Conservative' Family Campaign, embarrassingly reactionary, comes to mind) without any official backing. Having achieved their fifteen minutes of fame with some ludicrous pronouncement on immigration or working mothers they could slip back into obscurity leaving the party's image tarnished.

The structure remained antiquated until reforms were introduced by William Hague. His changes were controversial because they were centralising but at least they clarified the command structure. Back then, with no central membership lists and only a loose conglomeration of independent elements, the party's Central Office was not actually central to anything. When times were good the culture of loyalty that Conservatives claim to value so highly was enough to keep the broad church singing from the same hymn sheet, to use a favoured Tory cliché. But when things were more difficult and loyalties torn, there was no way of imposing discipline other than on MPs; on one occasion John Major chose to withdraw the whip from the Maastricht rebels. Yet this was a rather self-defeating sanction when the party had a small parliamentary majority.

Despite the many problems that beset John Major's leadership his perceived integrity remained a popular attribute. Though I have argued that the party was worryingly unsophisticated in its approach to presentation it is true that Major's refusal to be 'made over' (in itself a kind of 'non' image) did win him plaudits. However much he wanted the public to consider him an ordinary guy he was, at the same time, the prime minister, an extraordinary job that demands extraordinary attention to details of presentation, however irksome that might be.

One evening, just as we were all packing up to go home, Tim tentatively asked whether any one of us might do him a favour. When he expanded on the request, to pick out some shirts from Marks & Spencer, it seemed particularly odd. Tim would admit, I think, to being someone for whom sartorial elegance came a long way down his list of priorities after *Dr Who* and Pepsi Cola. But in fact the shirts were intended for a grander, potentially a starring, role. The next day John Major was due to film a party political broadcast. The shirts were for the prime minister to wear on the broadcast. So the press office secretary said she fancied a bit of late night shopping and would happily pick up a pink shirt for the PM. This was the fabled Central Office machine, renowned worldwide as a sophisticated propaganda operation, in reality cobbling together ideas as it went along, and reduced to pulling together a last-minute wardrobe from the high street for the prime minister. At an earlier meeting a decision had been made that perhaps a departure into pink shirts might add an exotic dash of colour to the broadcast. It might well have done but when the PM was groomed for the cameras he was not wearing pink. A selection had come back from Marks & Spencer but his collar size had been noted down incorrectly.

Before going to work at CCO I expected that, if needed, shirts for the prime minister's broadcasts would arrive automatically from Thomas Pink and Turnbull & Asser in every shade of pink with a variety of collars and cuff styles. But things no longer worked like that, if they ever had. The whole of Labour's front bench appeared to have had a Armani makeover, but we couldn't even manage to buy the PM a new shirt. Somewhere along the line the wheels had come off the Rolls-Royce machine. It seemed to me that this was the world's oldest political party struggling in more ways than one to keep up with changing fashions.

8

BY-ELECTIONS, BISEXUALS AND BIFOCALS

Christchurch, Dorset 1993

Despite earning my spurs as a press officer at the general election
I soon realised that the journey from rookie press officer to seasoned party worker cannot be completed without chalking up a
by-election campaign. As any political journalist, party volunteer
or apparatchik knows, a general election, as I was to find out, is a
mere walk in the park compared with the rigours of a by-election.
The by-election is the real baptism by fire, a sort of boot camp
induction into the fold that tests endurance, commitment and
sanity.

A party press officer sent on a by-election will encounter every
facet of our political culture all at once. The press officer is dispatched
from the party's London HQ for several weeks to live, work and
breathe alongside the enemy, and that's not even the other parties –
the first job is dealing with the enmity of their own local party officers
and grass-roots volunteers. The redoubtable constituency agent

who has weathered countless local storms is likely to resent the implicit suggestion that he or she cannot manage the demands of the campaign without help imposed from London. The candidate, if local, will probably share the agent's suspicions, and if not local, has probably already offended the half of the association that did not vote for him expressly because he was an out-of-towner. The resident press will expect, by virtue of it being their patch, the best scoops and will hang around menacingly with spiral notebooks primed for gossip. They will complain to the BBC when pushed out of the way by frantic cameramen pursuing babies groomed for kisses from the candidate. The Central Office campaign team will put together a battle plan, but it will not match the template developed by the local chairman. The local chairman will want to leaflet each street starting with the odd numbers; the central team will argue that the even numbers should come first.

In rare moments of teamwork nerves will be less frayed and jolly outings for late dinners suggested. The press officer, miles away from the blessed temptations of the capital, will perk up hoping for a bijou local brasserie but will find herself instead with chicken in a basket in ye olde theme pub festooned with unauthentically clean horse brasses that gleam suspiciously like the candidate's teeth. Before she has had the chance to eat this meal, ten minutes before she was planning to go to bed, the pager will have gone off twice, the mobile phone three times and that important lobby correspondent from the *Daily Telegraph* is loitering at the bar with a photographer to do the 'human interest' piece about a day in the life of the campaign. She will wish to tell them to 'F off' but realise she promised this three weeks ago and must now suffer the indignity of being photographed while juggling chips, mobile, contacts book, can of hairspray, lap top and uncharacteristic pint of shandy. 'Everyone say cheese.'

This multilayered challenge will be intensified if the party is in government, even more so if the government is in trouble.

And when my turn for by-election duty came round the government was certainly in trouble. Deep trouble. One year on

from the general election we should not have won I was dispatched to a by-election we could not have won – although it
wasn't in Glasgow or Newcastle or the Rhondda. It was in delightful, middle-class, retired-with-two-cars Dorset. Until spring
1993 the name Christchurch had meant only one thing to most of
the party's high command – an Oxford College. But thereafter for
the rest of us the name became synonymous with the place where
John Major received his second 'bloody nose' in almost as many
months.

The results of the recent Newbury by-election, a record twenty-
eight per cent swing from the Conservatives to the Lib Dems, had
barely been absorbed when I sallied forth to Dorset. In Newbury,
another genteel and small-c conservative town, the recent government decision to levy VAT on domestic fuel had received its first
electoral test. Not surprisingly, it had failed. Privately I thought
that it had deserved to, as VAT on essential items is a pretty
pernicious trick – especially from a prime minister recently elected
in the mantle of a tax-cutter. It went against Conservative first
principles and it reflected the government's own mismanagement
of the economy. But if Newbury was the first test, Christchurch
was to be the ultimate measure of the growing disenchantment.
Here the grey vote rules and since the old are most inclined to feel
the cold it was just about the worst constituency in which to sell
this policy.

According to the town motto, Christchurch is where 'time is
pleasant'. I was glad to be greeted with that thought when I arrived
for the first of what would be many evenings in exile from my natural habitat. True the air was remarkably clean, the town centre
spotless and the grass verges verdant but to live there for several
weeks? It was all fish and chips, K shoes and canasta evenings. No
sushi, Jimmy Choos or salsa dancing. Not that there would be time
for any extra-curricular activities. I knew that the schedule was
going to be hectic. I had been told to expect something like an
obstacle race, so it was with great relief that I was at least able to
clear the first hurdle facing me. The constituency agent was

renowned as a force to be reckoned with. If I did not hit it off with her this south coast sojourn would be even more of an ordeal than it was already promising to be.

The expression 'tough cookie' was invented for Judy Jamieson, the sort of woman who virtually single-handedly makes the case that men are the weaker sex. Even her military husband seemed like a malleable softy compared to magnificent Judy in full flight. I had been warned that she was quite a combative woman, that she might not take kindly to folks from the Big Smoke taking over her territory. But we hit it off right from the start.

Even sitting down behind a desk at the end of long office she looked tall. I approached with caution. She eyed me with a dismissive disregard, firing questions in a tone that suggested she was expecting me to fail her interview for the job I had already been appointed to. 'So what'ya got to say for yourself? Why did they send you? Know anything about this game? What's ya experience.' Given the severity of the test I was not sure I'd pass but when I said I'd had three years at the BBC (omitting to mention that it had been picking pop records) she said, 'Well, I never, someone from Central Office with experience of the media. Did you hear that everyone?' At which point several elderly party workers abandoned their envelope stuffing and came hobbling over, 'Did you hear that, someone from Central Office who's actually had a job in the media!'

So now apparently I was the specialist but even my exaggerated experience was to prove inadequate. This first trip was just an overnight stay to attend the final hustings meeting where the candidate was to be chosen by a vote of constituency members. I would stay to write a press release about the winner and deal with any press enquiries following the meeting. There were three contenders: a local farmer, a woman who had fought a seat during the general election, and a former MP who had lost his Bristol seat the previous year. The latter, Rob Hayward, was by far the best performer on the night. Knowing little more of the candidates than what I had seen that evening I was greatly relieved when he was announced the winner. I knew this election would provoke a great deal of media coverage and I was just pleased that we had a pro on board. At Newbury locals had selected a decent but inexperienced 'chap' who was just not sophisticated enough to deal with the pressure of the coverage. What with the background of VAT on fuel, an apparently callous post-1980s outbreak of pit closures, Norman Lamont admitting to singing 'Je ne regrette rien' in his bath (too much information) and his recent sacking from the cabinet, plus the continuing nightmare to ratify the Maastricht treaty rumbling on in Westminster, this was set to be a by-election that would receive unprecedented national media attention. On top of that the victors of Newbury, the 'coming' Liberal Democrats, were expected to repeat their success again here in a safe Tory seat.

At the end of the evening victorious Rob Hayward bounced over to say hi! We had previously met at CCO where as a psephologist he had been a frequent adviser. He was energetic and positive and had given a really good speech. 'Fancy dinner?' he asked. 'I'm going to take my gorgeous press officer to dinner.' He was just being enthusiastic but I declined in favour of writing my press release and also because it is all too easy for misplaced rumours to spread. On top of everything else the last thing I need, I thought to myself, is any whiff of scandal.

Rob's selection as candidate was early in June. Under less fraught circumstances the writ to announce the date of the election would have been called shortly afterwards, but at Westminster there was nothing but gloom. The timing of the election became an issue in itself with weeks of speculation about which date would provide the best opportunity for the government. Our efforts were deemed a damage limitation exercise before we had even begun to fight the campaign. Not having attended a by-election before I was really apprehensive. I wasn't sure if I was up to the job. It was clear that this little corner of the south coast was about to become the epicentre of the political universe. Japanese tourists may seem ubiquitous in London but when Japanese film crews turn up in Dorset you know you are in the middle of something big.

So I expected we were about to feel the force of a political tsunami, and although I was preparing myself for all sorts of problems I wasn't quite prepared for it to hit in quite the way it did. One of the Central Office campaign chiefs, a veteran of many such campaigns, took great pleasure in showing me to my new quarters. Knowing my penchant for all things metropolitan he positively relished introducing me to the King's Arms Hotel, which greeted me with an ominous toby jug sign of welcome and a room in the attic that would come to feel like a garret oasis from the mania about to unfold. Looking on the bright side, paisley carpets, saggy beds and flock wallpaper can all fade into inconsequence as long as one is equipped with a well-stocked hospitality tray. My mini kettle and leaky teapot were to see a great deal of action – with the 5 a.m. starts during the campaign itself, and the fevered late night conferences with my partner in crime Elaine Coomber, the appointed Central Office research officer. Together we formed a close alliance cemented by a mutual sense of creeping surrealism.

I knew that there is no such thing as a 'normal' by-election. Each has its own set of characters, issues and problems. The indication that even by these standards Christchurch would enter a world of its own came on my second night there. I was already in the saggy bed studying local statistics when the phone call from Andrew came. 'Oh, hi, darling, what's up?' I asked sleepily.

'Hmm. Just something you ought to know. There is a lot of stuff going around about Rob.'

'Well, of course, he's been an MP. He's had a life. He's divorced. But so what – what's the problem?' I asked with some irritation.

'No, seriously Jo-Anne, this is could cause you some problems. A number of people who should know say that a Sunday newspaper has stories about Rob and men and there are photographs.' Andrew's contacts were impeccable, his information usually watertight.

'But that's just ridiculous,' I countered without thinking. 'He's not gay. Actually he is quite flirtatious,' I said, clutching at straws. 'He's been married, for God's sake.' I heard the vacuity of my argument as I uttered it.

It seemed I was the last person in Westminster to have heard these rumours and normally I would have been one of the last to care, but it was naive to assume I could ignore this news. I lay in bed wondering what best to do. First of all if he was gay it was none of my business and shouldn't have been anyone else's, but if there was more to it than that, if there were some sort of scandal looming it would be a problem that I couldn't ignore. This was a by-election, the genre of British political engagement for which the term 'dirty tricks campaign' was invented. If there was an issue to be made of them I was sure that the candidates' sexual predilections would surface. This could put us at a disadvantage in such a constituency, which shared little of neighbouring Bournemouth's cosmopolitanism, especially given our competing candidates. The Liberals had selected a prematurely white-haired woman, who though much younger than the average Christchurch constituent nevertheless spookily resembled them. Labour was fielding a disarmingly posh young barrister who was the stuff of fantasy for those voters hoping he might one day choose a delightful constituency wife from their own stable of eligible granddaughters. In such circumstances I could not see that the time was right for the Tories to radicalise their image, much though I would have liked it. In Christchurch an 'outing' was a trip to a seafood stall on Bournemouth beach, not a by-word for a sexual revelation.

It was only ten years ago but then, despite a palpable gay presence at CCO and throughout Conservative circles at Westminster, Tories did not come out. That clearly irritated some campaigners and could be seen as hypocritical, but no one should have to wear their sexuality on their sleeve. So I concluded as I debated the issues with myself in the middle of the night. After all this was part of what we believed in, a fundamental principle, that we should be judged for what we think and do, not identified and assessed just by skin colour, religion, sexuality or gender. Sexuality may be one influence on a person but not the defining one, predetermining his judgement as he walks through the voting lobbies. But equally I could see that the shrill tone of party moralisers had left the Tories looking prejudiced and way out of step with liberal opinion. I sat up in bed as though to pull my thoughts out of the realm of philosophy and concentrate on the matter in hand: I might have a gay candidate. Was it up to me to find out? If he was, was it a problem? Not necessarily, but I wanted a line to take and I wanted a press strategy in case we were going to be held to ransom by a Sunday newspaper. Thankfully it was not up to me to make a final decision so eventually I slept on it.

In the morning I realised that it was best we knew about this and were prepared but that it was not necessarily a problem. I decided that the fewer people who discussed this around the office the better and it should be considered totally irrelevant unless it somehow became an issue. The second decision was not to tell anyone else on site lest I add to a rumour that may still be baseless. Instead I phoned the appropriate director at Central Office, told him what I had heard and left any further investigation and decision-making to him.

At the time I thought that I had made the right decison but I did find it hard to put the issue to the back of my mind even though the news from Westminster was so grim that it should have been enough to absorb me completely. Day after day we waited to be given the date of the election and the chance to start campaigning properly. Elaine and I pondered how we could put the best spin on the brickbats coming our way during this phoney war. The replacement of Norman 'Singing' Lamont with Ken 'Streetfighter' Clarke had provoked Lamont's spectacularly bitchy retort in the House of Commons ('In office but not in power') as well as comparisons with Geoffrey Howe's fatal blow to Margaret Thatcher. On top of that it aroused speculation about the possibility of tax rises, tax rises we had 'not expected' to have had to consider. Another economic solution might have been interest rate cuts – exactly the sort of thing which would send our mild-mannered Christchurch Tory octogenarians, dependent on their savings, screaming into the arms of the Liberal Democrats.

Locally, rail privatisation, or the possibility of it, was also a rich seam for exploitation by our opposite numbers. The late Tory MP Robert Adley whose death had caused the by-election had been a vehement opponent of any sort of rail privatisation and had saddled us with the unhelpful phrase 'a poll tax on wheels'. For me, being the sort of Conservative who would privatise anything, I found the constant repetition of his sentimental evocation of some sort of golden age of railways deeply irritating, but I could see my personal dislike of compromise was hardly the line to use when news broke that the rail service from Christchurch to London was being cut back. What else, I wondered, what else would they throw at us?

Despite the very real political hurdles facing us I remained concerned that the rumours Andrew had relayed to me might be true and that our frantic concerns about policy would not matter at all when the Sunday Scum revealed the lurid details. In my imagination these were becoming ever more vivid as I responded to the other stresses of the situation and to the bits of gossip and innuendo that were beginning to circulate among the assembling media, despite my best efforts. And I was far from reassured by the lack of contact from CCO. There had been no follow up to my call. Perhaps they had investigated and found nothing of concern, perhaps they had done nothing at all? Whatever they had decided I was certainly in the dark about it all.

Although June was proving a frustrating month with some press reports suggesting the election would be delayed until the autumn, at least the campaign team was shaping up. At the heart of it there was Judy and her association officers, including the regulation former colonel and a collection of elderly women each with enough 'backbone' to serve a brontosaurus. There were a lot of chiefs. From Central Office there was me, Elaine and several campaigning staff of various levels of experience. From the regional headquarters (since rendered defunct by Hague's review) came another layer of professional expertise in the shape of one of the party's longest serving agents, a bearded giant of a man who arrived intermittently to make a few pronouncements with biblical flourish. From a neighbouring constituency the experienced MP John Butterfill (now Sir) had been coaxed into becoming the candidate's minder. It was his role to stick closely to the candidate and coach him in the ways of handling an election. Rob was himself an old pro, but prone to becoming overexcited so it was best that he had a minder. John struck me as an old-style Tory MP who would impart the same sort of wisdom as a man of the cloth undertaking pastoral responsibilities, although I wasn't totally convinced that he had the killer instinct this campaign might yet require. But by way of back-up we also had a tame local newspaper reporter on side to travel with Rob and fill him in on the arcane parochial details.

Paranoid as I was about the possibility of rumours and leaks I kept my counsel about the suggestion of any scandal. Despite the wealth of experience around me I was not convinced that any of my colleagues would know how to advise me. Oddly perhaps I did not broach the issue with Rob himself, as I did not want to risk undermining a necessarily close working relationship on the back of as yet uncorroborated rumour. I assumed that I had done the right thing in referring the matter to the highest level, away from the hothouse of Christchurch, but having heard nothing back I was uneasy. A nagging concern continued, heightened by my observations of the Conservative machine over the previous year. If it had been the ruthless operation celebrated in the popular imagination of political thriller writers, Central Office may have used the delay between Rob's selection and the start of the formal campaign to conveniently 'eradicate' him. I imagined a bare room, a light bulb flashing on and off, John Major's voice broadcast on a continual loop, some sort of sensory deprivation (had my hotel room got to me?) and a political plank he would be forced to walk. But assuming that there was a scandal and this may have been necessary (I did not know if it was or not) I had seen no evidence that our HQ contained anyone approximating to the sort of Blofeld evil genius required for such a bloodless operation. There was no Tory Peter Mandelson. No Alastair Campbell.

It was, of course, ridiculously naive of me to think a rumour known to the Press Gallery, which had reached me in the manner it had, would remain contained in Westminster. To me, with all my precious metropolitan pretensions, Christchurch did seem like another world but it was not the sealed-off bubble I assumed anywhere this far from Parliament Square must be. As long as the Westminster media boys were up and down the M3 in quest of their 800-word pre-election scene setters, rumours would surface. It soon became obvious from the inappropriate giggles in the office to the misplaced double entendres among more senior staff that I was not the only person who had heard of the possible exotic entanglements of our candidate.

On a rare weekend off in mid-June Elaine and I returned to London, falling on the bright lights of the city like excited day-trippers. We had forty-eight hours to fill up on good coffee, carbon monoxide and the sight of people below retirement age. But there was some work to be done as well, so we went off to a meeting at Rob's south London home. Away from the claustrophobia of the campaign I reassured myself that I had just been worrying too much. After all, throughout the general election campaign there had been threats of exposés involving cabinet members and they had come to nothing. Indeed the Prime Minister was still involved in legal action over rumours about an illicit relationship with his cook and the government was trundling on regardless so I should stop panicking. Arriving *chez* Rob at the same time Elaine and I sensed each other's unease at being introduced to the flatmate. Oiled for the sun in Calvin Klein jockeys, his gleaming chest reflected the flickering summer sunlight and our mixture of embarrassment and envy at this Hockneyesque spectacle. Having a beautiful, semi-clad flatmate is, of course, no proof of any misdemeanour, real or imagined, but under the circumstances this encounter was eyebrow raising. By the time I returned to Christchurch my worries were rekindled.

What I suspected was that any issue involving sex would befuddle the campaign. Conservatives did have sex of course, witness David Mellor and Cecil Parkinson, but with an awkward, English, cricket-playing sensibility. Even Maggie at her most powerful had not quite known how to castigate her errant colleagues. She was tough enough to lead a nation into war but on matters sexual clearly thought that the less said the better. Although a radical she had in many ways cut a censorious figure whose dominance of the party from the mid 1970s had, I think, only served to prolong its isolation from the increasingly relaxed sexual mores of post-1960s Britain. The epicentre of this isolation was Central Office, which was populated with middle-aged men who seemed so uncomfortable when dressed — in their badly fitting suits and polyester shirts — that I doubted they could ever feel comfortable undressed. The adolescents seemed elderly and the elderly adolescent. And even a decade ago when I worked there the prevailing culture remained desperately unworldly. It might not have mattered if we were a firm of accountants, but politics is a people business and I feared a lot of our people were remnants of a bygone age. It was hardly surprising that so many Tory MPs, themselves drawn from a similar pool of talent, married their first girlfriends and only discovered sex in their late forties by which time power had given them pulling power quite out of proportion to their innate attractiveness or indeed their own earlier expectations.

Ironically, the constituency of Christchurch did offer some sort of precedent if the party had been looking for a seat in which to demonstrate a more sophisticated approach to sexuality, particularly to champion a gay candidate and challenge presumed prejudices head on. Nigel Nicolson, a previous Tory MP, was the product of a marriage between Vita Sackville-West and Harold Nicolson, a couple that famously flouted convention and challenged the prevailing morality. In the 1950s Nigel Nicolson stood down from the Conservative Party over the continued criminalisation of homosexuality. By 1993 that legislation was long since repealed but some of the prejudices and sentiments it encapsulated were proving disappointingly enduring.

Even though the rumour mill had started no formal mention of our 'issue' was made. The campaign office was soon a hotbed of gossip. Imagination was running far ahead of the likely reality. Friends of Rob would phone and leave perfectly innocent personal messages which, having gone through a process of Chinese whispers, were transmogrified into requests for salacious assignations. Each trip to Bournemouth for a fish supper was turned into a likely orgiastic feast at one of the south coast's premier gay nightspots. A pretty youth arrived to work on the campaign but left within days sparking more suspicious rumours. Even I began to resent Rob's cultivated moustache in case it invited unhelpful comments. Among the office staff there was fevered talk of bus drivers, firemen, tree surgeons calling by for Rob. Damn, I thought, we are about to go into battle for the future of this Tory seat with the flaming Village People!

One evening in the car park at the King's Arms I finally had the chance to open the subject with the most senior official on site. I found that it was not news to him either. He too had heard of the alleged photographs and the possibility of some sort of scandal. I was angry that having requested a meeting for days he could not have found any other time to have had, what I had indicated to him would be, a conversation of some importance. It was hardly the appropriate time or place to be discussing tactics, or for me to be dealing with his embarrassment.

'What do you think they do?' he asked like some sort of pubescent ingénue.

'I don't give a damn what "they" do. What are we going to do? We've got the massed ranks of the world's press camped here. They've come to see the spectacle of another Tory disaster. The economy is collapsing, the party is revolting, and we don't know if we should be backing our candidate to the hilt or advising him to get a lawyer. What if he has to step down after the first Sunday of the campaign?! Is anybody doing anything about any of this?' I asked in a series of angry whispers, unable to raise my voice to reflect my growing irritation in case the rustling bushes hid furtive members of the fourth estate.

Continued attempts to be discreet were by that stage fairly pointless. The routine jobs of leaflet production, telephone canvassing, envelope stuffing and poster preparation etc. went on amid a slightly hysterical atmosphere of guffawing and innuendo. Poor Rob, if he ever felt any resentment or diminished enthusiasm, he certainly did not show it. His Tiggerish energy was boundless, his hunger to start this doomed campaign a positive boost to the rest of us, his humour always positive. If anything I rather felt he was getting a bit of a kick out of the whole thing, rather enjoying the 'Carry On' frisson of suggestiveness that now seemed to permeate the whole event.

But it wasn't all fun, fun, fun. The beginning of the campaign, when it did eventually, come, was bad. It ill-behoved us all, a professional organisation that had had plenty of time to sort these things out (and I blamed myself as much as anyone else for having failed to discuss matters with Rob directly), that on the first day of the July campaign the lead players were holed up in legal meetings. A press conference had launched us off in the morning, promising scribblers and camera crews that they could join us in an afternoon of canvassing. Then, thankfully, there was rain. Rain which disguised the fact the Conservative Party was staying in for the afternoon. There was a meeting with lawyers. Issues which really ought to have been private were discussed but even then without clearing up the main contention. Was there a scandal looming or not? I still did not know. It was an undignified event which left me with more information than was ethically deniable, but still no clear line. There was still nothing to say the alleged newspaper story was true but equally nothing had been said to rule it out completely. I felt that it was as I had feared. The mere mention of sex had inspired some sort of sclerosis among my colleagues, certainly the male ones. Or perhaps the problems at Westminster had just rendered our problems too far down their list of priorities.

By then things were being discussed by lawyers but no one had taken a political decision, or at least had told me, as the person to whom the press would first turn, whether we needed a political decision.

My last chance for an authoritative steer came with the arrival of the party chairman who was among the many senior figures scheduled to join us on the campaign trail. I had the perfect opportunity to discuss tactics with him alone when I managed to engineer a joint car trip between two of the villages of this large rural constituency. I wasn't sure what I was going to tell him or indeed what I wanted him to say, but I felt he should at least be aware of what we might be facing. Sir Norman Fowler had been party chairman since the departure of Chris Patten to Hong Kong. He was pleasant and approachable, but was not the first man I'd want to talk to about sex. When it finally came to the conversation I was inhibited. First by the presence of the driver which meant the meeting was not as private as I would have liked. Second by the reality of Norman Fowler. After all, this was the man who, notoriously, while devising the AIDS campaign as health minister in the 1980s had had to ask his civil servants for an explanation of oral sex. Sitting in the back seat of the chauffeured Rover, while going up dale and down dale through the Dorset countryside I was finding it hard to find the right words for this conversation.

'You may be aware we have a possible "issue" here, Chairman. An issue that might blow up in our faces.'

'Oh yes,' he nodded sagely, 'there are issues, of course there are.'

'And everyone at Central Office knows about them and is prepared?'

'Quite prepared. No need to worry.'

To this day I've no idea if he knew what I was talking about but I wasn't prepared to be any more explicit in front of the driver and it was the last chance I had to raise the issue.

I thought I had done as much as I could and possible sex scandals apart there was quite enough 'real' politics to be worried about.

Fortunately it was the candidate's living-room skills rather than his bedroom skills that took precedence in our daily programme. Rob thrived on the fireside chat approach to politics, genuinely comfortable on a doorstep and even more so in the front rooms of inquisitive voters. A new style of campaigning evolved which we called 'at homes'. Here a local party member would host a coffee morning or an afternoon tea, invite around the neighbours and Rob would pop by to chat about anything on their minds. It was a diet of law and order, pension concerns, VAT complaints and patriotic sentiment served up with hob-nobs on doilies and vases of dried ferns.

I loved these events. They were all open to the press and the cameras. Rob was good at them. The people, although supportive, asked some genuinely tough questions. The media liked the unusual informality of them. And the best thing was that I could just sit there for an hour and half, a blessed relief two weeks into the campaign which began at five each day when Elaine and I started the preparation for the daily press conference. Here in the comfortable, double glazed bungalows of middle England I could munch my way through a surfeit of Jaffa Cakes and Mini Rolls while convincing myself I was playing a vital role in the dizzy dance of democracy. It was so completely preferable to all those afternoons on the campaign trail, going to door to door with camera crews, running along in high heels while trying to look out for unforeseen photo disasters like streets full of Liberal posters, dogs set to piss on the candidate, bird baths likely to be knocked down by over-enthusiastic canvassers, embarrassing street names and argumentative members of the public. No, the 'at homes' were a brilliant development, although here, in the front rooms of Dorset, with family photos on display, everyone was very polite. We were sheltered from the reality. We heard too little of the seething discontent that was putting such a smile on the face of the Liberal Democrats. God I hated those Liberals. They were everywhere in Christchurch, infecting this decent town with which I was coming to have some sort of affinity, with their plaits and sandals.

Wherever we went there they were. The Jehovah's Witnesses of politics. I imagined them with tambourines poised to sing 'Kum ba ya'. It was the campaign mania. I was pretty pissed off with VAT on fuel myself but, by God, this was a Conservative seat and we weren't going to go down without a fight.

When preparing for a fight the Conservative Party could always unleash its most terrifying weapon. Although since decommissioned, prior to perjury charges and consequent fall from grace, it was still the age of the Archer-mobile. In what many may now consider a golden age of campaigning a by-election was only really deemed to have started when Jeffrey Archer came to town, the Conservative Party's pied piper. In the first ten days of the campaign we had had to deal with the sudden move up the political agenda of the future of pension provision, and the news that ministers were considering cutting the number of free prescriptions: both heavy issues demanding long-term consideration, but did they have to start considering them while some of us were fighting an election in a constituency where pensions and prescriptions were the highest priority? Then came the Commons vote on VAT on fuel. It passed, narrowly. We were prepared for the possibility that it might not. The increasing vulnerability of the government was being exposed at all turns. But hell, we had millionaire bestselling novelist Jeffrey Archer. How bad could things be?

When I was spotted in the back of the Archer-mobile crumpled across the minder, John Butterfill, I was tempted to think things could not get much worse. It was a curious juxtaposition: the glamorous writer and peer and the *Only Fools and Horses* loudspeaker van in which he delivered his own particular contribution to the Christchurch experience. It was my first meeting with Archer. To me he seemed nuts, but by then we all did. If nutty, he was at least determined to get some sort of show on the road and I admired him for that. We had a day to tour the constituency. Me, Rob, John, and Jeffrey driving. 'Jeffrey Archer, this is Jeffrey Archer with your Conservative candidate Robert Hayward.' It was a practised script chanted with a sort of arresting yet mesmerising rhythm. 'This is Jeffrey Archer saying vote Conservative, vote Conservative.'

Twenty years previously I had stood transfixed in Putney High Street when the election battle bus had come to town. Now I was part of the show. But I was so tired that the hypnotic quality of Archer's relentless mantra caused me to nod off in the back of the van. The next thing I knew we had come to a stop and there I was with my head in the lap of the candidate's minder, the official sleaze buster of the campaign. Thank God no one can see me, I thought as I came to my senses and then there was a rap on the window and the smiling face of *Newsnight*'s Michael Crick beamed down at me, cameraman in the background.

Crick, whose more recent investigation of Iain Duncan Smith proves him a consistent scourge of the political class, is also a seasoned by-election follower and a professional Archer chaser (later he wrote Archer's revealing biography). Although generally an admirer of his work, his was not the first face I wanted to see at that moment. Thankfully it was all obviously innocent, though I could have done without that introduction. With Archer leading the way we were off into the land of carefully tended cul-de-sacs for another street canvass. Curiously, although he had discarded the loudspeaker, his delivery was just as commanding without it. I pitied all these poor pensioners whose lawns we were trampling over for that perfect photo opportunity. To be disturbed in one's own home and answer the door to Jeffrey Archer and a film crew, along with assembled party hangers-on must be unnerving, but amazingly people were very rarely rude. Archer was wearing an enormous blue rosette made even heavier by the layers of stickers, the latest of which bore the name Hayward. The thick pile underneath was testament to the number of by-elections he had graced and also to the number we had lost since William Hague had managed to keep Richmond for the Tories in 1989.

Archer and Crick circled each other with mutual suspicion and yet seemed at the same time curiously drawn to each other, the puppet and the puppet-master, though it wasn't always easy to tell who was pulling the strings. Archer clearly loved his celebrity. Without it, one imagined, he would be nothing, but he also managed to affect a mock disdain at the interest of the camera crew. He did have a certain seductive quality, determined and wily for sure, but my meeting with him did not convince me he was anything much more than the jester who had managed to convince far cleverer men and women than he that he deserved a place at court. The ultimate political player gained the misplaced confidence of people who were supposed to be intelligent enough to run the country. But as some of New Labour's scandals have again proved, politicians can be seduced surprisingly easily. For many, now including the once-professed 'whiter than white' New Labour establishment, it seems that the allure of a rich man is greater even than that of a cheap woman. If the story of the decline of the Tory Party is largely one of human frailties and misjudgements, as I believe it is, the plot line involving Archer is particularly revealing – not so much for what it says about him but for what it says about the judgement of others.

That afternoon, after another hectic schedule and the camera crew safely dispatched, I returned to the town centre HQ for the evening ritual of press release preparation, interview planning, journalist briefing and press conference organising. The day's festivities had distracted me from the wider political picture, but with Ken Clarke due in for a day's campaigning I needed to get up to speed. Various ministers were arriving regularly to sweep the shopping centres in 'walkabouts' with Rob. I had read the write-ups in newspapers where reporters seemed to have been attending different events. Most described the festering anger of the betrayed elderly middle class, but in truth, they were simply too well behaved to let it out. This was not a tomato throwing constituency. Clearly when cornered by journalists the people of Christchurch admitted to their disappointment, even gave full vent to their irritations, but it was not in their nature to harangue the candidate. So we were having a very strange election, constantly being told how bad it was by everyone except those who would have the final say.

And for me, with the possibility of a potential exposé still hanging around, although some Sundays had come and gone without event, it was certainly a surreal election.

Dragging my feet up the stairs to the large office we had taken over above a community hall, I sensed something was wrong. An angry looking stranger had brushed me on his way down the staircase but on reaching the office all seemed calm. Rob had taken a different route and had arrived before me. He was sitting chatting to Judy and John. There were various helpers poring over maps and making instant coffee. The large sash window at the far end of the room was open and bits of newspaper and crisp bags were circling in eddies of air as though recently disturbed. Judy's husband smiled at me with a grin he could barely conceal. 'What's going on?' I demanded petulantly. 'What are you guys not telling me?'

'There's been an incident. You've just missed it.'

'What sort of incident?'

Evidently my concerns about exotic sexual scandals were a worry too far. Apparently we had a common or garden one right here in the heart of the campaign. Moments earlier the furious husband of a woman, with whom one of the local (also married) Tories was having an affair, had turned up in the mood for a fight.

'Oh my God, what happened?' I asked, knowing that despite their lack of celebrity it was enough to make the papers in the current climate.

'He went that way,' said Judy referring to the avenging husband and pointing toward the middle of the room, 'and he' — referring to our colleague — 'went that way,' she said, pointing at the open window.

We were two floors up.

The local Tory, who was reasonably well known in the area, had decided not to take on his furious opposite number and had in a moment of madness leapt from the open window, landing in the sacks of rubbish below. I gather he was unharmed.

Perhaps it was very funny, but I was not amused.

This is a farce, a bloody farce, I thought to myself but for a moment said nothing, then after a deliberately dramatic pause during which I ruminated on my own enforced celibacy (if I was going without for the sake of the party why wasn't anyone else?) I left no one in any doubt of my irritation.

'What the hell is the matter with all you bloody men!' I demanded. 'Can't any of you keep your trousers on? From now on keep your pants zipped, keep your mouths zipped as we are all heading for the great political rubbish dump and I would rather we did it with a bit of fucking dignity.'

Perhaps my outburst acted as some sort of emotional enema because after that the gossiping and the speculative rumours seemed to die down as the 'real' politics of the increasingly narrow votes in the Commons became the ever-pressing concern. The impending vote on Maastricht was a sort of global disaster hovering over us ominously, but on the way there were countless other diversions. What would strike the right note with our electorate here in Christchurch? Certainly not the noises off from Westminster about health, pensions and VAT, but a dollop of law and order, a soupçon of Euroscepticism, a smattering of traditionalism, were all thrown into the mix to entice our core voters not to join the exodus to the soft-focus Liberal Democrats.

Unfortunately, by-elections are not forums for the most sophisticated political discourse. The hyped-up scourge of New Age travellers, the disciplinarian promise of a new variety of truncheon, the danger of computer-generated pornography, even the fake claims to local status of our opposing candidates were all straws we clutched at with increasing desperation. You name it, we tried it, even succumbing to the all time low of playing the death penalty card. When Rob let it be known that he had voted for the return of the death penalty (something I oppose vehemently) I was pretty keen to start a distracting sex scandal myself. Ministers came and went, journalists came and went, polls got worse and worse. The people of Christchurch grew used to their town centre soap opera, a setting for camera crews and parading ministers with faces they vaguely recognised but were too polite to acknowledge. Disruption was occasionally a problem but only really upset the traffic the day the wheelchair protesters came to town.

Rob, as I found out, did have a past. Not the seedy one as alleged but there was a political skeleton in his cupboard. As a former MP his voting record was public knowledge and in one case that came back to haunt us, a political liability. His role in talking out a private members' bill that proposed extending legal rights for the disabled had been noted. A visit by Michael Howard, as Home Secretary, was to prove the ideal high profile opportunity for a radical group of protesters to disrupt proceedings in the full glare of the assembled media. It really did not look good to see the candidate jeered and hustled by the fifty or so wheelchair-using protesters, and given the demography of Christchurch it was momentarily difficult to tell who were the protesters and who were just the normal residents out and about shopping. Did the protest make any difference to our chances here in Christchurch? I doubt it, although for some looking to have their prejudices rein-forced the sight of the Tory candidate tackled by disabled people added convenient proof of our nastiness. In reality the bill which Rob had talked out had been quickly replaced with government legislation that went far further than any previously in providing statutory rights to the disabled. If anything the visit from the Direct Action Network rather distracted attention from yet another con-stituency the government was managing to upset. Michael Howard had come to push a few buttons on law and order but found him-self up against criticism for the recently published Sheehy Report into reforming the police. The middle class, the elderly, and now the police as well were beginning to hate us. Perhaps the promised classless society was one in which all classes were united in their rejection of the Conservatives?

As we entered the final days of the campaign the scene was certainly set for our very public humiliation. But surviving the vote in Christchurch was a mere trifle compared with the possibility that the government may not survive a vote in the House of Commons. Throughout the two months I had spent in Christchurch it had been obvious that staunch Euroscepticism informed the opinions of those activists still prepared to call themselves Conservatives. It was equally obvious, however, that Europe was not the first concern raised, certainly by 'normal' voters and even by the activists themselves. They understood the difference between having an opinion and having a priority. The generation that had lived through the last war necessarily cared deeply about defending British sovereignty, but more pressing on their lists of daily concerns were the health service and the economy. It was a distinction the Conservative Party would only come to understand once it had chalked up defeats far greater than the one they faced here, and ironically once it had adopted its most explicitly Eurosceptical leader.

In 1993 Iain Duncan Smith was one of the backbench rebels whose antipathy to the European project would constantly chip away at the consensus John Major tried so determinedly to maintain. Despite the havoc they were causing I had more than a grudging admiration for people who were prepared to put principle before party, but most of the awkward squad did not come across as principled so much as vainglorious and in some cases plain potty. The legitimate campaign against a single currency was to become deeply tarnished by their unremitting ghastliness, as indeed was the whole Conservative cause. Even before these party wars were to reach their mid-term nadir the spectacle of the government fighting for its life during the final days of our campaign in Christchurch was not a reassuring one for our Dorset voters, regardless of whether they felt strongly about Europe or not. It was hardly reassuring either for those of us holed up in the Tory campaign HQ. On 22 July the government lost a key vote by eight votes. It was possible that we were facing not just a by-election within days but perhaps another General Election?

Elaine and I were frantically trying to devise lines to take for the next day's morning press conference that would inevitably turn into another grilling on the whole of the government's record. We

had some news to announce – the name of our guest for the final
campaign rally. I felt that in its choice of 'big draw' speaker for the
Christchurch grand finale CCO may have been trying to tell us
something about the likely fate of the party and the government.
As if things were not bad enough we were to be saddled with Ted
Heath on the same night that the Liberal Democrats were to welcome their virile, action man leader, Paddy Ashdown, to entertain
his happy-clappy troops. 'A former prime minister!' I was told by
the speakers department as though to taunt me with the prospect
of something really quite exciting. For a fleeting moment I had
imagined a visit from Lady T but given that she had already started
to vote against the government in the Lords it was hardly likely.
Ted Heath, Ted Heath? Ted bloody Heath? Faced with that prospect
I would have welcomed back Jeffrey Archer with open arms. I
wondered what the press would make of it. The Libs get real life
war hero, action man, virile Ashdown we get Ted Heath? The symbolism was not great and it was not lost on me – they get
'dynamic', we get 'dinosaur'. They get livewire, we get liver spots.

   In the end the government survived a confidence vote forced by
the Maastricht defeat and I survived Ted Heath – although only
just, as sweeping in to take his place on the podium he closed a
heavy swing door on to my face, perhaps sensing my lack of enthusiasm about his presence. Ted Heath's visit seemed to tell us what
we of course already knew, that we were about to lose and lose big.
There was to be no last-minute rally of the vote as during the general election but we were set to make history, albeit in more
negative terms. The piles of slips mounting up in the Liberal
corner of the count told their own story. By 2.30 a.m. on Friday
29th the result had been announced. Christchurch was the worst
ever result for the Conservatives in a by-election. A Conservative
majority of over 23,000 became a Lib Dem majority of over
16,000. We had known it was coming but having been shielded
from the worst of the canvass returns, fought on in the vain hope
of some positive news. In the end it was hard to see any. In June
John Major had told us the he 'was fit, was here and was staying',

but by the end of July it seemed the 'bastards' were getting him down. When he had let slip that expletive hours before the Christchurch poll he had been describing three of his own cabinet, not the Liberal Democrats.

Unlike Newbury two months previously which remains a Liberal Democrat seat, Christchurch did prove to be a protest vote. And what a protest it was; in 1997 the seat returned to the party fold just as the rest of the country was registering its withering opinion of the Conservatives. In that first year of the re-elected Major government preceding the Christchurch vote all the elements that contributed to the 1997 defeat had already revealed themselves: the factionalism, the sleaze (real as in 'Arms to Iraq' or exaggerated), the economic mismanagement that improved but was never forgotten. And behind the scenes, too, there were signs of the creaking machine and a culture that had grown rarefied, distanced by years in power from the liberalising trends in attitudes that were the natural corollary of its own structural reforms during the 1980s. The party that had swept changes through industry, the city and trades unions, was planning on doing the same to public services, had failed to apply this stringency on itself. With results like Christchurch there came also an increasing association of the Conservatives with failure, a phenomenon that was to run and run throughout the following four years and beyond just as the professionalised, modernised, un-ideologised Labour party was capturing the Zeitgeist. A generation of political wannabes and talented apparatchiks who might have hitched their horse to the Tory Party a decade earlier could see no future in it and having found a welcome in New Labour they still swell its ranks today.

I doubt very much that Christchurch, Tories or otherwise, could have weathered an openly gay candidate in 1993. As long as that prejudice keeps candidates in the closet it is something that the party, all parties, should devise selection rules to overcome but to force disclosure where individuals would prefer discretion hardly seems like much of a step forward. It's good to note that openly gay candidates are now being selected as the party chooses its slate for the next general election. In the end all the rumours and the fretting about potential scandals did not come to anything. I never found out if there was any truth to them, or if it had just been an outbreak of homophobia. Rob's personal life never became the issue – it didn't need to, as in the end the far bigger story was the collapse of Conservative middle England.

Some time later Rob came out and now referees for Britain's only all-gay rugby team.

Judy Jamieson went on to represent the National Association of Conservative Agents and to see Christchurch turn blue again in 1997 with Chris Chope as MP.

I returned to Central Office, where within days of the party's biggest ever by-election defeat I was overheard discussing my experiences at Christchurch.

'I didn't know you were at Oxford. What did you read?' interjected a senior party director.

Something told me it was time to move on.

9

Dying Embers, Fading Members

Autumn 1993

Just as John Major was taking the Tories 'Back to Basics' I was heading back to the BBC, and back into the increasingly attractive arms of the 'liberal elite'. The return from Christchurch had been my cue to leave Central Office and finally to pursue journalism from which I had taken a lengthy detour after leaving York.

In my new role as a political journalist, and particularly at the BBC, it went without saying that I would have to put my personal views to one side. But there was no need to worry that I would find that hard to do. The Conservative Party went out of its way to help me acquire the required objectivity. Wrapping myself in the mantle of cool professional distance or even adding to it a Paxmanesque raised eyebrow about the governing party was made so much easier after 1993 by its apparent desire to irritate everyone. Even for the few of us who might have felt inclined to accentuate the positive it was impossible to eliminate the negative news about the Conservatives – there was just so much of it.

Back to Basics began as a perfectly reasonable attempt to move education to the top of the political agenda but with a catchphrase wide open to other people's projections. And with an increasingly ill-fated and overly libidinous administration it was hardly surprising that it appeared at times as though the government's real priority was back to bonking. The ill-fated and, in its own words, backward looking initiative came during the same conference season that saw Labour make a tremendous leap forward with the totemic introduction of One Member One Vote – a giant step for Mandelsonkind.

So instead of the 3 Rs on which John Major had intended to place new stress with Back to Basics we had instead 3 Bs: Bonking, Barking and Bitterness, that characterised the remainder of his government. From David Mellor to Piers Merchant the 'bonking' was a running sore, embarrassing and distracting. The 'barking' (both as in the place and the condition) manifested itself as a byword for the 'Essex tendency', that particularly intense distillation – almost distortion – of Eurosceptical Thatcherism, and also handily describes that special type of madness that often seemed to afflict its proponents. And then, the 'bitterness'. It had been tangible and acrid since the removal of Thatcher, returning to the fore in Norman Lamont's resignation speech, and was set to spit on regularly throughout the following five years. One of its most notable outbursts occurred in summer 1995 when John Major turned thorny in the Number 10 Rose Garden and resigned his leadership of the Conservative Party.

By luck as much as design I turned journalist poacher from party gamekeeper at just the right time, for although a distressing period for a Conservative supporter, it was certainly a time of lush pickings for a political correspondent. Even so, the pettiness of so much of what passed for political news – there were so many 'scandals' that it is hard now to remember them all (Gary Waller – who he?) – must have dismayed many observers. At times it was as though Westminster had become just another branch of the entertainment industry. But in among the gossip there were substantial exposés that had lasting significance: the Pergau Dam deal, the Matrix Churchill affair, the enquiries into Westminster Council's Homes for Votes, and the Cash for Questions scandal. These may have faded now but they created an impression of a corrupt or, at best, lazily complacent regime that has left lasting stains on the Tory image. Archer, Aitken, Hamilton and Lady Shirley Porter rank up there in the party's hall of fame and, with friends like that . . . And then even Mr Major, whose failure to inspire was optimistically overlooked by so many because of his much-trumpeted honesty and integrity, was revealed as a less straightforward man than even his fans had allowed for. The thought of John Major popping out for a quick curry no longer endears him to us in quite the way it used to.

In many ways, the mid-1990s could be seen as a depressing time for anyone interested in domestic politics. Apart from the progress of the peace talks in Northern Ireland, for which Major deserves considerable credit, much of the news from Westminster was as, I have said, petty and tiresome. Where it was serious, as in the scandals listed, there was an accompanying sense that the malaise went beyond that of the Tory Party and that the whole body politic was being undermined. The government's weaknesses did make it particularly easy for the Opposition to claim the moral high ground. Much of the criticism from the press and the opposition parties was valid, but there was also a burgeoning neo-puritanism distorting the extent of the problem and intent on convincing us that our system was corrupt to the point of collapse. Even given the clear vulnerabilities of the government this was an exaggeration. It was nonetheless a potent and effective criticism for opponents to make although the hyperbole has since, of course, returned to haunt Labour who are now unable to match the high standards it then propounded.

So it was, in some ways, a dispiriting time to be involved in covering politics, whether a Tory or not. But this was only half the picture. Beyond the cycle of decay in which the government had become mired, and which made all politics seem moribund, this was also a very dynamic period. The aftershocks of the late 1980s were settling down to reveal how the political landscape might develop in the future. Unfortunately, Margaret Thatcher's own party proved unable to, and still struggles now, to grasp the liberalising implications of her legacy. The opposition, however, showed that it had learned the lessons of recent history; profound and significant changes took place within the Labour Party. A small coterie of reformers who wanted to modernise the party (what they called The Project) were suddenly boosted by the unexpected and sad event that propelled Tony Blair to the leadership.

From my perspective, the transition from old to New Labour was a fascinating paradox; the very real revolution in the Labour Party was a direct result of the Thatcherite 'revolution' that had brought me and a whole generation of 'new right' into politics two decades previously. In that sense Labour's revolution was hardly revolutionary at all, but rather required both an admission of its past failure and an acceptance of the new market-driven status quo. Added to that, there was the obvious irony that while new Labour was grasping the implications of these changes the party that had been responsible for them was unable to divine where they should lead next.

I had begun another phase of my BBC career working on a television programme that followed the political scene of London and the South East. It was an excellent setting from which to observe all the changes and contradictory currents as the region was then the best barometer of national opinion. Bluntly, to savagely misquote Sinatra, 'New Labour, New Labour – if they can make it in the South East, they can make it anywhere.' And making it they increasingly were.

I was with a group of similar TV newcomers sitting in *Newsnight*'s Shepherds Bush studio when the news came through about the death of John Smith. We were trainees just starting out on a crash course on producing live television. Chief among these challenges is to learn to expect the unexpected. So when our instructor first appeared with early information from the wires suggesting that the Labour leader had had a heart-attack, we weren't sure if this was actually true or an imagined crisis which we were to respond to as part of the day's workshop. We were hardly veterans of the Westminster scene and yet there was tangible shock and sorrow, as it became obvious that the news was true and that John Smith would not recover.

Although Smith had not been leader of his party long it was a testament to his natural authority that he seemed very much like Labour's backbone. His shadow budget had hindered Labour's chances of success at the General Election, yet his totemic One Member One Vote at Conference 1993 had paved the way for bigger reforms to come. Even so, without knowing then just how enfeebled the Tories would become over the period of the parliament, I was not convinced that Smith would beat Major at the next election. Even before the news was fully out, we wannabe journos were busy analysing the implications of John Smith's death with all the brutal speed of our more experienced colleagues. There was only really one name that emerged as his obvious, vote-winning, successor.

Tony Blair's brilliant 'tough on crime, tough on the causes of crime' rhetoric convinced me that he would be equally as tough on Labour's failure and the causes of Labour's failure. For while it was very obvious that Labour would have to continue in its transition to being a party at ease with the market, Blair's agenda was perhaps more radical, and would also challenge other deep-seated, negative perceptions of his party. As Shadow Home Secretary he had opposed Michael Howard with skill and, more importantly, a telegenic charisma. His 'crime' soundbite was a short cut to Third Way thinking – intellectually hollow but apparently bold and inventive. It neatly encapsulated Labour's repositioning as pragmatic, sensible and middle class, no longer in hock either to that traditional brand of socialism that disapproved of property ownership, or to those that apparently sympathised with the criminal more than the victim. Yet at the same time he was indicating that Labour would be compassionate and thorough.

Home Affairs was the perfect brief for Blair as it clearly showcased his particular flair for undermining the Conservatives and for outsmarting them on territory they considered their own. Aside from the issue of the European Union, which was always a red flag to the bluest of blue bulls, crime had always offered ministers the chance to push the cheapest buttons at Tory conferences and to bring on a chorus of 'hang 'em and flog 'em', Union Jack-waving hysterics. Throughout the 1980s Tory ministers had become hooked on a crime mantra that was completely at odds with the message of Blair's soundbite. They promised that they were tough on crime, of course, but the causes of crime were reduced to one thing – intrinsic evil. Conservatives refused to admit that circumstances might have some bearing on crime lest they seemed to be branding all those people living in the same circumstances as criminals. Philosophically, it is a completely defensible position, but when it came to the realities of everyday life it didn't seem to ring true. For those of us watching politicians on *Newsnight*, or even interviewing them for similar programmes, it seemed only reasonable to suggest that poverty, for example, was a factor in the crime figures. The high-minded Tory purists were not wrong but neither were they absolutely right; they simply seemed out of touch, preoccupied with arcane details of language and definition rather than addressing the practical problem.

Blair, by contrast, had captured the mood. His signature soundbite was as plain speaking as Howard's 'Prison works' yet it also suggested that Labour had a strategy based on more than just punishment. The impression was given that Labour was intelligently and rationally engaging with the problem while Tories merely played to the basest of gut instincts. This was all part of Labour's repositioning as a party that could appeal both to the acquisitive lower-middle class who had swung to Thatcher in 1979 and to the more established middle class who, losing faith in Tory efficiency, still needed assurance that Labour were fit to govern.

Later, in one of his less-reported speeches, William Hague, when new leader of the Tory Party, conceded this point to Labour. As I sat listening to his 1997 speech delivered in the splendour of one of Westminster's grandest meeting rooms, I was really excited. It looked as though Hague would live up to the hopes of those who had elected him – to modernise his party with the same combination of intelligence and ruthlessness that Blair had his. But unfortunately the pressure of an impending election saw Hague taking his inspiration from Tony Martin rather than Tony Blair and, mistakenly, modernity lost out to reaction.

The election of Tony Blair as Labour leader in 1994 gave the Labour Party the perfect figurehead to finesse its seduction of the capital and home-counties. Tony Blair and Peter Mandelson may have represented northern constituencies but their appearance and demeanour were every inch sophisticated and metropolitan. British politics was about to embrace the importance of image and aesthetics as never before.

The cosmopolitan mile-long strip of restaurants, bars and boutiques that is Islington's Upper Street became the perfect visual metaphor for New Labour. It was youthful, aspirational and style-conscious. It had minimalist cafés serving Tuscan cuisine to wannabe Labour leaders who lived on neighbouring streets in newly gentrified Victorian villas they had bought during the property slump and had filled with political biographies and Swedish furniture. In television, if we wanted to illustrate features about the changing face of the Labour Party, its recent accommodation with free enterprise, its pronounced pro-Europeanism, its informality and its 'femininity', Islington gave us just the right pictures for the job. The once working-class north London borough, home to the Marx Library, had flourished off the back of money made in the nearby City. In place of international communism it now offered international cuisine. To me this seemed to be a victory for the forces of the free market but it was a victory the market's strongest proponents seemed set on handing over to their more contemporary, Paul Smith-wearing interlopers. For while the exuberant images of Upper Street so often seemed like the appropriate wallpaper for documentaries about New Labour, the ongoing Tory story threw up a far less inviting set of images.

The disintegration of the government was slow and torturous. For me and my camera crew there were almost weekly reasons to visit former Tory strongholds for 'vox pops' testing the mood of local associations. Essex was a popular location, both because it was home to the country's bluest rednecks and because most of the MPs tormenting John Major over Europe hailed from Thatcher's favoured county. It was where the story was. Although it was not deliberate I can see that it might be possible to argue that broadcasters were trying to influence opinion. Whereas programmes about Labour offered up colourful panoramas of pavement cafés or stylish interiors, those about the Tories were a melange of blue rinses, bulldogs and fading association offices. We must have done a full round of Conservative clubs and offices over the years of the Major government. We interviewed local party members about their views on the latest errant MP, the Party's leadership and, most often, Europe and the Maastricht treaty.

We would turn up in the early evening at a town centre office or favoured local pub to be greeted by half a dozen of the party's most committed activists, generally maverick and elderly, busily sorting their In Touch leaflets into piles for delivery. It was much the same as when I joined the Party fifteen years previously, albeit with a different set of pensioners, a different set of leaflets, and, more tellingly, the assurance of being the 'natural party of government' having given way to an air of resignation. And even there in Essex, Maggie's bluest belt, I found that enthusiasms were muted, the universal passion among party members seemed not so much to be the fear of an external enemy but a bitter frustration at the fragmentation of the parliamentary party and the apparent drift of the government. These people felt left out and let down.

The common assumption was that the membership of the party

was to the right of Attila the Hun; in reality it was not that simple. Although there were the retired army majors and the second generation small businessmen who had moved north of East London's suburbs because 'Enoch Powell was right', there were also former teachers and nurses who had reservations about Care in the Community and Virginia Bottomley's round of hospital closures. There were people with a social conscience whose Conservatism had always been compassionate.

It was my job to sound out groups like this on the phone and check they had something interesting to say before we jumped in the crew van and headed off for yet another straw poll of Tory opinion. It was not unusual for the most trenchant of views communicated over the telephone to wither later in the presence of a camera and a microphone. I felt this was probably due to deep-seated party loyalty and that, arguably, the original anger reflected a desire for clear leadership.

On one occasion I identified a group of game Essex activists who were willing to let the cameras into one of their weekly meetings. I was told to ask for a Mr Curtayne. 'Unusual name,' I replied, 'how is it spelt?' 'C U R T A I N,' came the reply. On the telephone Mr Curtain had been bold and outspoken, suggesting his colleagues were a band of militant Major critics but by the time we arrived they seemed more concerned with keeping up appearances. I had promised my programme editor a feature that would prove Tory activists were Europhobic and baying for Mr Major's blood. The truth was far less sensational. By instinct this group was definitely unhappy about increasing talk of European political and monetary union. They were sceptical about the whole European project and confused by talk of hard and soft ECUs, and when and whether there should be a referendum. But they were not ranting Europhobes. They seemed bemused by the ongoing rows in the party rather than desperate to take up sides against the prime minister. Their allegiance to local Eurosceptic MPs seemed as much based on an attraction to their certitude as sympathy with their views. And criticisms of the government appeared to stem from disapproval of its apparent indecision. They liked Mr Major, they just wanted him to be tougher, more decisive and they wanted a united line on Europe and the Euro just as on other issues. As the cameras rolled, the videotape recorded a party that if not predictably right wing was certainly very far from being at ease with itself.

The craving for clear leadership is something of a psychological impulse among grass-roots Tories. But if not from John Major, from where could they get it? The 'big beasts' had already largely disqualified themselves from the role of alternative leader by marking out their pro-European credentials. The man who could have been, should have been and latterly would have been party leader suffered from his own crisis of indecision when presented with the challenge to back or sack Major.

Michael Portillo's provocative conference speeches ('Let's stop the rot from Brussels') had played to the latent little-Englanderism that unfortunately hovers around the edges of reasonable Euroscepticism.

I had always considered myself a reasonable Eurosceptic. That is, I was and I remain opposed to Britain joining the Euro and completing the programme of political convergence because it's less democratic, less transparent and less accountable than the system we already have. But I would often cringe at the vulgarisation of this cause. Just as much of the Conservative programme was often painfully misrepresented by its ugliest ambassadors, this was never more so than in the case of Euroscepticism. There is an economic argument against the Euro and an even stronger constitutional one that has nothing at all to do with disliking foreigners, Luddism or an inflated sense of Britain's contemporary role. But unfortunately there were some vocal Tories for whom 'keeping the pound' seemed to be bywords for resuscitating a very narrow and limited sense of Englishness.

Playing to the cheap seats should have been below Michael Portillo, but I suspect through vanity, or possibly insecurity, he found it all too easy to appease his devoted tribe of followers by pushing those buttons marked X for xenophobia. I understand that the most passionate patriots can be those who have chosen their nationality; in common with Michael Portillo, I had a father who had chosen to be British. So apart from being dismayed about the state of modern Conservatism there were reasons why I felt personally let down by his flirtation with nationalism. 'Who dares wins,' he went on to tell the Conservative party conference in 1995, controversially associating himself with the machismo of the nation's most revered army corps even though he had failed to take up Major's dare to challenge for the leadership.

It was yet another story about Tory disharmony in summer 1995 that took me to a back garden in the west London suburb of Ealing. Damian Green was then a relatively new Conservative MP. A former TV reporter and a staple of the wet Tory Reform Group, young and pin-stripe free, he was an 'acceptable face' of the party. Damian would give us BBC types what we wanted. Good soundbites and a firm defence of John Major. It was another week of rows and counter-rows and I was on the road again with my camera crew to record the latest twists in what was really beginning to feel like the very strange death of Conservative England. As it was a lovely June day we had set the interview up in Damian's garden. No old school tie, no family heirlooms, no crusty pictures of Maggie. A sunlight-filled garden strewn with kids' toys was ironically almost the perfect setting for a New Labour interview, but just as we were about to start rolling things came to a dramatic pause. 'Stop, stop, stop,' called the Greens' au pair who ran into the garden looking concerned. 'The prime minister has resigned!'

If anything was set to stop the interview in its tracks that was it. It took a few minutes and some frantic phone calls by both Damian and me to establish exactly what had happened in an equally sunny garden a few miles east in Westminster. For a fleeting moment we both thought that a General Election was imminent, but as it became clear that John Major had resigned as party leader, not as prime minister, it was the much-heralded leadership election that loomed into view. The interview changed direction. Who would stand? What would party members think about this? Was it a courageous move or an irresponsible gesture?

If the stunt had caused consternation in a West London garden how much more it must have caused in the corridors of Whitehall where certain ministers were suddenly forced to consider the immediate implications of their criticisms of Major? For all his swagger and poise, piratical Portillo stopped short of mutiny and resisted the entreaties of his passionate fans. Phone lines were installed in a putative campaign HQ but when Portillo hesitated, 'BTgate' was averted. But there was meat to throw to the Essex bulldogs in the form of Portillo's harder, purer, weirder 'Vulcan' competitor.

John Redwood was gutsy in responding to Major's challenge but courage is not the motif that sticks in the mind about his leadership bid. He has the brains, the ideas and the conviction to offer real intellectual backbone to any administration. But he also has the curiously vacant stare, the apparently condescending tone and the ivory tower demeanour, probably born of shyness, that best predisposed him to a job behind the scenes. If I think Redwood leadership campaign I don't think courage; I recall the party's least attractive collection of odd bods and misfits spouting a curiously uninspiring and inconsistent manifesto. Taken one at a time these MPs could be excused as mavericks, perhaps even be considered valued eccentrics we traditionally love to indulge, but en masse they hardly inspired confidence. Once a true radical, Redwood had 'invented' privatisation while in the Number 10 Policy Unit under Margaret Thatcher. Now as potential leader his big idea was not selling off the Royal Yacht *Britannia*.

As a lifelong Tory, this was up there as a supreme 'They're nothing to do with me, honest, guv' moment. When John Redwood launched his campaign, with David Evans, Nicholas Winterton, Theresa Gorman as the faces of his crack team, it was almost enough to send me running screaming into the seductive arms of New Labour and the polenta palaces of Islington. Initially, Major's manoeuvre secured his leadership but by focusing attention on his most electorally challenged opponents it also served to remind voters of the many reasons they disliked and distrusted the Tories. It was hardly the time, mid-parliament, for a party to have a public debate about its reasons for governing, but actually that is what the rows really stemmed from – what the party should stand for.

There is little doubt that John Redwood, despite his lapse into a populist anti-crime, saving hospitals agenda, was far better able to answer these big philosophical questions than just about anyone else in the party. But he was not the man to sell these ideas to the public – he could barely sell them to those of us who were predisposed to liking them. Michael Portillo on the other hand had been blessed with the natural ability to make the unromantic logic of a lot of Tory thinking sound palatable and sensible but he had been busy squandering that talent during his ill-advised flight into the politics of posturing. Although it was Redwood that had dared to stand he could never have won as he had already savaged his own career the moment he was filmed miming the Welsh national anthem. The left (both inside and outside the Tory Party) did not like him, but they couldn't quite take him seriously enough to demonise him in the way they did Michael Portillo. His was the scalp Old Labour, New Labour and the Tory wets most wanted and they wouldn't have to wait too long to claim it.

The week that followed the rose garden challenge confirmed again that making programmes for the BBC was exciting and fun. For a party that had once prided itself on its discretion and professionalism, the values of the stiff upper lip appeared to give way to confession and the public airing of dirty linen. The well-trodden triangle of grass of Westminster's College Green quickly sprouted cameras, mobile lighting kits and temporary studios to follow the hourly drama of the latest Tory soap opera. The cast of walk-ons just kept walking on – lesser-known back-benchers unable to resist the lure of temporary celebrity. There was a break out of Mad Conservative Disease even before the ghastly spectre of BSE revealed its frightening human consequences and provoked the government's final damaging rows with the EU. For a brief moment these bit-part Tories felt important again. The sun shone, the journalists were in attendance and the Conservatives were the lead news item, not the glamorous new Labour Party. It was a much-needed psychological boost that heightened their dangerous taste for leadership elections.

The Prime Minister's invitation had been a brilliant tactic, one urged by press commentators who advised that he should ward off months of corrosive speculation about a challenge to his leadership. But it was really a wasted opportunity because the circus that descended on College Green told us nothing substantive about the potential of the Conservative Party, only of its personality flaws. Given how unlikely it was that the exercise would safeguard the government at the next election it would at least have been encouraging if we had gleaned the semblance of a programme for the future. Instead, the immediate crisis was averted only to be replaced with a longer, slower retreat from power during which the Conservatives allowed Labour to set up shop as the party of business, of sound finance, of selective education (in selective cases), of law and order, of home owners, of patriots, of the consumer, of women, of the market, of farmers, of devolution and, so they claimed, of the people.

The leadership election had revived my taste for Westminster. For the two years after I left Smith Square I was based at BBC Elstree in Hertfordshire. Along with the programme I made the studios were also home to *Top of the Pops* and *EastEnders*. Bumping into Ricky and Bianca in the canteen was an entertaining distraction, not least because their everyday tale of real folk seemed blissfully impervious to the everyday worries of real real folk. There were no Eurosceptics, house repossessions, infected beefburgers or Blairite campaigners roaming Albert Square, but in my job I wanted to be back in the centre of things, back in Parliament Square. In the autumn I moved to a job at BBC Westminster and said goodbye to my weekly tour of the M25 – leaving behind a region that had been changing political colour before my very eyes. For me nowhere was this colour change from blue to red more significant and more extraordinary than in my own little bit of the South East. By 1997 even Wombles were voting Labour.

The BBC's election night coverage is an awesome operation that calls on an army of staff to make sure that it is all right on the night. Up on the sixth floor of the BBC's Westminster HQ those of us working on the weekly *On the Record* programme were having it relatively easy. We were producing a series of long interviews with the party leaders that would run for the three Sundays of the election campaign. Unlike the usual rush when making filmed items, preparing for these programmes was a forensic but civilised research job. Come the night of the vote most of us were to be recruited as producers to manage the live operation at various vote counts around the country. By chance I was allotted responsibility for the London Borough of Merton, comprising the two seats of Mitcham and Wimbledon. It was my home turf. The thinking was that Mitcham would swing back to Labour after so many years of Tory rule. It was another of those emblematic seats — where Thatcherism had won over a previously Labour electorate, which would mark the nation's change of heart.

But Mitcham had long been a marginal seat and by 1997 its significance as a national indicator would have been most marked had the Conservatives managed to hang on to it. An early positive result from Mitcham would have suggested the possibility of a last-minute rally in the Tory vote. That, however, was not what we were expecting – although the final outcome in Merton still managed to confound a forgone conclusion.

The South Wimbledon sports hall that held the count was buzzing with activity from early in the evening even though nothing much could happen until the close of polls. The BBC and ITN had set up live links to their respective Dimbleby-chaired programmes. The wires were gaffer-taped down, the satellites in place and the reporters briefed about the local peculiarities and the personalities involved.

Our focus, Mitcham, featured a prominent Tory dame,

Thatcherite Angela Rumbold, expected to lose her seat to a prominent 'Blair Babe', Siobhain McDonagh. Over in Wimbledon,
where I cut my teeth canvassing in 1983, a rather faceless Tory
doctor was considered a safe bet to hold his seat against a challenge
from an equally faceless New Labour lecturer. At the count I was
also trying to remain faceless given that I had recognised a couple
of the long-serving local Conservative activists and was keen to
maintain my professional neutrality. Unfortunately I was spotted
and enthusiastically greeted by Wimbledon Conservative
Association's grandest grandmother. Suddenly I was being introduced to the faceless doctor as a longstanding supporter and
former stalwart of his party. In full view of the reporter, camera
crew and assembled press this was a little awkward. But then quick
as a flash my credibility was restored because looking down at my
ID this charming Tory matriarch realised she was mothering the
wrong woman. Clearly she concluded I was not the girl I had once
been. I had defected – not to New Labour, but even worse for a
Tory, to the BBC!

The evening was to get even worse for her. True to expectation
it did not take long after the ballot boxes were opened for the
Labour piles to grow tellingly high at the Mitcham count. Unlike
the election night five years previously when had I watched the
results with colleagues at Central Office it was soon clear that the
newly adjusted opinion polls had accurately predicted Labour's
victory. There had been no last-minute change in luck for the
Tories – there was no Basildon. If anything the polls, like many
Tories, had underestimated the degree of Blair's success. Although
it was hard to grasp, I could soon see that the real story of the
evening in Merton was not Labour's much-predicted victory in
Mitcham but the astonishing number of votes piling up for Labour
at the Wimbledon end of the count. I wanted to warn the production gallery over at the live show in TV centre that the real story
was Wimbledon. But with similar shockers coming in from all
over the country they were spoilt for choice as to which counts to
cut to for live updates. In fact we were lucky to get on air at all –

and that was to relay the news of the Mitcham count when it predictably added to the stream of results that even early in the night already invited the epithet 'landslide'.

And it was no exaggeration. All around us the land was sliding from under Conservative feet. Mitcham first, then yes, astonishingly, neighbouring Wimbledon returned a Labour MP. No one was more astonished than the Labour victor himself. In fact Merton's richer, more well-to-do constituency had shown a greater swing to Labour. To the east, Labour's avalanche mowed down the bonking David Mellor in Putney. On the TV monitor I watched in the live-link van he bowed out gracelessly, reserving his strongest bile not for the victor but for James Goldsmith whose Eurosceptic referendum party had brought its single issue campaign down on Mellor and helped to usher in a Labour MP. To the west, the bitter Norman Lamont had been deemed sufficiently sceptical to avoid the attentions of Goldsmith's clansmen but slid away anyway beneath a yellow peril that brought a swathe of Liberal Democrats to former Tory strongholds in Kingston, Sutton and Richmond. As I drove home from the count I was navigating familiar streets but suddenly I was in very unfamiliar territory.

Had the Tories deserved so thorough an ousting? On substance of policy I could hardly say yes. Major's wait-and-see on Europe had been ambivalent but it was certainly preferable to New Labour's unfettered enthusiasm for a European project. Did I relish the introduction of proportional representation? No, absolutely not. Did we need devolution? Well, yes, but a real devolution based on redressing the necessary centralisation of the 1980s and empowering parents, patients and local communities. That should and could have been a Tory platform preferable and more effective than Labour's scheme to create more politicians. Had the Tories run out of ideas? Not completely. Peter Lilley's badly timed Pensions Plus was a brave, bold and necessary plan to face up to long-term problems.

But had the Tories really deserved to win? To that also I could hardly say yes. True the economy was sound (once again) but they

seemed hardly fit to govern. Barking, bonking and bitterness had
led them from Back to Basics straight down a back alley. I had
voted Conservative with a mixture of tribal instinct, nostalgia,
defensiveness and hope, but with nothing like the excitement,
optimism and enthusiasm that palpably glowed from the crowds
swarming Labour's HQ at Millbank that evening. The
Conservatives were distrusted, disliked, even loathed, and for the
majority of voters we personified a myriad of cultural dislikes.
Poor Michael Portillo. He had let himself down but he did not
deserve so thorough a roasting. As I drove glued to Radio 4 I heard
him bow out with generous courtesy. To the Tories' most charm-
less opponents his defeat had been the public lynching they had
required to mark their coronation. But his grace under fire already
showed that he had grasped the extent of his party's problems, and
the part he had played in them, more thoroughly than most.

At Westminster a carnival was going on. And it was colourful
and exuberant and exciting. But for a life-long Tory it felt ominously as though things could only get worse.

PART 3

THIS IS NOW

ME: opinionated thirtysomething, London female journalist, no rock – no lock, metropolitan, argumentative, occasionally neurotic LOVES: shoes, sushi, red wine, films, dance music, coffee bars, conversation and the great indoors
SEEKS: dynamic, contemporary, authority figure, willing to shake off traditional constraints and rekindle that torch – all mod cons welcome

10

DESPERATELY SEEKING SOLUTIONS

The Gulf Coast, January 2000

Early in 2000 I had a phone call from the BBC. It was not long since I had left the corporation for a freelance life. 'Would I get on the next plane to Florida?' 'Would I? Absolutely!'

The unexpected proposal was particularly interesting as it offered the prospect of introducing me to a man I had been sizing up, professionally speaking, for well over two years. Courtesy of Auntie I was being given the equivalent of a journalistic blind date, and as such things go it was very promising: at short notice, an obscure exotic location, a sunset seaside dinner, the beginning of a new millennium and the man? Very good on paper – matched the specified requirements, but how would he measure up in person? There were all the right qualifications; young, bright, articulate, experienced and thoroughly steeped in politics. He had seemed the best choice for the job. And I had certainly done my homework in advance of the meeting. Whenever he had appeared in public there

I'd be with my notebook; his television appearances – I watched them all. One day, I was certain, he would be mine! Well my subject for a book that is.

Writing a biography can feel like a bit of an obsession, but when that obsession is William Hague I found it was best not to make the preoccupation too public. I had first thought of the project during the Conservative Party leadership campaign that followed the election defeat of 1997. I liked what I heard from this relative unknown during those frantic weeks of post-election hysteria when the party's remaining MPs, yet again, tried to reassure themselves that the attention paid to yet another leadership contest meant that they still mattered. Despite the largely unedifying spectacle of Tory vs Tory, Hague seemed to be talking my language. He sounded as though he might have what was needed to relight the interest of people like me, who were increasingly frustrated and disenchanted by the state of the party, and also more importantly to reach out to new supporters. So as a Tory I was intrigued. Like most people I knew very little about the man who was set to be leader of the Opposition, and a potential prime minister. And as a journalist I saw a challenge and an opportunity in writing about him but I was not to meet him until the Beeb brought us together thousands of miles from Westminster.

The job was to produce a live interview with Hague for *On the Record* – BBC1's now departed weekly politics programme. He was already halfway through a parliament, facing dreadful opinion polls (the party was 'flatlining' – showing no improvement since the mid-1990s) and was already considered a liability by many (the *Sun*'s 'Dead Parrot'). He was set for a grilling from John Humphrys. But he was also committed to addressing a conference in Florida that same weekend so his contribution had to be beamed in live from the States. Our obscure destination, Punta Gorda, a neat, pastel-housed, picket-fenced, retirement town, was nowhere near a TV studio and so I was dispatched to ensure that it all went smoothly.

On arrival it was clear that the conference was set to be a blast from the past. The International Democratic Union had been set up by Thatcher and Reagan to further the cause of their shared credo across the globe. This was a meeting of its youngest members, so called 'future leaders of the world's right'. As I walked into the welcome reception I was transported back in time – just for a moment that Essex Moat House hotel had been reborn in the USA. It was a cross between the Young Conservatives circa 1983 and in that tropical location a Club 18–30 holiday, though apparently without the sex and like so many Conservative gatherings I had attended, without the women. Twenty years on, it all still looked very familiar. Youthful right-wingers had apparently taken globalisation to heart. Like McDonald's or Nike the apprentice Conservative is an instantly recognisable brand. The intense fervour and unnerving swivel-eyed enthusiasms had not been peculiar to Thatcherite Romford. But it was comforting to know there was still a determined vanguard out there somewhere. Admirable, especially as things weren't looking good for many of the right-wing parties attending, unlike before at the inception of IDU. Some at the conference had encouraging stories about the possibility of renewal and recovery; the Canadian Conservatives had suffered a similar humiliation to their British cousins but were fighting back with their own brand of 'Common Sense Conservatism'. Texan representatives could talk about George W. Bush's 'compassionate Conservatism'. But Hague was the star attraction, *the* admired role model, the ultimate. He was of their generation and he was already a leader – literally so, whose talents were highly appreciated in this friendly arena even if, as the reasons for the BBC interview testified, they were less easily recognised by the British public.

And it was clear that Hague himself was completely at ease with this audience, and all its wannabe Hagues. The conference summoned up the former glory days when Young Conservatives and their student counterparts were in the ascendancy and revelling in their market-driven revolution. That had been the era of Hague's own university activism, which was to leave an indelible mark on the character of his leadership. Unlike some of his contemporaries who were inspired by ideas, Hague's student days were marked by his love of the game and his skill at the necessary political machinations that would take him to the top. In the early 1980s he had risen to the top of the Oxford tree, as chairman of the Conservative Association and president of the Oxford Union. Twenty years later he was at the pinnacle of his party and also president of the IDU. Casually dressed in a DKNY sweatshirt and chinos, Hague looked like one of the crowd, infinitely more at home and authoritative in this arena than in the contrived baseball-capped photo-opportunities of his first weeks as Tory leader. He did not seem so different in conversation either, easy-going and friendly.

He was then, as I found him always, unfazed. He invited me to join his table of close colleagues for a buffet supper. My immediate impressions were of someone who was comfortable in his own skin, unusually self-possessed, but he did not have that particular sheen of power I had seen on a few of his colleagues. I found him generally open and discursive, although only up to a point; he was at the same time discreet and on his guard. Although apparently down to earth and likeable, it was clear that small talk was not his strongpoint, observations later confirmed by his closest friends. We chatted about the requirements of the interview and then a little about the state of the party. I suggested that its spokespeople were still struggling to find the right language, that Tories could still seem haughty and rarefied in comparison with the casual 'blokiness' of the government. He took an interest in my opinion, although I was guarded in my approach, both because I was there to do a job for the BBC and because I did not want to derail my book project before it had even started. It didn't necessarily need Hague's official blessing but had he chosen not to cooperate it would have been a different sort of project.

So we were both being tactful and political. However, my reluctance to venture too much of an opinion was more than tactical; I was undecided about Hague and had grown more so over recent months. There were many reasons to be impressed by him, but I also had reservations, reservations that were shared by a largely unimpressed public. The failure of the party to make any improvement in its poll ratings suggested that 1997 might not have been its lowest ebb.

I was certainly pretty low the next morning, having to rise some time before the crack of dawn to get our show on the road. The time difference between London and Florida meant that an interview being broadcast live at lunchtime in the UK required Hague in the hot seat by 6 a.m. Gulf Coast time. Early mornings, particularly after long-haul flights, are not my speciality. Even the local TV crew were, like me, bleary eyed but Hague, by marked contrast, was clearly in his element. Sharp-suited, relaxed, fully briefed. It was a taxing interview with John Humphrys at his most unforgiving best, but Hague's was a characteristically strong performance, once again revealing the particular strengths of a man at ease in the inquisitional hot seat.

When the interview was over and I was sufficiently awake only to crawl to the hotel café for breakfast, Hague embraced his next early morning challenge with intimidating zeal. He went training with Sebastian Coe. As I downed a bottomless cup of coffee and a stack of blueberry pancakes hoping that would induce alertness, my view of the seafront was interrupted by the sporty duo sprinting along the boardwalk. It was barely seven in the morning. Hague had already been groomed, briefed, given a tough half-hour interview, now he was training hard, and shortly he would open the conference with a keynote speech. It's no wonder people don't relate to him, I thought. He's superpolitico.

So in that first meeting were all the clues to the person I would uncover over the next few months, and also to the reasons why his leadership was not as successful as all his other ventures had been. There within the camaraderie of the conference Hague could once again revel in the excitement of the early 1980s. But the Conservative Party had been losing momentum ever since and in his leadership of the party Hague had not yet demonstrated that he knew how to regain it. What went wrong?

Back in 1997, on his election as Conservative leader, Hague had pledged himself to be a moderniser when the party was crying out for one. It had needed a leader who would profes-sionalise the stale machine that was already way past its best by 1992, refocus the logic of liberal economics on the ailing public services and would identify and attack the emerging weaknesses and inconsistencies of Blairism. But also a leader who recognised what had made New Labour appealing and had ideas about how the Tories might similarly portray more of a human face. Given the importance of the European project to the identity of the newly elected Labour government I thought it was also vital, if only as a point of distinction, that the Tories had an articulate, Eurosceptic leader, but that of course was also my ideological preference.

During a short stint in Cabinet Hague's communication skills had shone. Unlike others on the right he avoided vulgarising his message for popular effect. So Hague, with his youth, political conviction, management expertise and commitment to reform, was simply the best man available for the job of leader in 1997. Michael Howard was then too old school, Ken Clarke too ideologically pro the Euro, John Redwood too odd, Peter Lilley too traumatised by defeat, Stephen Dorrell too anonymous and Michael Portillo too unavailable. And aided by the dramatic last-minute chalk and cheese pact of Ken Clarke and John Redwood (yet another thoroughly implausible twist in the Tory soap opera) the young pretender was able to stop pretending.

In comparison with his colleagues, Hague and his campaign had been a breath of fresh air. There were moments when the struggle to sound distinctive provoked slogans that sounded more like ads for spot lotions – 'Fresh open and clear', but that was as close as he could get to declaring a New Tory party without using the word 'New', as successfully monopolised by Labour. But we knew what he meant, and for those of us who admired Labour's remake

Hague's professional campaign style and undeniable energy won through. Here at last, I thought, was a leader offering the beleaguered Tories an opportunity to adopt a thorough and determined approach, such as might have occurred if the party had lost in 1992.

In the months that followed Hague's accession to leadership, doubts about his suitability began to bother me. While these concerns made him a more interesting subject to write about, they undermined my confidence in him as a leader. The nation it seemed, well the media anyway, were not prepared to forgive him for 'that childhood speech' to the Conservative Party conference in 1977. Given how frightful I must have been as a teenager I could only sympathise with him for the relentless teasing he received as a result of his early activism. Even so, I did cringe along with the rest of the country to see him in forced poses at the Notting Hill Carnival. But these were worries about superficial things. I really did want him to succeed yet I remained to be convinced that he had sufficiently grasped the way in which the political landscape had changed. He just didn't seem to be living in the same world as most of the other young urban professionals I knew.

Hague was certainly qualified, literally so as a former high-flying management consultant, to modernise the Tory operation, but he seemed less sure-footed when dealing with other more amorphous issues that require a politician's consideration. Unfortunately his first such challenge was about as dramatic as they come, revealing Britain's changing character and his lack of empathy with it. The death of the Princess of Wales, only weeks after Hague's election as Tory leader, shocked a nation and the world beyond it. The way we reacted to her death challenged traditional assumptions about 'Britishness' and British behaviour. If the stuttering decline of John Major's government had seemed to mark the strange death of Conservative England, arguably the unprecedented public outpouring of grief for Diana marked even more the passing of small-c conservative England.

At that moment it was Tony Blair who keyed in to the mood.

Spontaneous and affectionate, he seemed to personify our move away from deference to a more informal and evolving set of social mores. Blair emoted for Britain. His were the values of 'Cool Britannia' and 'dress down Friday' and 'calling teachers by their first name' versus those of the 'old school tie', the 'stiff upper lip' and the 'Sunday roast' with which Hague, regardless of the accuracy of that perception, was associated. For Conservatives these new gods seemed suspiciously modish, attempts to reinvent rusting but renewable wheels. But although we might not have liked it we were in different times. Established institutions, including the Tory party, the Church, royalty and even M & S had been crumbling, largely due to the changes the Conservatives had set in train. Society was increasingly diverse, choices increasingly numerous, and issues of identity and community increasingly complex. Consumerism had become the most observed 'ism' of the age, and taking its lead from the high street New Labour had grasped the importance of packaging and presentation, of 'rebranding'. Hague's low-key tribute to Princess Diana revealed a man who, quite reasonably, did not want to claim the right to grieve publicly for a woman he barely knew. But his restraint seemed anachronistic, and worse, uncaring, recalling Nicholas Soames's pre-election criticisms of Diana's worthwhile crusade against landmines. And that brand of patriarchal Toryism was certainly out of favour. Outdated and hard-hearted – two characteristics that research proved were still indelibly and damagingly associated with Tories in an age when perception was all. Tony Blair, actually the public schoolboy, was 'blokeish' and appealing, whereas Hague, the comprehensive pupil, was assumed to be elitist and detached.

This one incident pointed so graphically to the ways in which the political battleground had evolved. In the 1997 election New Labour had shown, with devastating effect, that it understood, and had largely defined, this new territory. Labour had stopped fighting the battles it could no longer win and conceded the case for privatisation, low taxation, a sound economy and strong defence. They selected instead to fight culture wars (urban versus country, youth versus age, inclusive versus exclusive, broadminded versus narrow-minded, Oasis versus opera, etc.) and to fill in the gaps that Thatcherism had not thought worth addressing. Equipped with the solid economy bequeathed by a Conservative government New Labour had appeared to offer the public a way to have it all – a 'third way' – that allowed us both to be acquisitive and compassionate.

Ironically this was not such a revolutionary concept. I never have believed that low tax, low-spend economics and caring were mutually exclusive. But it didn't matter what I thought, or what other Tories thought; even if somewhat jaded we were already the party's core vote. What mattered was that the majority of people did not see it that way. And in the aftermath of Diana's death this change of tone seemed to crystallise and each side of the argument to be embodied in the party leader. This was a conundrum for the Conservatives – or at least for those who recognised how things had changed, as Hague while running for leadership indicated that he had. On the one hand Labour had risen to power on the back of Tory economic policies, so where was the need for Conservatives either to change or to apologise? On the other Tories were clearly hated so surely they must concede some public penitence and illustrate a changed agenda?

With no immediate or obvious agreement on this dilemma, Hague decided to spend some time feeling for a resolution. The profound nature of the party's defeat had hit very deeply, producing something of a psychological trauma for many involved. The more the party command came to grasp the depth of its problems the more this seemed to militate against making any significant decisions about direction. In practice, William Hague took a sort of non-decision, choosing in the early months after defeat to keep the party's profile low, concentrating on internal reform and addressing only its immediate problems, such as the continued disagreements on the Euro policy. It was a pragmatic approach but would in time give the impression of a party taking a frustratingly piecemeal approach to opposition. It reflected the party's lack of big thinkers, in contrast with the last time it had been in opposition, when the brilliant, brave voices of the early Thatcherites had heralded the revolution that had re-fired the imagination of my parents' generation, and later that of so many of my peers. It reflected also the extent of the problem facing a young and inexperienced leader, who despite his starred career, was not, as he was later to tell me, quite as confident as he seemed about confronting some of the obstacles to progress.

In certain cases those obstacles to progress came in the shape of some of the party's most familiar faces. Whereas the Diana affair was one of those unexpected 'events' for which preparation can never be made, it was rather more disconcerting to see Hague slip up over more predictable problems.

My brief encounter with Jeffrey Archer during the Christchurch by-election had been enough to make me wonder how it was that serious people took him seriously. Admittedly, putting aside his controversial record, Archer's charisma was not in doubt, but his political skills were not so obvious that they demanded others suspend their critical judgement. I was given the chance to meet Archer again while working for the BBC, and this second meeting convinced me that he was a political lightweight and above all, a rather nasty man, hardly an appropriate figurehead for relaunching the party in its most testing arena.

For Hague's generation of Thatcherites, myself included, the abolition of the GLC had been a legitimate strike against bloated Labour local government. And at a highpoint of the old Labour/new right struggle it had also been, for us, a piece of sheer tribal indulgence. But the justifiable good sense of the move was subsequently undermined by the complex and inefficient governing structures for London that developed in its wake. Things did not work out in as streamlined a way as we had envisioned. New Labour's promise of a Mayor and new assembly was welcomed, according to the results of the London referendum shortly after Labour came to power, so the Conservatives had to bite the bullet and enter the race for Mayor.

Although Conservatives would not have chosen to reinstate London government the move offered the party a brilliant opportunity. Here in sophisticated London the Tories had a chance to field an urbane, perhaps counter-intuitive, candidate, someone who would rise above the limited appeal of his party. It was a vital balance also to the 'Yorkshireness' flaunted by William Hague, which did not play well with my city-loving contemporaries who found the 'professional Yorkshireman' routine parochial and irritating. Sure it was a contrast to New Labour, but as New Labour's sophistication had been an electoral plus, clothing the Tories in the garb of the yokel hardly looked like a cunning plan for future success. So here, in the race for London Mayor, was the perfect platform to fight Labour in its own spiritual home.

If the party really was serious about recovery the right candidate was vital. And there were many reasons to conclude that Jeffrey Archer was not that person, despite his determination, chutzpah, and his indisputable recognition factor. Long before an official process of selection had begun Archer had charged up his own Mayoral bandwagon. One morning in late summer a colleague and I were granted a colourful initiation into the Archer world. It was certainly a more glamorous meeting than usually preceded a TV interview with a politician. The private lift in the lobby of his luxury, Thameside penthouse opens straight into his apartment where we were met by the butler. Archer was definitely on a charm offensive but we also had something to gain from this meeting. His aim was publicity. Ours was the chance of shooting some exclusive footage with him and Rudi Giuliani in New York for a programme we were making about mayors.

We were given the Rolls-Royce treatment: a full tour of the awesome apartment with its breathtaking collection of paintings, including, as Archer made a particular feature of pointing out to us, a large portrait of Mary in pride of place in the bedroom. Despite his image Archer's taste was elegant and surprisingly understated. The triple-height living room was furnished with low-slung cream sofas and vast coffee tables piled high with first-edition art books. Grinning and spinning, Archer danced around the room, pointing out the location where he had recently shot an advert for BT. Bumptious he certainly still was, but undeniably seductive in a rather unsettling way. He could beguile. Twenty floors above London on the curve of the river at Vauxhall Bridge offers a tremendous view across the capital with the Palace of Westminster in the foreground. It was a dream world and here it wasn't hard to see how an ambitious politician with all the imagination of a top-selling novelist could look out over this vital landscape and feel inspired. He gestured expansively over his longed-for dominion as though suggesting that one day it would be all his.

Buoyed up by Archer's incredible energy and hard sell we returned to the office both impressed. In that moment we could see him as Mayor even though he had not actually told us what his plans for the role were. And, crucially, we had our programme in the bag; we were off to New York to film with him. But up close and personal with Jeffrey Archer in the Big Apple proved that the charm with which he had won us over in London was as easily turned off as turned on. His fact-finding mission to New York seemed less about finding facts than about associating himself with the highly successful Giuliani. By turns Archer was oily, patronising, bossy and manipulative. I was sure that he didn't recognise me from our previous meeting several years before at the Christchurch by-election but someone in his staff had tipped him off about my Conservative background. Consequently he was charming to me, but he seemed to take pleasure wherever possible in criticising my crew (although he was keen to get the publicity), even on one occasion screaming abuse at a colleague who was filming, with permission, in the Republican Party's headquarters. The attack was unprovoked, embarrassing even his own staff, and appeared contrived to impress his powerful new friends. He gave the impression of a man, who despite revelling in his fame and success, still needed to bolster his own sense of importance by belittling others, those who were expendable to him.

But unpleasant politicians, even corrupt politicians, womanisers and social inadequates are the stuff of Westminster. Most importantly, Archer did not seem to be a convincing candidate for the role of Mayor of Europe's first city, let alone a person appropriate for public office, especially for a party with an image problem. His questionable behaviour was already very well documented. But even if the accusations against Archer were then only conjecture, there were enough of them from enough good sources to have suggested that Hague should have kept greater distance, and certainly should not have used the peer's private gym for his judo sessions.

It was eighteen months after the New York trip that the Sunday papers proved Archer's perjury and his removal from the Conservative candidacy for Mayor followed. That was a great night but as I cheered inwardly at his downfall I reflected on the damage this whole incident was causing the party, raking up yet again those negative associations of sleaze and greed. I was dismayed at the sheer ineptitude of this self-inflicted wound. Although Hague had given party members the right to the final say in the selection of candidates Archer could have been stopped before he had even got that far. An older, more experienced, leader might have taken Archer aside and simply asked him not to run. But Hague did not yet have the confidence in himself or in his role to realise that kind of authority. It was a bad sign. And worse even than that was the fact that Hague had been let down by colleagues at Central Office who had not alerted him to warnings they had received about the troublesome peer. An inexperienced leader with an inefficient HQ; it did not augur well for taking on the already distrusted, but undeniably effective, New Labour machine in the run up to an election.

Archer had recently met his just deserts and the Diana affair was long gone by the time I had that first meeting with William Hague in the unlikely setting of Punta Gorda. His first two years as leader had been shaky but by then he had scored one significant public success. He had led the party to a national victory at the 1999 European elections. This had given a boost to his already troubled leadership and had vindicated his judgement in clarifying the party's sceptical line on the Euro and further integration. Even acknowledging the achievements there was, however, one undeniable and overriding concern that became increasingly marked throughout this period: it simply was not clear what sort of party Hague wanted to lead, or what sort of leader he wanted to be. The early mood music about modernisation had not evolved into an identifiable policy agenda or strategy, and over the following year several moves would suggest that it had been rejected outright.

I did not think then that we had seen a lurch to the right, as the headlines accused. But throughout 1999 there certainly had been a change in tone and emphasis that confused and diffused the initial impression of an out-reaching, broad-minded Conservatism that Hague had rightly sought to articulate in his first months as leader.

His early speeches had been faultless, measured and intelligent, explaining the necessity of the party to broaden its address to 'quality of life' issues. Standing at the back of the room after Hague concluded a talk about Conservatism and society a prominent New Labour adviser whispered to me, 'Great speech, couldn't disagree with any of it.' That, I thought, was valuable praise indeed. Not because, as some Tories would criticise, the speech was merely aping New Labour but because for the revival of the party it was essential to explain Conservative solutions to problems on which Labour had correctly, and successfully, focused. This was essential both for attracting back voters, old and new, and for reviving the interest of political thinkers and strategists who would otherwise take their talents to a Labour Party unencumbered by ideology.

What it had seemed Hague was trying to do as a new leader was to begin to correct many of the negative impressions about his party.

At some points this meant (controversially) apologising, as he did about the ERM fiasco, to mark a public penance. At others it meant being seen to listen rather than preach. In some cases it was about demythologising testaments of the Tory faith, such as tax cuts, explaining why these can be benign rather than opportunist, how it can be possible to cut taxes and yet improve public services. And of course it meant addressing those areas, most notably the public services, that concerned voters in a far more immediate way than the Tories pre-election preoccupation with the threat to the Union and the nation. But delivered to select audiences during the prolonged New Labour honeymoon, these arguments were never likely to register much with the general public now relieved of its recent constant diet of politics. That was not, however, sufficient reason to set aside the logic of their message.

Given the real length of the Tory decline, from the poll tax through to 1997, it was always the case that 'rebranding' the Conservatives would be a long job, just as it had been for Labour. The route map, in so far as there was one, was in the model New Labour had developed. At the heart of that were a few brilliant and ruthless political operators with a common aim and a seriously disciplined, long-term agenda. Blair's pollster Philip Gould wrote an insider account of this coup, which was required reading at Central Office in the early months of Hague's leadership. It was clear though from the subsequent changes in direction that the central message, 'it's a long haul', had not made sufficient impact.

Hague was hardly the first politician, and certainly not the first Tory leader, to claim resolutely that he paid no attention to opinion poll results, but clearly after two and half years of his leadership the pressure was on for him to score some obvious successes. By switching his focus away from the long-term 'vision thing' to reacting more forcefully to the immediate concerns of any given day, Hague did raise his profile and at points the poll ratings of his party. But his so called 'lurch to the right' with its particular preoccupations – Clause 28, Tony Martin and Asylum issues – raised the spectre of a very different kind of Hague leadership – and not a very attractive one. Just as peripatetic as John Major's but rather 'nastier'.

Curiously, the editorial pages of the *Independent* and the *Guardian*, epicentres of Hague's despised 'liberal elites', maintained that Hague's bandwagon campaigns were purely opportunistic and belied his true socially liberal instincts. But as I ventured further into my research and traced the genesis of Hague's beliefs I realised that they were wrong. In fact I felt that the man who championed the conventional Tory issues, be it law and order or defence of the nation state, was really the unadulterated Hague, appealing to his own political convictions. And the rather more erudite, philosophical figure of his early leadership was the more experimental face of a man whose gut instincts were considerably less nebulous than the musing might have suggested. It struck me as an interesting contrast; on the one hand the party's lost leader Michael Portillo had spent his time in exile outside the Commons taking a very public journey towards redefining his politics in a more nuanced and subtle way. On the other hand, the party's actual leader gave very short shrift to such indulgent preoccupation. 'How would you define your Conservatism,' I asked Hague in one of our early interviews, 'economically dry, socially liberal, pragmatic but authoritarian?'

'I am a Conservative,' he told me, 'there's no need for further definition.'

It was a frustrating answer but I could see his point. It really was not his role to narrowly define or to analyse himself. That was my job. And aside from the requirements of the book I was anyway intrigued. In theory Hague was not someone with whom I would naturally bond – I was, after all, trying damn hard to get into the liberal elite! But nevertheless we shared the same political allegiance. At a time when the future of the Conservative Party seemed very unsure and the definitions of political identity were becoming ever more fluid à la Blair's 'social – ism' I was wondering what it was that bound us together.

First stop on this journey of discovery was South Yorkshire and the coal-mining, steel-producing, farming villages that had been the home of early 1970s industrial militancy and William Hague's childhood. As I mentioned, I recognised far more of me than I felt completely comfortable with (and certainly that I'd have confessed to in the BBC canteen) in the teenage Hague who had decorated his room with Maggie posters and taken over the local branch of the YCs. The sense of decay and drift that I had perceived as part of our national identity during my childhood in the late 1970s Hague had witnessed first-hand, almost literally at the 'coal face' of the disputes that precipitated the rejection of the postwar economic consensus. I recognised in Hague's family, and their comfortable but modest lifestyle, much of the 'northern grit' that had shaped my mother's upbringing, a stoic, common-sense approach valuing hard work and independence. But I also saw strong elements of reaction and conventionality to which I did not relate to so easily and which lent Hague's Conservatism a certain crude edge undermining his efforts to broaden the appeal of his party.

The issue around which these tensions were most obviously laid bare, and an issue that has become a barometer of 'modernisation' was Section 28. Having heard Hague's early speeches as leader it would have been reasonable to surmise that he would ditch the party's stance on Section 28. Whatever justification the law may have had during the battle to control irresponsible and profligate councils in the 1980s, continued support for it had long become, without doubt, a legitimate stick with which liberals could beat the Tory Party. The party's unchanging stance on Section 28 forced away an enterprising and individualistic constituency among gays and lesbians, who might otherwise have been Conservative supporters. It was one of those culture wars that Hague needn't have let New Labour win, and his continued commitment to it revealed just how keenly he still felt the drives of the 1980s; he remained, at heart, an unreconstructed Thatcherite at a time when reconstruction was vital for the party's long term survival.

Unfortunately, the pressure to score some points over the

government went against Hague's initial patient strategy. With Section 28, Hague hit the headlines, and reassured a particular right-wing tabloid audience. When he went back to his roots he campaigned on issues that chimed with his own strongest convictions. It proved an irresistible urge for him. On law and order Hague bristled with indignation at the shame of a lax criminal justice system, but in championing Tony Martin, the Norfolk farmer who shot an intruder, he was too obviously appealing to a cheap and easy sense of moral outrage. Martin, by some accounts a paranoid, had taken the law into his own hands using an illegal firearm in what could be considered a disproportionate response. He did not deserve to become a cult hero – and he certainly shouldn't have been helped into that role by the leader of a national political party, whose own speeches had so recently striven to steer the Tories away from the cheap use of the politics of punishment.

My feelings as I watched this all unravel were mixed and uncomfortable. The temporary boosts in poll ratings suggested that Hague was making an impact. That might help sell books! But as Hague grew more notorious he looked less like the leader the party had elected in 1997. Apart from the bandwagon issues that got the party noticed, I could not see what was being offered to anyone who had abandoned it in 1997. There was still far too little on schools and hospitals and transport. New Labour was revealing its cracks and its crackpots, but although it spun too much and delivered too little, there was no obvious reason for a floating voter to move to the Tories. The most high profile of Hague's colleagues, Ann Widdecombe and John Redwood, although in certain instances very effective, were not always the best faces for a Tory outreach project. Many of my friends in the party were by now thoroughly disenchanted. Their views hadn't changed, but the user-'unfriendliness' of the party, its machine and its image, had turned them off careers in politics. Lobbying, PR, business and banking all seemed easier options. Added to which, New Labour think-tanks spoke of breaking taboos that even the Tories were reluctant to consider, like extending privatisation in the provision

of education and health. Now that was exciting. That was interesting. And that was more like the flurry of ideas that had brought
many of my generation into the Tory Party in the first place. There
was still a great deal about New Labour that we did not like – its
superficiality, its inconsistency and its disregard for established
British institutions, but unfortunately there was quite a lot about
the Conservative Party we did not like also. The cringe factor was
still an issue. When half the shadow cabinet felt the need to confess
their pot-smoking pasts, as a counterweight to Ann Widdecombe's
one-woman drive against permissiveness (conference 2000), they
had inadvertently hit on a far more effective anti-drugs' message
than the 'just say no' campaign. If smoking dope is likely to turn
you into a Tory MP it might just seem a risk too far for most
people.

In the run up to another general election there was one significant issue that still held the potential to reinvigorate our commitment.
There were significant differences between us and New Labour on
the future of British relations with Europe. My Conservative
friends are Eurosceptics, as are the majority of Conservatives. We
may disagree about matters of 'family' policy or the legalisation of
soft drugs, but there's little disagreement about the Euro. We
don't think it's right for Britain. We think the project centralises
power too dramatically and removes flexibility from the control of
our economy. It takes power further away from its source, the
people. It turns on its head the idea that Labour is committed to
decentralisation and devolution. But as much as we agreed about
the importance of the issue, we didn't relish the Conservative
campaign, or what we had thus far seen of it.

Strangely, given Hague's cool composure and rational nature, he
chose to inject a distracting emotional tone into his campaign
against Labour's stance on the Euro. Rather than concentrate on
the economics or the political issues, the 'Save the Pound' campaign clothed his approach in the Union Jack and focused on the
danger of losing the Queen's head from our notes and coins. The
flat-bed lorry campaign, reminiscent of John Major's DIY soapbox,

took Hague around the country like a sort of travelling Al Murray.
It had all the appearance of sheer desperation, even though Hague
is certainly a good public speaker. His brightest and best moments
as leader were his wounding performances at the dispatch box, but
the town-centre stand-up routine looked amateurish. It was simply
naff. This attempt to stir up sentimental patriotism, rather than
address coolly the substantial reasons for opposing Euro entry,
also looked likely to play to a less benign strain of nationalism.
Similarly, the party's preoccupation with immigration and asylum
issues would play into the hands of its opponents, eager to reinforce old stereotypes about narrow little Englanders. Perhaps
Hague was brave and acted with foresight in raising issues that
now bedevil the Labour government, but to give it higher priority
than public services in the year running up to an election was self-
defeating. Hadn't we done that before? This miscalculation was
most obvious to me in the controversial speech Hague made to the
Tories' half-year conference in Harrogate, the notorious 'foreign
lands' speech.

Unlike the annual party conference in the autumn the half-year
spring event in Harrogate is a low-key affair. Traditionally it has
been the conference organised by and held for the party's members, mainly to discuss issues like training and recruitment rather
than debate matters of policy. It is not the prestige event but it does
give a good, in fact a truer, taste of what's actually going on at the
grass roots than the show-biz events of Blackpool or Bournemouth.
Harrogate 2001 was likely to be the last chance Hague would have
to make a key-note speech to the party faithful before he would
lead them into the general election. I sat among the party members, rather than in the press stand, as Hague delivered a curious
speech. It struck me first as underwhelming, rather than disastrous
or contentious as the press were to report. Even ignoring for a
moment the 'foreign lands' reference, it felt like a speech designed
to woo the audience in the hall rather than a wider electorate. As
has been said of Tory audiences, these were the patient pensioners,
the long-suffering councillors, and the well-meaning local

volunteers whose vote Hague already had, and even their response was muted but polite applause.

But this was meant to be a campaign speech, not a pep talk to the troops, and as such its scope was curiously narrow and its ambitions limited. I shook my head in disbelief – still no schools and hospitals – despite the fact that poll after poll (and common sense) indicated these were the issues uppermost in the minds of voters.

There was a legitimate issue to raise about abuse of the asylum system, but to make it a key theme distorted its significance and distracted attention from the sensible policies on public services that Hague's front bench had been quietly developing. Indeed most of Hague's schools' policy has since been absorbed into Labour's during their second term, but who now would know where the thinking had been developed?

There in genteel Harrogate with its teashops, spa water and York stone solidity there were more than enough concrete examples of our national heritage to help conjure up the more abstract elements of it – our freedoms and our history. New Labour seemed intent on undermining all this in its forays into a new economic and constitutional settlement with Europe. A new legal system, a new currency, a new central bank . . . Labour's vision for Britain may indeed resemble a 'foreign land', as Hague's speech contended. Certainly in the conference hall, in the context of the whole speech, that seemed to be the point he was making. But in the press office, during the press briefing, these subtleties were ignored. Instead references to the 'foreign land' were conflated with sections about asylum to win headlines in the *Daily Mail*. It was ten years since Norman Tebbit – whom I had loved in his union-bashing days – had saddled us with his comments about the 'cricket test'. I had agonised about it then, the suggestion that allegiance to a sporting side is the real test of a citizen's loyalty, was simply too proscriptive and too narrow particularly for a first-generation immigrant. It did not ring true to my own observations; my father, no sports fan, had worn English shirts but always filled the fridge with Polish sausage. Surely a true Brit can have different cultural loyalties? Cricket isn't war after all.

Now, in the run up to Hague's most vital test of public opinion, here he was, or at least here his team was, undoing all that good work he had explicitly commissioned to expand the mix of his party. Nothing he had ever said to me had even the slightest tinge of racism about it so this was a particularly opportunist escapade, but at least it proved self-defeating – giving misplaced succour to the odd 'maverick' MP like John Townend who felt emboldened to give a pre-election address about Labour's intention for a 'mongrel race'. Rightly there was an outcry. Wrongly Hague prevaricated about disciplining the MP who, thankfully, was serving out his last parliamentary term. It was a minor incident during the 2001 election campaign but somehow it struck me as a motif for the missed opportunities of the Hague leadership.

In the moment that William Hague resigned with such elegance and self-deprecation on the front drive of Central Office in the early hours of 8 June he instantly rewrote his own political obituaries. It was not long into the Duncan Smith leadership that calls for Hague's return began to grace the letters page of the *Daily Mail*. Even media people mused on the lost talent that was William Hague. This indefatigable, ever-resilient man who had rejoiced in laughing off his political ill-fortune (rather than understanding why it kept coming) and in celebrating his Yorkshire grit had suddenly, dramatically subverted his own unique selling point. By making himself the ultimate victim of the 2001 result, prepared to sacrifice all he had ever wanted for the good of his party, he had finally appeared vulnerable, human. Away from the disastrous and contrived efforts to create a 'likeable' image of a beer-swilling, judo-practising 'normal guy' we had finally been allowed a glimpse of the private man. It looked as though he had cracked the paradox of modern democratic leadership, to be extraordinary but to appear ordinary. Three speeches had defined his public image so far, one made as a teenage devotee at the feet of Margaret

Thatcher, one made years later but displaying the same characteristic invulnerability at the death of Princess Diana and then this one
in the jaws of defeat showing too late that the man had come of age.
The textbook politico who had never put a foot wrong on the
route to party leadership had failed big but nothing had become
him so well as defeat.

I had been broadcasting through the night at Television Centre
and had taken a cab back through town to Westminster in the early
hours of the morning. With the result a foregone conclusion, the
night was a predictably lacklustre event following a short and uninspiring campaign. There was no sense of tension or expectation.
Labour was rightly concerned not to appear triumphal so there was
to be no repeat of the revelry of four years previously. Westminster
was dead. A few droopy eyed journalists and party officials hung on
in the Atrium restaurant watching TV coverage. I bumped into a
couple of Labour Party friends, whose lack of excitement suggested they were suitably 'on message' with the 'no gloat' dictate.
A few journalists wandered back and forth over the few metres
from this temporary Millbank HQ to the media room at Central
Office where the only story of the night was exactly how bad the
Tory rout would be.

I felt for the legion of Central Office workers squirrelled away
in the rest of the building. Unlike 1992 when I had been one of
them myself, these committed apparatchiks were having a night of
unremitting gloom. And it was more grim even than 1997 because
no improvement in the party's performance meant in reality that
things had got worse. Throughout the previous four weeks of election 2001 Conservative officials had told us that it was better than
1997. 'People don't hate us any more,' they said. But it seemed
to me that the transition from hatred to indifference was absolutely
damning. The end of a love affair such as the one that British
had with Maggie in the 1980s does not come when disillusion
sets in and the heart is broken, but is only when you simply don't
care any more. What Tory officials had wanted to squeeze some
crumb of comfort from revealed in fact the very pitiful indictment

that their party could no longer muster any passion, positive or negative.

This sense of pathos was encapsulated in Hague's dramatic resignation. It was his first admission of failure – indeed, in a starred life and career, it was his first failure. The most raw I had seen him, or indeed anyone had seen him, was that morning in the act of resigning. Perhaps it had broadened his experience sufficiently to have made him a more successful leader. The plan to go had been made with characteristic foresight several months before, in the event of a poor result, but acting on that plan was unmistakably painful. Until then William Hague had been that unlikely politician – the one who could rightly claim that what you see is what you get. His image makers had mistakenly patronised us with the idea that people would grow to love him if only they could get to see the real man. But we had seen the real man, up close he was the same man I assumed him to be even before I met him. We had seen that he was intimidatingly witty, ambitious and focused, but almost too invulnerable, too self-reliant, and generally we hadn't taken to it. Something had seemed to be missing – perhaps humility, perhaps perspective, perhaps imagination. And those are the things that experience, not PR, brings.

Hague's departure was impressive and it was moving. Every jaded journalist looking for their sacrificial Tory lamb that June morning had it served up on a plate. In the event it was impossible even for the most cynical not to find new reserves of admiration for the architect of the doomed Conservative revival. I was looking on as personal admirer, and by this stage, a really disappointed supporter. Had he applied the same long-term strategic approach and discipline toward marshalling a Tory recovery as he had to his own career this selfless gesture would not have been necessary. His resignation announcement may have been refreshingly candid but in so doing it revealed even more than was intended. Its focus on Hague's personality and his own admission that people had not taken to him indicated the real failure of the Tories to have made any impact with policies or ideas. True, there was no doubt that William Hague did not strike a natural chord with voters but his personality would not have become the central issue if the party's message itself had been more coherent and attractive. In blaming his defeat on his personality Hague was selling himself short but also disguising the more damaging truth: that he had failed not because he lacked charisma but because he lacked a consistent strategy.

11

ON THE ANTLERS OF A DILEMMA

London and Scotland, Autumn 2001

In the aftermath of a second dreadful defeat Conservatives were yet again forced into another round of recrimination and introspection, desperate to find new direction as well as answers to what had gone wrong. The New Labour government, into the second term, continued to blur the boundaries between right and left. It was not uncommon to hear the suggestion, even from Tory voters, that Tony Blair was the best prime minister a Conservative could hope for, and that was even before the prospect of military action in Iraq. Certainly his enthusiasm for the market was encouraging and exciting for those of us on the right, but in other respects, particularly with regard to the constitutional changes of the previous four years (devolution, reform of the House of Lords, promotion of the Euro) he had shown that he was anything but a Conservative.

Many of my right-wing contemporaries considered themselves radical Thatcherites rather than conventional Tories, and I too had never really found it easy to relate to the old-school establishment on which my party was founded. For my generation there was a time when the real test of allegiance to institutions such as the Federation of Conservative Students and the radicalised Young Conservatives had been to advocate abolishing the House of Lords, privatising the monarchy and disestablishing the Church of England. For most of us, proximity to the party in the years since these youthful provocations had muted our experimental enthusiasms and we had come to see the sense in tradition and that very Tory concept of evolution rather than revolution. The ill-thought-out changes that Blair had begun forced me into ever-closer sympathy with my party's patricians and its old guard, so when I received an invitation to play 'Tory toff' for a week I was more open to the idea than I had ever had been before, even though the company and the proposal were far removed from my natural territory.

Would I like to go stalking? Stalking? As a lone female living in central London even the word had malign connotations. It conjured up images of street corner loiterers in soiled macs, and footsteps behind you that mysteriously stop when you put your key in the lock. The stalking on offer to me was something completely different but for an unashamed urbanite the reality was nearly as bizarre. I was new to the idea of stalking as a sport. The invitation was actually a call of the wild, or more accurately a cull of the wild: the cull of wild deer which takes place during the shooting season in the Scottish Highlands. I was being offered a journey into the still-beating heart of the Tory squirearchy and, given this period of Conservative soul-searching, I felt a certain responsibility to take this chance to immerse myself, if only for a few days, in this rather alien aspect of my party's culture.

For some years one of my friends, a journalist who loves claret and loathes political correctness in equal and passionate measure, and is the personification of the kind of Tory everyone loves to hate (or in some cases just hate) had been extolling the joys of stalking.

I had always dismissed these bucolic invocations as the post-pran-
dial preaching of a Scot yearning for home. In the moments when
the claret induced him to wander through the heather-flecked
recesses of his memory he will go misty-eyed in recalling a particular shoot. He would sound almost poetic in conjuring up the
image of the once-proud beast staggering as it took the force of the
bullet and collapsing in its dying throes as the smoke from the rifle
cleared.

On reflection, I could see that these shooting parties were a brilliant combination of animal husbandry, profit-making and
bloodlust. By appealing to the primeval instincts of emasculated
city dwellers, the owners of large Scottish estates have found a way
to finance the necessary cull of animals that would otherwise die of
starvation during the winter. By offering guns and supervised
shooting at a price the canny Scots have made this autumn Highland
ritual an expensive sport for those who can afford to buy a slice of
country life alongside some grand living, a sort of *City Slickers* for
the UK. The donning of tweeds, hipflask and rifle complete the
transformation from passive city worker to stalker, the determined
hunter pitting himself against the beasts in a battle of wits. But
while I don't sentimentalise animals, the idea that I might kill a
magnificent deer still did not appeal, no matter closely countryside
pursuits had become associated with the Tory Party.

I knew deep down that my instinctive hostility to the idea of
joining the stalk wasn't really about a meaningful attachment to
pre-venison deer. My remaining reticence was purely cultural and
more than a little tribal, even tribal within my own tribe. Stalking
is of the country and I am of the city, and since in opposition I felt
that the city-loving caucus among us Conservatives had had an
increasingly dismal time of it.

My militant cityism – or more specifically Londonism – had
hardened considerably in recent years in direct reaction to the
posture of my party. John Major, although a Londoner himself, had
famously branded the Conservatives the party of old maids on
bicycles passing cricket matches on manicured lawns of villages in

bloom. An association so anodyne and outdated was hardly stirring stuff for anyone who appreciates the vibrancy of a city, or to be fair, anyone who really gets their hands dirty in the working country-side.

If I thought that was bad, and I did, it was a mere flirtation compared with the full-on love affair between the Conservatives and the countryside after 1997. William Hague, in his early incar-nation as shiny, happy moderniser, was elected as the Barbarella of the Conservatives. But as we had seen, he too quickly became the Barbour-wearer, wedded to organic reaction and recycling policies of the rotting right. Undoubtedly there was a crisis in the coun-tryside worsening in the summer of 1997 but I am afraid that like many city dwellers I wondered when farmers in particular might take some responsibility for their own dilemmas. The culture of subsidy that Conservatives rightly opposed in the European Union, we apparently accepted at home — but not for mineworkers or car workers, only for farmers. These were the people who had brought us poisoned chickens, rancid eggs and killer beef but had blamed the politicians. I admit I was prejudiced and I found it hard to be sympathetic.

I had always agreed with Oscar Wilde's description of fox hunters as the 'unspeakable in full pursuit of the uneatable' so when Conservatives had marched hand in hand with the Countryside rally down Park Lane, politely waving their banners past the Porsche dealership and the Metropolitan Hotel I felt little allegiance. The horsepower I was cheering was man made and the livestock served rare with wasabi overlooking Hyde Park. I agreed with the hunters' right to defend their way of life against New Labour's last remaining spasm of class retribution, but my lifestyle is far more in league with the chattering critics of hunt-ing rather than its ruddy-faced practitioners. But, of course, I was beginning to accept that you can't be a Conservative without acknowledging the historic role of landowners in the develop-ment of the party. Essentially the party was born of the countryside but it was also a party that had harnessed the potential of the Industrial Revolution, developed the best of our cities and evolved as power moved from land to commerce. And for Thatcher's children like me the recent history of Conservatism was a far more emotional pull than the distant past, which fascinates so many Tories.

Ted Heath, a 'commoner', had already led the party of toffs but Thatcher seemed to blow a hole in the idea that you had to be 'someone' to be a Conservative. It wasn't where you came from that mattered to her, but where you were going. That's particularly what had caught and held my imagination since childhood. It should have punctured the myth that Conservatism was all about privilege. In a different age her people might have been Marxists, indeed some of them had been. They were the intellectuals, ideas people, self-made people, non-conformists – in short not the county set or the landed gentry. And look at the people who had hated her. They were the shire Tories and the inheritors of wealth and titles. They were the wets. And that is how I saw the country, wet.

My own little crusade was to stand up for cosmopolitan Conservatism, that cocktail of intellect and reason versus soggy shire sentimentalism and people whose houses smell of dogs. Was I abandoning my principled objections with the possibility of heading north for stalking? No, I should accept the invitation and confront my prejudices down the barrel of a gun.

The journey from the station at Pitlochry was comfortable, hospitable and text-book country. My carriage: a Range Rover; my driver: in puffa jacket and cords. The fellow guest who greeted me at the station was a young man head to toe in tweed complete with waistcoat and knee-length woollen socks. 'Oh no,' I thought, 'no one told me it was fancy dress.' When I arrived at the lodge to find several others kitted out the same way I thought I'd arrived at a Sherlock Holmes convention. In black trousers, a designer T-shirt from Selfridges and a charcoal rubber mac I was clearly the novice. I had on the least practical of two pairs of boots I had brought with me, but not yet the open-backed steel-heeled stilettos, which I had packed just in case this trip was to offer me the opportunity for a little after-dinner stalking.

Although the lodge was remote it was a supremely comfortable introduction to country living, perhaps I would adapt more easily than I had hoped? This was five hundred miles away from my flat – it could have been light years. My preference for the uniform city chic of chrome, glass and acres of white suddenly seemed soulless and ephemeral. Stepping into a house like this felt like an immediate encounter with history, with a family and its lineage. The oil paintings of hunting scenes, the large worn sofas, the dining table for twenty people, the heavy curtain swags, the sets of antlers in the hallway, the overlapping antique rugs and roaring fires reflecting in every facet of the cut-glass whisky decanters all spoke of longevity, solidity and duty just as much as privilege. I knew that the family which owns the lodge, now largely run as a commercial concern for holidays such as mine, had played their part in politics. And even before I had set my eyes on the estate – the very many square miles of it – I had a new insight into that world of traditional Toryism that had always bothered me.

It is a large house, but not a grand one, full of things valuable because of their age more than their flashiness. This is a house that would have had, and still does have, a role in the centre of a community, a house around which people tend the land, make a living and understand their place in the scheme of things. Until then I had thought there could be no worse thing to say to someone than 'Do you know your place?' but perhaps knowing one's place was a damn good place to start? Over the years I had met many of the party's grandees and I had tried not to be too impressed by their lineage, but I could see more clearly here that that had been something of an affectation on my behalf. Along with innovation and radicalism there had to be balance and respect for established traditions, especially when the government seemed intent on tearing up bits of British life without thinking through the implications. Who would know better about the ways of adapting traditions, whether in terms of our government or in rural life, than those people whose families had lived it for centuries? I was feeling a lot more at home with the Tory in me – something I'd always dismissed as nothing to do with the cool-headed, rationalist inspired by metropolitan politicos.

Inspiration in a completely different form came the next day. Gordon Macgregor, the lead stalker, was all man. At breakfast, frighteningly early for a holiday, I had eaten porridge. Then in the gun room I was confronted by the man from the front of the Scots porridge Oats packet. In London, men seem to fall apart when having to decide whether they want their roasted pepper sandwich on focaccia or ciabatta; here was a man who would eat his lunch straight from the carcass. That was it, I was determined that I was going to do well. This shooting business held no fears for me. I was beginning to sense blood as the organic Tory in me was contemplating the orgasmic Tory in me.

First stop was the target range, although no one had thought to tell me. I was temporarily thrown when Gordon issued the instructions, 'Lie down and get your hands round this.' Then he handed me a rifle and I suddenly grasped the reality of the situation.

I was face down in a muddy puddle with several of the other guests and a passing bull looking on as I was set to take my first ever shot at a hardboard stag across the field. I was simply not prepared. A wardrobe of combat chic was hardly appropriate training for the military precision I was going to have to pull out of nowhere at that moment.

It took a while to focus on the sight as my mascara-heavy eyelashes kept obscuring the view. And the feel of a gun in my hands was alien. No amount of exposure to the ubiquitous 'lock stock' celluloid gun culture, had prepared me for the reality of handling a gun. It wasn't an AK 47, an Uzi 9 millimetre or even a perfect handbag Beretta. It was just a run of the mill rifle, but that was weird enough for a girl who had always preferred colouring-in to cowboys and indians. I was an ammunition virgin and I was expected to go all the way without a safety catch. Everyone, particularly me, expected I would fail. So when I obeyed orders and squeezed on the trigger I was the last one to hear the verdict. The shock of the recoil and the deafening boom as I fired the bullet left me oblivious to the judgement. 'Perfect, it's a perfect shot.' The words came over the walkie-talkie from the Land Rover dispensed to check on the target. It was the first perfect shot of the season. Oh damn, I was a natural – a natural with the right footwear and a borrowed Rohan jacket, so there was no excuse. They were doing a good job of bringing out the traditional Tory in me. They were going to make a killer out of me as well.

The previous night I had drunk a lot of whisky. But I only began to feel its consequences as we set off across the estate in a doorless Land Rover. Such were the after-effects of Scotland's finest spirit that I was even grateful when the terrain became too testing for the off-roader and we had to start the ascent by foot.

I gathered we were to stalk in small groups so as not to alert the stags of our threatening presence. My group comprised me, Gordon and an extraordinary young man whose campness easily rivalled Graham Norton. There I was, hungover, on a steep, bleak and very wet hillside sandwiched between two extremes of man-hood and not a stag in sight.

Though I was still deaf from the earlier shot and queasy from the night before, I was not so out of it that I couldn't feel the invasive damp from the ever-thickening mist. As we climbed higher the view – which I had been told was stunning – grew more elusive. I didn't know much about stalking but I had grasped enough to realise that not being able to see past the person in front hardly constituted prime hunting conditions. And I also quickly under-stood why I had needed sensible shoes. These were serious hills, which required much scrambling, grabbing of gorse bushes, pick-ing feet out of potholes, avoiding of rocks and walking with feet at right angles to legs. As soon as we reached the top of one hill, another summit loomed. This was very hard work. After an hour and a half my head began to clear but the view became more obscure. After three hours of considerable physical exertion I began to ask myself if I had unknowingly made myself the victim of an elaborate practical joke. After all, this was supposed to be fun. I was supposed to be enjoying this and frankly, it was hell.

Against initial doubts I had been successfully inveigled into this expedition. My inveiglers had lured me with promises that the joy of a stalk was not so much about the kill but about the whole experience: the views, the fresh air, the invigorating exercise and the majesty of nature. Four hours into a wet, vertical hike I realised I had been had. The considerable discomfort of this day suggested to me that there was something peculiarly British and more particularly Scottish about the psychology of calling it fun. All in all I got very wet, went up a mountain and ate a sandwich. And that is about as heroic as it got.

The rest of the day continued in much the same vein. By about half-past three the mists began to clear and it was indeed a stunning view. Each hill of loamy green reached a bare peak and then beyond another and another until the green and the grey and the brown and the blue all merged at the edges. There are not many places in the British Isles where you can stand and for as far as the eye can see there are no traces of anything man made. Of course to my mind that isn't automatically a recommendation but it is certainly in marked contrast to my normal habitat. And I'll admit that I was awestruck. Partly because of the beauty, though it is a very intimidating beauty, the very scale of which makes a human feel very insignificant, but more accurately because of the responsibilities this view implied.

This was one estate. For as far as I could see, the land stretching out across these purple hills belonged to one family and, I suppose, ultimately to one man. If I were a socialist I would have been appalled as this was so clearly an example of inherited wealth and with it inherited status. If I were a social climber I might perhaps have been envious or acquisitive. But as a perfectly contented member of the urban middle classes, I was impressed, relieved and humbled. To have one's identity and destiny limited by the circumstances of birth must feel restrictive whether born into great poverty or great wealth. Though it would certainly be preferable to being born into poverty, I doubted that I would want to wake up one day to the duties of this kind of inheritance. After all, from where I was standing I could not see any cultivatable land, yet all of it, and its animals and properties, had to be cared for.

Later back at the house I asked a fellow guest how such a place makes money. 'Ahh,' he said, 'you can make a tiny fortune out of a Scottish estate.'

'How?' I asked.

'Inherit a large one.'

A whole community revolved around great estates like this one and that meant a burden of huge responsibilities as well as wealth. Being born into privilege might not have been as easy a ride as the 'property is theft' brigade, and the old-hiding-behind-New Labourites would have us believe. Certainly if my one day of stalking was anything to go by life could be pretty uncomfortable for the posh. I was secretly relieved that the day had gone as it had. I had managed to prove myself a perfect shot without actually having to kill something, and although I can't deny that I felt myself falling for the subversive charms of the rifle I don't know how I would have felt in the act of slaughtering Bambi.

In what must be a local interpretation of the no-pain, no-gain philosophy I discovered that the Scottish version – no pain, no grain, was the recipe for the best part of the day. Damp and aching we made it back to the gun room for the traditional post-stalk dram and cake. Now this was a habit I could adopt at home. My eyes shone with excitement at the possibility of establishing a Marylebone writers' salon that would meet for late-afternoon whisky and buns. But I don't suppose it would taste so good without the preceding seven-hour uphill walk. A member of the Scottish Parliament had joined our party during the day. He was the personification of a 'jolly fellow', slightly ruddy complexion and a dab hand at impromptu Scottish karaoke. In between songs we chatted about the day's events and I asked him what he had done before becoming an MSP. 'Oh, just a bit of fishing,' he replied casually. Given that he was over fifty it struck me as odd that he seemed never to have had a proper job (although I dare say that being a journalist hardly equips me to make such a judgement). After a little more enquiry it turned out that far from being a late developer or an inveterate pub singer he was an ideal example of the breed I was beginning to admire. Mr MSP's idea of 'just a bit of fishing' had been a lifetime running his own estate, of which the main business had been fishing. I marvelled at his elegant under-statement. That was real class, not the sort of thing Thatcher's nouveau riche would have been able to pull off.

I was adapting easily to the best Scotland had to offer: fine foods and unrefined men, spectacular scenery, whisky and cake and then the Highland version of a siesta, the pre-dinner soak and snooze. The hunting lodge had colossal cast-iron tubs and great water pres-sure so that within moments you could run a very hot, very bubbly bath. Apart from easing out the after-effects of the day's exertions it was an opportunity to collect my thoughts. Lying around in the lap of luxury with unlimited haggis and champagne on tap was hardly an encounter with everyday Scottish or country life. This was after all, a lifestyle holiday, as much a taste of the real Highlands as Madonna's wedding in a Scottish castle had been. This was no initiation into those parts of the working countryside that had taken to the streets of London to protest that government policies did not take its crisis into account. But there is a connec-tion between those busloads of angry farmers and this privileged world – and it was a fundamental connection sealed through their related roles in an established but dying ecosystem I had always been too quick to dismiss. I was hardly about to eschew my keenly defended London lifestyle, but I had to admit that my easy dis-missal of the Tory squireachy had been glib and premature.

Those Tories who, when not stalking their family estates, stalked the corridors of Westminster by virtue of their ancestry had always unsettled the meritocrat in me. But Tony Blair's alternatives for the House of Lords had already convinced me that the hereditary prin-ciple was just as likely to offer up appropriate legislators as his arbitrary judgement. An all-appointed second chamber is far more open to corruption than the system he has replaced. It's a curious type of democratising reform that replaces one unelected, but effective body, with an unelected but untried one. Blair's plans inadvertently offered the Conservatives an opportunity to outflank him with something more radical, more democratic. But even though I might once have enthused about modern Conservatives taking up such a baton, I was now only convinced of its political expediency rather than its real value.

From where I was lying, surrounded by bubbles and plaid wall-paper, the countryside and all that meant to me was beginning to take on a positive glow, even without a pair of rose-tinted Gucci sunglasses. The turnip-chewing, self-interested farmers I had previously condemned I now saw as heroic, selfless champions of the British countryside and its heritage. The snobby, chinless wonders who marry their own cousins I re-evaluated as an endangered species, a burdened elite without whom the country and the party would lose a vital link with history. All these things were noble, admirable and undoubtedly very conservative, with a small and a big C. Unfortunately these most conservative elements of the party have not helped to endear it to the young, the professional or the city dweller, but I was now in the mood to celebrate this rich stream of tradition and bonding.

My reverie was rudely interrupted by some commotion outside. It sounded as though I was missing the party. I wrapped myself in a towel and went to the window. 'Ahh, Miss Nadler,' called up my host, a talented right-wing MP, 'did you hear that I shot a royal today. Wait there and I'll show you the head.'

Oh, my God, I thought. I knew that this MP had bravely advocated legalising drugs but surely this was taking the modernising spirit of revolution a bit too far. Just as I was beginning to really get into this blue blood thing, surely we weren't going to outflank Labour by advocating a republic? Republicanism had always appealed to some libertarians but shooting royals just isn't cricket. Alan had momentarily disappeared behind a tree and re-emerged with a newly severed head, so fresh that red blood was now much more in evidence than blue. This I understood was a royal but a different kind: King Deer.

A small audience of fellow guests had assembled to congratulate him on the prestige killing. I was learning fast. A royal denotes a stag with a certain number of points on his antlers, second only to an imperial whose antlers hang on the walls of the most successful stalkers. Even taking into account all the rational reasons and irrational prejudices I had used to justify my preparedness to take up a rifle, this was a gruesome sight. The head was impressive, and although the antlers suited Alan, I couldn't help feeling they might have looked more impressive on its own body. I knew the animal would have otherwise died a slow, painful death from starvation but it was grim to see its great head with ribbons of sinew hanging where there should have been a body. If I had shot it I would have had to be initiated into the ancient club of killers with a streak of blood to the face. That was one rush of blood to the head I was not too keen to acquire.

It was a very graphic tableau to behold fresh from the bath. Although I wouldn't claim that country life and country pursuits are exclusively the domain of Tories, I could only imagine the indignation such a scene would cause a socialist, or a prissy new Blairite. The friends who had labelled me 'too nice to be a Tory' would certainly have had their doubts at this moment. I'm sure they would have been horrified at my association with this uncivilised barbarity and there was a time when I would have agreed. But although I had not actually shot anything I had nonetheless, in a curious way, been blooded. My allegiance to the invisible hand of the market had never been in question, but now I felt suddenly a much stronger kinship with the party's traditions as well. That this scene would provoke consternation in a class of people who spend their holidays cycling around Cuba was a definite plus for me but, despite the mellowing of my views on the countryside, secretly I did harbour a residual concern of my own. Maybe I am just too squeamish to be a Tory? Particularly in a party that seemed increasingly to relish inflicting wounds on itself. As I slipped into something more uncomfortable for dinner I felt reassuringly, urbanely, me again. I was comfortable with the idea that this heritage deserved my new-found respect but relieved of hiking boots and back in my own shoes again I was keen to indulge in my favoured 'capital-ism' as soon as I could climb on board the next train to London.

12

JACKETS OFF

Having made my peace with Tory toff-dom on the spectacular Scottish hillside I headed back south with a renewed sense of commitment to the party. Up there in the fertile undergrowth I had learned a little about the art of hunting, but it had been tame stuff compared with the blacker arts that had been practised in Westminster's rather more furtive undergrowth throughout that summer.

I may have been new to the idea of stalking but, as a seasoned Tory, not to the concept of the stalking horse. These near-mythical figures were the disgruntled backbenchers whose rumoured grievances with the leadership had made them in recent years an ever-present threat. Most legendary, of course, had been Sir Anthony Meyer whose challenge to Margaret Thatcher in 1989 had opened the starting gates for the leadership race that eventually saw her deposed a year later. That any disenchanted MP could challenge the leader and provoke a destabilising contest for the top job had caused constant insecurity whenever, as there often were, difficulties for the leadership. William Hague had attempted sensibly to tighten up the rules on such challenges, but in practice his new constitution failed to make Iain Duncan Smith's leadership any more secure than his had been – in fact it provided for another set of grievances as MPs resented having to allow party members the final say in the choice of leader. Although Hague himself had been dogged by the constant rumours of leadership challenges, in the end he dictated the timing of the 2001 leadership election by resigning. And in July of that year, much as Hague had done four years previously, Iain Duncan Smith emerged as leader out of the blue. Indeed out of dark and rather sinister blues according to his ominously vocal detractors.

Even by the time Hague stood down I had almost lost count of the number of leadership elections, or at least of threatened elections, that had bedevilled the Conservatives for as long as I could remember. They had become like 'Groundhog Day' for Westminster observers: alarm clock goes off, *Today* programme eases us into consciousness, Tory grandee denies splits in the party, another Tory grandee confirms splits in the party, sure enough a leadership campaign is underway.

But although long anticipated and much predicted, the protracted event that was the leadership election in 2001 was different from previous affairs. Firstly and most obviously because it was the first time that the most-talked-about contender, Michael Portillo, had actually entered a leadership race. His electoral defeat in 1997 had prevented him from living up to the hype and the hopes of his devoted fans who had been preparing for this move since first installing extra phonelines in a putative campaign HQ during John Major's 1995 back me or sack me. But Portillo had hesitated, hoping perhaps that his display of loyalty to the prime minister would play well for him in a post-general election contest, a contest that he was then unable to enter because of that memorable defeat to Stephen Twigg.

The second reason why the leadership election of 2001 was particularly notable was that for the first time it was an election, allowing party members to vote in the final ballot. This was Hague's legacy.

His democratising party reforms had echoed Labour's vital modernisation with its totemic celebration of One Member, One Vote. Conservative reformers argued with good logic that involving the membership more directly in their party's most important decision-making would motivate the deeply disenchanted grass roots and offer potential new members more of a reason to be involved. But Labour modernisers had specifically designed their reforms as a bulwark to the more reactionary elements of the Labour family. By extending the franchise on leadership selection they were counteracting the influence of the Trade Unions and their block votes. Given the profile and size of the remaining Conservative membership, however, Hague's replica reforms were likely to have quite the opposite effect, giving the final say over the leadership to the party's most cautious constituency, many of whom had never forgiven MPs for dumping Maggie against their wishes. By effectively emasculating the parliamentary party, it was probably only a question of time before the MPs chose to reassert their authority.

Five candidates offered themselves as the replacement for William Hague. Such a choice! But curiously, although this was an encouraging number – suggesting there was life left in the old dog after all – none gave the impression of really wanting the job, except perhaps for the ambitious, but then largely anonymous, David Davis.

Davis's campaign launch was cool, efficient and businesslike. He was early into the fray with a campaign specifically labelled 'modern', slick press conference set and dedicated website. Davis, a former minister, had snubbed William Hague's front bench and concentrated instead on building himself a strong reputation on the backbenches. But his relatively low profile did not mean that Davis was any less of a Westminster 'player' than his better-known adversaries. Far from it. Any journalist that had nurtured a contact with Davis would testify that he had long had his sights on leadership and had been scathing about Hague's strategy. As a BBC reporter I had once visited his North Yorkshire home to film an interview. He was

articulate and thoughtful but his house was curiously soulless.
From the outside it was traditional and seasoned, typical of the
area's oldest farmhouses, yet on the inside it resembled a Barrett
home, boxy and featureless with no personal effects and the sort of
un-aged furniture usually found in chain hotels. It could have
been a safe house for someone in a witness protection scheme, and
was nothing like the pleasantly cluttered, book-filled, photograph-
lined homes I normally found when visiting politicians. It was
strangely sterile, revealing no clues to the passions that drive him,
except perhaps that it was a blank canvas on which he could only
reflect himself. His sharp-suited, professional campaign launch
had been similarly obtuse. It seemed designed to stress the buzzword 'modernity' as though it automatically communicated a
specific set of ideas and priorities. I liked the buzzword because I
had a particular interpretation of it, but that was only my interpretation. It would be hard, for example, for me to reconcile
modernity with a leader who would not have disciplined John
Townend for those ghastly statements about a mongrel race – as
Davis was on record for saying he would not have done. As much
as I agreed with what Davis had to say about the bigger issues of the
public services, I was not convinced he would tackle those cultural
sticking points within the party that kept it anchored in the dark
ages.

On the other hand, the self-proclaimed modernisers' champion
Michael Portillo showed almost too great an enthusiasm for imposing his own sort of cultural revolution on the party. The 'Will
he? Won't he?' debate as to whether the Tory's most charismatic
candidate would actually stand was ultimately resolved in his glitzy
campaign launch, deliberately outside Westminster, deliberately in
a swish and fashionable restaurant, deliberately deliberate. In the
manner of contemporary brand management, Portillo had taken
the concept of third party endorsement to heart. Even before the
great man had deigned to address the mass of assembled, and hand-
picked, media we had heard testimonials to him from all wings of
the party. Washed down with espresso and delicate pastries this

was all very show biz but, even for my taste, rather too exclusive. By now the country was tiring of New Labour glitz – we did not need to replicate it. Image aside, however, Portillo, in all his reformed splendour, was still grand and impressive, as well as thoughtful and nuanced. His rhetoric had passion and flourish and I did find myself motivated, though not altogether sure what I was being motivated toward.

Enter stage left, Michael Ancram, the Tory toff whose dramatic entrance into the contest destabilised my newly kindled enthusiasm for that section of the Conservative fold. The best characteristics of the old-school Tory were loyalty, self deprecation and an ability to rise above the fray, à la Willie Whitelaw. Ancram, then Hague's most recent party chairman, a charming guitar-playing lawyer, had in the past renounced his own inherited title so that he could stand for parliament, but in his paper-thin disguised attack on Portillo he fell short of Whitelaw's reliable standards of tact and diplomacy. I have no doubt that Michael Portillo's alleged plots against William Hague were highly exaggerated and reflected differences in politics and personality between the key players rather than revealing a planned coup. Ancram clearly felt that Portillo, or his close friends, had been working to undermine William Hague, although the truth was that nothing had undermined William Hague so much as some of the dafter decisions made under his leadership, to which Ancram, as much as, if not more than, Portillo, had contributed. So Ancram's own best-selling point in standing as a potential leader in 2002 was that he was not Michael Portillo. As if to underline this point his rushed press launch, on the lawns of Victoria Gardens, featured the full parade of his undeniably gorgeous family and his fully expressed vitriol at an anonymous 'stardust' campaigner. This was the *Dad's Army* answer to the Conservative's problems; pontificate a great deal, sound responsible and considered but do absolutely nothing. Ancram advised against considering too many changes. Don't panic, Don't panic, came the message: it's never too late to stick your head in the sand.

Where Davis added interest and Ancram entertainment value, there was really only one man whose candidacy was sure to add excitement and tension to this contest. In the real battle of the big boys only Kenneth Clarke was in line to take on Michael Portillo. But Clarke, like Portillo, was slow to enter the race and did himself no favours with party members by seeming to give his commitments to British American Tobacco greater priority than his desire to lead.

Clarke's launch was the grandest and most traditionally political of the five candidates. There were no petit fours or newly designed logos but there was weight and gravitas, communicated by the grandeur of the Pall Mall club where it was held and the numbers of press scribbling, snapping and filming away throughout his characteristically bold address. Now things were getting really tricky for those people with a vote – in the first instance the MPs who would narrow down a choice to a final vote of the membership. Here was most obviously the candidate who could knock Tony Blair into a cocked hat. He had the experience, he had the chutzpah, he had unparalleled popularity ratings, but there remained one overriding problem. How could he oppose Tony Blair, if on one of the most inflammatory issues of the day, he agreed with New Labour policy? Indeed throughout the first term of the Blair government Clarke had been a more enthusiastic supporter of European integration than even the government had dared to be. Though Clarke is not the 'wet' his detractors would have him, and was after all the man who did the most to upset the establishment in health and education during the 1980s and even bravely attempted to extend Thatcherite logic to the running of the police, he is far to the left of the rest of his party on the pivotal issue of Europe. And having been the firebrand of public service reform while in government, he had grown lazy about considering where next it should go. He didn't indicate any particular strategy or any priorities, other than to stress he would not bow to the party's right-wing majority view over Europe. Similarly, he expressed no interest in updating or rebuilding the party's inadequate machine, particularly in Central Office. That was dreary stuff but it needed doing. Clarke was the most natural and the most combative performer standing for the party's highest office, but how would he muster the energy required for this fight if, as it appeared, his heart was no longer really in it? And although the press loved his insouciant cord jackets and his jazzy suede shoes – they weren't really blue enough for most of the party faithful.

For absolutely no effort at all expended on presentation or media management full marks had to go to the unlikely candidacy of Iain Duncan Smith. Duncan Smith's campaign launch had in fact been the first but it was, like the man, quiet and understated and had gone virtually unnoticed. It was easily the most dour and the most ascetic of all the campaign starts, hardly an augury of great things to come, and at eight in the morning in a featureless room in Church House, it was almost deliberately designed to put off the normally nocturnal Westminster journalist. There was definitely no stardust, certainly no chutzpah, admirably no ego and apparently no 'modernisation'. There was instead a long, dull and rather worthy address. But there was also, looking beyond the total lack of political presence, a serious and significant attempt to map out a sense of purpose for the Conservative Party, rightly stressing the need to concentrate on practical reform in the public services ahead of arcane preoccupation with Europe.

I was fond of Iain and well disposed towards him. I had known him reasonably well as a contact throughout my time in Westminster and had always found him charmingly open and warmer and more engaging than his image suggested. And against expectations he was one of the most human of his colleagues. We had had some interesting lunches talking about painting and food and the human condition, just as much as the finer points of the Maastricht Treaty or social service reform. These conversations had convinced me that he was not the right-wing loon of his caricature and that although he shared none of the slick charisma of Tony Blair, he did have one thing in common with the prime minister. In both cases their religious faith gives them a keen ethical framework for their different political convictions. While politicians are well advised to keep religion out of day-to-day politics it can explain what drives someone to take part in what is often an unpleasant world, and as drivers go it's far preferable to the raw ambition, crazed egotism, insecurity and vanity that is so obviously the inspiration for many politicians. What I thought I had seen in Duncan Smith was a rather old-fashioned motivation – simply to do the right thing. That was attractive of course, but not in itself enough to give him the ruthlessness required for high office. And, was he sufficiently bright? He hadn't struck me as an intellectual powerhouse but then again William Hague had, and that hadn't got him far enough. As his unprepossessing campaign launch had confirmed, Duncan Smith was certainly no typical politician. But was he enough of a politician to convince people he was up to the job?

When David Davis and Michael Ancram dropped out of the second round of the contest, both transferring their support and supporters to the by then initialised IDS, what had looked like a two-horse race was looking increasingly like a three-horse race. In fact Kenneth Clarke had only come third in the first ballot of MPs with Michael Portillo several furlongs in the lead and IDS in a very respectable second place. But it was way too soon to place serious bets. Tory MPs are notoriously duplicitous throughout leadership elections and they had already had plenty of them to hone these questionable skills.

Things were getting interesting. And things were also getting local. Given that the party members would have the final say in this contest, choosing between the two candidates that made it through to a third round, it was time for the competitors to appeal to them directly. And it was time for me to go back to the grass roots I had once tended. Wimbledon was winking at me again. The association, now almost resigned to opposition, had issued invites to all the remaining candidates. Would they come to speak to and answer questions at a meeting drawn from the members of the local constituencies?

Of the three approached, only two agreed to visit the south-west London Q & A. First up was Michael Portillo. Although Portillo had spent his two years of parliamentary exile 'being normal' by doing things like working as a hospital porter, he still had not shaken off that certain star quality that has the power to mesmerise. So when he arrived at the Beverley, a nondescript 1930s red-brick pub, on an even more nondescript mini round-about, in a betwixt and between series of rambling low-rise streets not quite in Wimbledon, Raynes Park, Kingston or Surbiton, he looked anything but normal.

This was a show-biz tour, and for one night and one night only the star was about to take up residence across the road at the unin-spiring Merton Assembly Halls. Lightly tanned from a recent Moroccan sojourn and sporting a softly tailored, deep lilac suit with coordinating open-necked mauve shirt (gone were the Hermes power ties) Portillo looked every inch the fashion plate, but I was not sure he would appeal to the particular tastes of his audience. In the pub he remained rather aloof while his posse warmed up the room for him. His lead bouncer, Steve 'Nozza' Norris was busy pressing flesh like the pro that he is. Soon the younger members at the event, who had perhaps more naturally coalesced around the bar for a pre-meeting drink, had had it with the support act and were impatient for the main attraction.

As such things go this was a sell-out event. The small hall, which still smelled of the fresh lime-green paint recently applied, was decked out with those ubiquitous metal-framed stacking chairs – at least a hundred of them, but that evening the walls were also lined with members who could stand. For the record this was probably about as mixed a selection of Conservative Party members as it's possible to find. Here were several Asian faces, several young members, plenty of women, but axiomatically the majority were elderly people with regulation chintz frocks, stretch slacks, walk-ing sticks and white hair. After a glowing introduction from Nozza we were into the main man. No podium, no notes, although quite a lot of pacing and gesticulation, but as if to reassure the audience that the informality would not get dangerously out of hand on what was a rare hot evening, a sign above Portillo's head read 'All music in this hall must stop by 11.30 p.m'.

The opera-loving Portillo brought an enthralling aria to sub-suburban London, dramatic, plaintive and contemplative by turns. But his largely Perry Como audience seemed underwhelmed or perhaps simply shellshocked. 'Whatever we do we cannot stay as we are.' No audience response. 'There is nothing automatic about recovery.' There was silence in the room although these activists must by now have known that he was right. Throughout my child-hood all the surrounding seats had been solidly Tory. Now none are and the general election that summer had only increased the stran-glehold of Labour and the Liberal Democrats – supreme also throughout the area's local councils. 'In the last ten years people only saw the Tories passionate about Europe,' Portillo continued. 'We've become like the pub bore. Members of Parliament drifted off to another planet.' The room was not yet singing along to his tune, but for me he was hitting so many of the right notes that I wanted to leap up and start a hallelujah chorus.

It was only when the question and answer session was underway that I felt a check on my enthusiasm. Almost all that Portillo said I agreed with but his going for broke approach, though brave, was more likely to lose him votes than if he tried a more subtle appeal. Was he trying to hijack his own campaign? At moments it looked as though he might have been. After all, when Tony Blair had con-tested Labour's leadership his hunger for the role was not in question, so he had studiously avoided frightening off his voters by making too much of his plans to rewrite Labour's most holy of holies, Clause 4. While I was enthralled by Portillo's candour I could see that for some it was just too iconoclastic and at times I understood why.

He was right to stress that things might indeed get worse for the Conservative Party and that it had been self-delusional in its com-placency and several degrees removed from reality. But he was presenting a kind of party that most people in this room could barely recognise as the one in which they had, in many cases, long participated. Quite rightly also he said that he would kick future John Townends out of the party, but then a nod to positive discrimination to broaden candidate selection took the point too far. Conservatives had always opposed positive discrimination; believing it can reinforce rather than overcome prejudice. Certainly there was no doubting the need for action to broaden the candidates' list but before suggesting such a divisive issue there was plenty of scope for straightforward best practice. Despite the good intentions of William Hague the party had still to employ the basic professional recruitment techniques taken for granted by businesses and public service. And since doing so more rigorously the profile of candidates selected to fight a future general election has changed.

'Counter-intuitive' is good as far as changing the public perception of the Conservative Party. I'm all for it, but to push the point too far at that stage of an election process was to counteract the crucial, no change no chance message (how many times had we been there?) that, of the all potential leaders, Portillo preached with the most conviction. And it was certainly counter-intuitive, at the very least, to sympathise with the Seattle protesters. A question from the floor about globalisation prompted an extraordinary response from Portillo, typically thoughtful and interesting but all too easily open to misinterpretation. I agreed that for too long the Conservatives in government had seemed like the natural friends of big business, too often at the expense of the 'little man', and it was important to correct this impression in the long run. We had allowed our free market mantra to become misrepresented. We did have a responsibility to explain that our preference for competition can and should militate against the build up of monopolies. We needed to have more guts about stressing the need for liberalising legislation, and that free markets have to operate within the rule of law and not, as is too easily assumed, according to the 'rules of the jungle'. So in this sense, yes, perhaps it was possible that Conservatives could find common cause with certain aspects of the anti-globalisation movement, those who rationally confront legitimate cases of multinational abuse of power. But to give the possible impression of condoning the mindlessness and violence of recent international protests was a dramatic gesture too far for this arena.

Nevertheless his had been a virtuoso performance: stimulating, intelligent and uncompromising, but it was a solo performance and its reception almost too polite and respectful, ominously so. This audience had a lot to consider before requesting an encore. I feared Portillo's evolving political persona was proving too difficult for his traditional fans to pin down, even though I was sure it was far closer to the real man than the exaggerated right winger of his ministerial days. Over the last two years he had accepted the minimum wage, ruled out automatic tax cuts, changed his tone over Europe as well as publicly admitting to sexual experimentation. Here he was repackaged, refocused and demanding from the outset that MPs and members see it all his way. Had he gone from being the right's darling to its diva?

And then there was Europe. I agreed that the party had been too shrill and too insistent on that running sore and I marvelled at Portillo's willingness to admit to his own past culpability in that. Merton's concerned Tories listened intently but their response was as inscrutable as that of MPs in Westminster who had yet to narrow the field to two for the final members' vote. The first ripple of applause throughout the evening had been for Portillo's tribute to William Hague's spirited campaigning, the second and loudest of the evening was for a questioner who feared that Portillo's pledge to 'turn down the volume on Europe' risked brushing the whole issue under the carpet. Portillo promised that were he to lead the party he would not allow any discussion of Europe from the platform at a future party conference. But no matter how badly Conservatives had presented their case on Europe, it was still a massive issue. These grass-roots Tories remained rightly concerned about the government's unchecked enthusiasm for federal solutions. If Portillo was to win their trust he had to convince them that, despite his newly sotto voce approach to Europe, he still shared their natural scepticism on the substance of the matter. After all, most of us were expecting that the membership would soon face a final showdown between Portillo and Clarke. The water between them was looking rather murky and not especially blue.

Michael Portillo had proved a crowd puller but at the end of the evening it was far from clear how many of the interested spectators would go on to support him, if indeed they were called on to do so. A few days later I returned to the same claustrophobic grid of streets and its modest community hall to watch the contest's wild, or more appropriately mild, card in action. Where Portillo had brought operatic flourish, IDS brought soporific rationalism. This time the hall was half-empty and the audience homogenously white and elderly. Just as well really because at first sight there was little to hold a more mixed group. In navy-blue suit and brogues IDS had the trappings of power-dressing without the conceit to carry it off. Oddly, for a former guardsman, his bearing was unobtrusive, almost diffident, as though he expected at any moment a bigger, bolder figure would come in and take over. At some point he must have pinched himself and realised there was no one else – he really was running for leader and he ought to look as though he believed it and believed in himself. But his tone was never more than to suggest that, 'It's a tough job. Someone has to do it. It might as well be me.'

He acted as his own warm-up act, regaling us with an over-practised shaggy dog story about campaigning with Norman Tebbit. The length of the anecdote was memorable. Its punchline was not. I was worried that Chingford (their mutual constituency) had gone to his head, and that Duncan Smith had morphed from unexpectedly urbane man into fully fledged Essex man. Would his message even travel as far as south-west London? But despite the effort necessary to engage with this presentation (one old chap next to me nodded off) there was something worth hearing.

Duncan Smith's message was unmistakably Conservative, much

to the reassurance of the long-serving audience, but it was not the unreconstructed, reactionary bilge his image led some people to assume that it would be. Yes, the party did have to change. Yes, there would have to be more female candidates. Yes, there had to be far less emphasis on Europe but coming from one of the party's most notorious Maastricht rebels this was more easily digestible for this audience. There was no doubting where IDS actually stood on these issues even if he rightly agreed they should no longer dominate the agenda. Yes, he went on, there had to be some new thinking on the public services. Here he was more specific than any of the other candidates. Decision-making had to be devolved to parents and patients. Conservatives should be braver about championing radical schemes like education vouchers and aiding the not-for-profits sector in health care. Perhaps in opposition the party could afford to take a few risks and concentrate on long-term strategy? This was surely the right approach.

Given Clarke's unyielding position on Europe I was coming to the view that a final vote between Portillo and IDS would certainly be the best outcome. I wanted Portillo to win but I felt that the substance of Duncan Smith's arguments deserved to be aired and that his sober approach might inject some well-needed humility into the whole proceedings. The Tory Party had after all just lost another general election because many people just didn't care for, or about it. A noisy, bitchy leadership contest, dominating the front pages during the relatively quiet summer months, was likely only to reinforce these feelings. And much though I was excited by Portillo I was concerned that his approach concentrated too much on drawing attention to what was wrong with the party (on all of which I agreed) rather than quietly accepting that and getting on with changing it. The words were great, but ultimately it was action that would count. There was also the increasing likelihood that if Portillo continued to fashion himself the radical moderniser he would simply frighten off the constituency that most needed to accept the change he advocated. If the reactionary right was going to move into the twenty-first century it was going to have to trust the man who took it there. Nixon went to China but could Portillo go to Chingford?

In IDS there was none of the finesse of Portillo or the combativeness of Clarke, but there was the gene of something practical and effective, and a sense of recognition from the patient and somewhat bewildered members of what had become this rather shambolic party, that he was one of them. They nodded in appreciation at his attack, if that is the right word for so polite an assault, on the government and clapped at an uncharacteristic display of bile in criticism of the Liberal Democrats. He promised to set up a unit at Central Office specifically to target the Lib Dems. It was a wise thing to tell these people for whom the yellow peril was the biggest menace. Putney and Wimbledon had fallen to New Labour, but in Surrey the Liberals were the main opposition and their year-round pavement politics had proved a successful campaigning technique. Targeting the opposition was unusual stuff for a Conservative leadership campaign: mostly we were used to the candidates targeting each other. Actually it seemed that William Hague had done the party a valuable service in forcing the leadership candidates out into the field. At least here in the community centres and church halls people were discussing the 'issues'. They could leave the 'sophisticated' electorate of MPs to concentrate on the big boys' politics; killing off careers and ruining reputations.

At the start of the contest there had been five candidates – well, five and a half if you count Ann Widdecombe, who had briefly sought to canvas backers in a pre-campaign photo opportunity on a council estate. Unfortunately she was judged to have something of the lightweight about her and the bid did not survive beyond this first flush. In some respects this was unfair as she certainly had something concrete to say about the priorities of the Conservative Party. Her argument that the party should concentrate on finding solutions to difficult social problems was right, both in substance and for its media-worthy counter-intuitiveness.

Taking the fight to old Labour territory was bold. But it was the fight between Tory candidates that most interested many of us journalists and we knew that part of Widdecombe's fire came from her disgust at the thought that Portillo might lead the party. Given her particular convictions and his particular confessions there were at least real issues of substance behind her reaction. That David Davis, thinly disguised, and Michael Ancram, totally blatantly, also harboured such visceral contempt for Portillo was a greater indication of how little Tory MPs seemed to have learned during their four years of opposition. Or perhaps in studying the success of Tony Blair's reformed party that they had learned the wrong lessons from Labour, whose feuds had always been based on personality rather than the policy splits that had troubled the Conservatives on and off since 1979.

The result of the MPs second ballot was due for the afternoon of 17 July, a very wet summer afternoon. Whereas the meetings I had attended in the outskirts of south-west London had been respectful and serious, back at Westminster the atmosphere that afternoon could not have been more different. By late afternoon journalists and parliamentarians were crammed into the corridor outside the committee rooms where vote counting had taken place all day. Some were there to root for their man, some to be first with the news, others to take a vicarious thrill from the ludicrous spectacle of Tories pink with excitement at this all too frequent escapade. Peter Mandelson, tall and professorial, was gliding spookily through the throng, as though surveying the wreckage of an explosion for which he had long ago lit the touchpaper. Just as Thatcher's legacy had changed the Labour Party for ever, so the evolution of New Labour was still working out its effects on the defeated Conservatives.

The news that Michael Portillo's leadership ambitions were vanquished and by one vote only, could not have been more dramatic. It would have tested the credibility even of a Michael Dobbs's or a Jeffrey Archer potboiler. In their florid prose they might have wondered as I was tempted to do whether the one vote had actually been his own. Throughout this contest Portillo had seemed ambivalent about wanting to lead. Of course I understood that ambivalence only too acutely, but it wasn't the most reassuring message for leadership. Portillo was easily the most presidential of the candidates, personifying, as Blair had, the 'values' he intended to bring to the Conservatives. In that sense his vision was clear but what was less so was whether he could graft it on to a party in which he no longer seemed comfortable.

The final choice was to rest with the grass roots, where a pragmatic desire for victory may have overcome small-c conservatism and rendered Portillo the winning candidate despite his controversial agenda. But, ironically, that choice was denied the majority because of the machinations of MPs, many of whom simply hated the dashing, emotional, sensual man they would never themselves be. Envy, disapproval, distrust, homophobia, xenophobia or legitimate political difference, each was a particular driver for the anti-Portillo sentiment. The sense of *Schadenfreude* hung heavily in the air, along with the storm clouds that added pathos to the rain-soaked spectacle out on College Green. Here Tories had rushed from the House to face the waiting cameras with their immediate reactions. Portillo's lieutenants were dismal, his opponents gleeful. One well-known Christian irreligiously squealed with relieved tension, punching the air with excitement. Back at the campaign HQ of Iain Duncan Smith a leadership contender from a previous election was rubbing his hands together with glee as the news about Portillo was beamed in live by satellite from just around the corner. 'Now we can concentrate on getting a proper Conservative elected,' he said with more than a hint of a cackle.

The presence of people like that at the heart of the IDS campaign was enough to make me wonder whether he would be able to fashion a sufficiently broad-minded coalition to fulfil his own potential for widening his and his party's apeal. Even though Iain himself belied his own stuffy image there was no doubt that he did attract the old school, and that was going to make trusting him a leap of faith too far for many of the Portillo supporters. IDS had been perhaps the least barking of the Barking tendency that had caused so much disruption to John Major's government, but his fellow travellers were back in full-effect at his leadership offices and just as in their heyday they were not a pretty sight. I was assured by one of his less-old-school supporters that the new campaign manager, recently drafted in from the David Davis camp, was reassuringly normal. The evidence for this apparently was his penchant for wearing short-sleeved silk shirts. I had to admit that this outbreak of casual dressing didn't fit the impression I had of David Maclean, the former home office minister. I was struck by an image of him ten years previously at the Christchurch by-election when he had performed a near assault on a police officer in an attempt to demonstrate a brutal new truncheon, symbolic of the Tories' tough stance on law and order. The idea that the former truncheon-wielding, three-piece-suit-wearing 'prison works' advocate was now a open-neck-shirted modernist out to counter the reactionaries in the IDS camp was intriguing – as were the meanings everyone was drawing from the sartorial fancies of each player. But the IDS campaign was set to be a skilful exercise in power brokering, with his closest managers anxious not to make too many concessions to their own awkward squad. It might well require truncheon wielding as well as soft-shirted diplomacy.

When IDS himself arrived, in regulation navy blue, for a congratulatory drink, his message was businesslike and appropriate, avoiding the personal indulgences of some of his crew. He stressed once again the need to broaden the composition and appeal of the party. Now it was down to him to explain to the party members why he was better equipped to do that than Kenneth Clarke.

Clarke had won the ballot of MPs but he was always set to face a tougher time out in the country. If IDS had become, by default, Margaret Thatcher's anointed choice for that contest so Clarke was the nearest to representing a Heseltine dynasty. During Blair's first term, both Heseltine and Clarke had joined the prime minister on a platform campaigning for the Euro, and that had only served to exacerbate resentment at their perceived disloyalty to the Conservative's cause. Some would excuse Clarke, perhaps even admire him, for his consistent and principled pro-Europeanism but most would judge it wrong. Of course IDS had been disloyal in voting against Maastricht, but in so doing he more accurately reflected the convictions of most Tory Party members than Clarke. Europe would certainly put Clarke at a serious disadvantage among the members. In his favour was the argument that Clarke was the man who would appeal beyond the party membership. And this was a fundamental requirement. For me it was the most persuasive argument in his favour. If indeed it was true; it was something I thought about a lot as I sought to justify my own preference for IDS. Now, of course, that preference might seem bizarre but without knowing then how Iain would fail to match his potential there were good reasons to give him, as the party members did, the benefit of the doubt.

I had no doubt that the calculations about Clarke's popularity were true in the short term. The election of an ebullient and familiar personality like Clarke would have given the party an immediate boost. In the medium term the picture was not so clear. It was right that the Tories should stop obsessing about Europe, but that seemed less likely if they were to elect a leader who was more obsessed about it than anyone else in the party. And in the event of a referendum on the Euro was it really practicable to expect the Tory leader to take a different view from the majority of his shadow cabinet, parliamentary colleagues and party members? On issues other than Europe the relative merits of Clarke and IDS refused to present themselves in straightforward terms. Looking beyond the stereotyping this was not a simple choice between left and right, nor was it an obvious case of modernity versus reaction, or liberalism versus authoritarianism. In different ways both Clarke and IDS had image problems. While each was his own man neither was obviously attractive to those constituencies, particularly youth and women, who were least interested in the party. Was the red-faced, cigar-puffing chuffer automatically 'sexier' than the stiff-upper-lipped former soldier? It was a hard call. The only positive thing about this unwelcome dilemma was that it forced people to look beyond the personality to the substance of the arguments being offered by each candidate.

And on those grounds the choice was more straightforward. Ironically, it was those who took for granted the inevitability of an eventual return to power for the Tories who were more likely to vote for Clarke. Whereas those who understood that the party had to prove its credibility in order to win back voters would have chosen IDS. Despite his charms, Clarke showed little sign of interest in the coming debates about public service provision. He had been ahead of the game during his time in office, introducing the internal market into the NHS, reforms which, despite its rhetoric, had been incorporated into New Labour practice. Clarke's concerns about the market seemed, like Labour's, to be centred on making delivery more efficient, while maintaining centralised control, than as a way of empowering patients by devolving decision making and delivery. I felt that the Tory Party would only recover by offering a real alternative to New Labour, thinking more creatively and unconventionally about the day-to-day issues which all the candidates had learned was now the so-called common ground.

Most of the Clarke team argued that the Conservative Party had failed because it had moved too far to the right. They maintained that a Clarke leadership would return it to, what they called, the 'centre ground' where any future general election would be contested. This was a dangerous confusion. I certainly agreed that the Hague bandwagon effect and his election campaign had concentrated far too heavily on issues most voters deemed marginal. But refocusing on central concerns was not the same as moving to the left. It appeared from what IDS was saying throughout his campaign that he understood this distinction and was the candidate most likely to adopt the sort of sober, long-term approach that the party now desperately needed. I hoped the party would get a quietly effective leader who could yet surprise his critics. It wasn't ideal but it seemed then the better of two flawed options.

I was relieved to see that along with the dinosaurs, who felt their natural home was in the IDS camp, there were also far more liberal

voices, some of whom had moved over from the Portillo camp.
Portillo had rightly stressed the significance of certain social issues
in defining the character of a renewed Tory Party. Whereas Portillo
had wanted a revolution I hoped that with an IDS leadership we
would at least see an evolution away from the more reactionary
influences in his own campaign. They were pressing him to reiter-
ate a traditional line on Clause 28, and would have benefited from
the earlier tabloid headlines sensationalising Portillo's stance on gay
marriage. IDS was naturally more conservative about these social
issues than I would have liked in the perfect Tory leader, but I also
knew that he was not a preachy or judgemental kind of a man. This
moderate tone was clear in the interviews he gave throughout the
campaign. And ultimately the logic of the sort of market reforms
he was suggesting, extending competition, local accountability and
extending choice, empowers the individual, and militates against
central authority. Despite the moral authoritarians in the IDS campaign there was reason for a liberal to back his campaign.

Convinced of these arguments, I agreed to appear on a *Newsnight*
programme debating with a couple of other journalists the relative
merits of the two remaining candidates. I went to the studio
straight from a family barbecue and was casually dressed. On the
way home afterwards I realised that it hadn't really been necessary
for me to say anything at all. The other two right-wing journalists,
one of whom argued for Clarke, the other that Portillo should be
reinstated, were balding, middle-aged men in tweed jackets, opinionated and patronising. If they were representing the progressive
wings of Conservatism it wasn't obvious in their manner. I may
have been equally shrill but apparently that hardly mattered. I
switched my mobile phone back on to find a text message from the
IDS campaign's most anxious moderniser. Bernard Jenkin, the
most suave of the Essex MPs, and son of Patrick, had chosen to
back IDS rather than his former hero Michael Portillo. In view of
the switch I was not quite sure where Bernard now placed himself
on the right-wing spectrum, but as I understood it he wanted to
bring a good dash of modernity to the proceedings. That I hoped

meant a voice to counter the arch-traditionalists, but on this occasion it was a voice to counter the traditionalist's dress code. 'You were fabulous. Loved the denim jacket. Just the right image. Need more of those.'

'Oh no,' I thought; policy apart, surely one of the best reasons to vote for IDS was that we might be saved a repeat of Hague's famous bonding session when MPs had been made over in casual dress for a 'man at C & A'-style photo opportunity. Ominously, C & A had gone bust shortly afterwards. John Redwood in combat pants had been a frightening sight and the thought now of Bill Cash and Nicholas Winterton in regulation IDS denim jackets might make me think again about the future of the party. That it needed to change its image was not in question, but it had to be more than another case of the emperor's new clothes. We would have to see whether IDS would do more than dress down. I hoped he'd roll up his sleeves and press on with making the real changes his party needed.

13

'TOTTY' AND 'BOTTY'

Shortly after IDS had been confirmed as party leader a new Tory MP, who had only entered the House at the 2001 general election, made headlines with his love-life. For once it wasn't the perversity of his predilections, it wasn't an unhealthy longing for oranges, stockings, threesomes or nubile research assistants that brought this otherwise unknown to the attention of the national press. Instead it was the sheer ordinariness of his desires; merely searching for a girlfriend, or perhaps a wife, had marked Adrian Flook out as the Bridget – or Brian – Jones of the Palace of Westminster. But it was the relatively unorthodox method of his search, placing a wanted ad in Westminster's *House Magazine*, that ensured his plight would become well known.

It was, he said, difficult for MPs to meet people and to find enough time to develop a relationship. He might have added that being a Tory MP was also likely to have limited his eligibility. Where once there was a promise of power and its associate glamour for a certain kind of county girl set on marrying a Conservative MP, in recent years there has only been the mundane reality of opposition. And with it the knowledge that for some time at least it is still unlikely that ministerial boxes or offices in Whitehall will compensate for all the financial and practical inconveniences of such a union. Far better then to marry a banker or a lawyer. There is also the likelihood these days that the county girl is herself a banker or lawyer — unable or perhaps unwilling to step into the unreconstructed role of constituency wife that so many Tory selection committees prefer. Then there are all those negative associations of Toryness that, regardless of his status as an MP, would not endear Mr Flook to so many of the available single women. After all, his literary counterpart — the real Bridget Jones — is prepared to put up with all sorts of 'emotional fuckwittage' but when a potential boyfriend is revealed as a Conservative it is simply beyond the pale. For Bridget even celibacy is preferable to Conservatism.

I read of Mr Flook's plight with a certain sympathy, but it occurred to me that the search for love, although hard for a Tory boy, is probably even harder for a free-market female. Not only do we put off any left-wing suitors the moment conversation turns to politics, we then have to negotiate our way around the worst excesses of the right-wing male. The demographics tell the story with cool rational detachment — i.e., that of all the groups to have abandoned the Tories the trend is most marked among young, professional women — and if they won't vote for a Tory they are hardly likely to date one. Anecdotal evidence supports these trends in more vivid terms. At a recent dinner party a smart, intelligent female psychotherapist whose job is to counsel the severely troubled (wife beaters, substance abusers, various neurotics all welcome) told me without a hint of irony that she would treat anyone except a Tory MP. So they really are poor beleaguered things — Bridget Jones won't sleep with them and shrinks won't treat them, all of which seems to leave me as a definite trend-bucker. I am slap-bang in the middle of that disenchanted group, the educated young professional woman, and yet I'll still admit to being a Conservative and, on top of that, I have tried, with mixed results, to keep my sex life in line with my politics!

In one sense a wanted ad placed by a Tory MP looking for love is just a sensible way of approaching a contemporary problem, now that the relatively straightforward days of meeting a spouse at a Young Conservative ball have passed. And yet Mr Flook's enquiry seemed even more than that – a metaphor for the state of his party. Pondering his circumstances with all the Carrie Bradshaw questioning I could muster I wondered, 'Could the Tory Party ever become sexy again?'

Thus far I've written about the stigma that has always, in my experience, come as part of the package of being a Tory. Historically, it is about Empire, elitism, inherited privilege and the not always unreasonable accusation of being the 'stupid party'. Equally in my lifetime it was about the perceived harshness of Thatcherism and later the perceived corruption of the Major years – the not always unreasonable accusation of being, in Theresa May's words, the 'nasty party'. But although he had never been my cup of tea, Alan B'stard, as the personification of these presumed Tory vices still had some kind of sex appeal. Harshness and corruption though not endearing were never as miserably unattractive as failure, anonymity and self-absorption. Sadly, exempting the recent signs of recovery, the party's constant flat-lining in the polls since the mid 1990s suggests a collective case of brewer's droop. With the best will in the world it's hard to associate virility with the Hague and IDS leaderships – though I'm hoping Michael Howard can yet supply the necessary dose of political Viagra. But even I, veteran of several Tory romances, can't help thinking now that Mr Flook and his Tory Boys are looking like the unfortunate few left at the end of the singles party –'market clearance' to throw in a cruel colloquialism. The thing is that as much as people hated them the sexy sheen of authority did give the Tories pulling power – but while in low-profile opposition the Tories just seemed impotent – in more ways than one.

By now I would hope that our loveless MP has found his match, and that the Howard effect has boosted his appeal, but if not perhaps he could benefit from some tips drawn from my own experience of romancing the right. The search for a partner is difficult enough these days without the added requirement of political compatibility, so if Mr Flook will contemplate sleeping with the enemy he immediately ups his chances of success. However, I do sympathise with him if he feels more comfortable with a political fellow-traveller. After all, there is nothing more likely to disturb a warm afterglow than a fierce political argument, even if a spot of intellectual jousting can be quite a spicy prelim. But foreplay can still come to a rapid halt if a serious difference of worldview emerges — I'll always put the glass of wine down and walk away when I hear 'That George Bush, he's no better than Saddam Hussein you know.'

I too had entered my thirties a 'Flookie'. With romance over, Andrew and I had decided to go our separate ways and I was a newly available girl about town. The search was on again for Mr Right or in my case Mr Right Wing. It might seem rather fussy but the alternative can be just too problematic. Take for instance the case of the antique dealer. He was undoubtedly handsome, sort of half Al Pacino half Antonio Banderas, and undoubtedly romantic, as he would send me frequent notes handwritten in gold ink on the torn-out pages of antiquarian books. Against my better judgement, I had tried to steer any conversation as far away from politics as possible sensing that if I were to reveal myself a Tory the moment might pass. But as much as I tried to avoid the inevitable it was bound to come out, and one night in a Mayfair tapas bar the 'C' word sealed my fate. In fact, in the end, I don't think Mr Antiques minded my politics but I just couldn't stomach his. After a long impassioned debate about education policy we parted (well, looking ahead, how would we agree on a school for the kids?) and all I had to remember him by was the bill and plate of shrivelled chorizo. So take heed, Mr Flook and follow your convictions from the start.

Next, I moved on to what seemed like safer ground — a Republican. I met Mr Banker in the gym. It was not easy to keep up much of a conversation while running on a treadmill but there is nothing like a challenge to sharpen the mind. On the other hand,

a gym left little to the imagination – if there was more
...n met the eye that was certainly an added bonus. And the
...as that yes, he was a Conservative – that is, an American
...lican – the downside was that he lived in Chicago.
...rtheless, with the benefit of business travel a transatlantic
...anglement was established which was to reach its apex in a
...lorida holiday.

As the water from the designer swimming pool lapped over my
toes in the exotic garden of Madonna's favoured Delano Hotel, Mr
Right Wing was certainly looking like Mr Right Now. But then,
true to form, I had to go and put my foot in it. What started as an
innocent conversation about the merits of keeping children out of
luxury hotels developed into a no-holds-barred argument about
property rights. I felt it was down to the hotelier to be able to dis-
criminate about who to accommodate in his own hotel, he felt that
the state (that is the state of Florida as opposed to the state in general) had the right to regulate. Actually it was a revealing insight
into the different attitudes that two apparently similar *laissez faire*
nations have to the notion of the free market (we tend to forget
how much regulation Americans accept). But whatever the merits
of this discussion, as an academic exercise it was only to prove a
passion killer. So another lesson, Mr Flook, on that occasion I was
the political bore and I rightly paid the price.

Back in Blighty I continued to practise the politics of dating. A
couple of times I thought I had struck gold when potential para-
mours quickly revealed their own right-wing tendencies to me in
our own stylised mating dance. 'I always was a great admirer of
Michael Howard,' was music to my ears especially when followed
up with, 'He is so much nicer in reality that he ever seems on TV.'
But Tory Boys like that one do tend towards the conventional, and
I can understand why so many of my female contemporaries would
automatically give them a wide berth.

In observing the curious mating rituals of the right-wing male
in his own environment I've noticed that many exhibit a rather
unsophisticated set of requirements for their significant other:

their chief targets being – in their lingo – 'Totty' or 'Botty'. Being the wrong gender, means I hold no interest for the Botty boys, those dapper gay Tories who proliferate in the political consultancies of Westminster. Do I qualify as Totty? Doubtful that I do or that I'd want to. One evening spent with the kind of Tory man who covets 'Totty' was an unmitigated disaster. Charming, eligible, attractive and intelligent Mr MP seemed like the perfect date but all that urbane charisma masked an unreconstructed heart that beat with considerable venom. Oysters washed down with a lively deconstruction of Gordon Brown's post-endogenous growth theory made a surprisingly harmonious hors d'oeuvre, but by the time the bill came things had turned sour. When the waiter accidentally knocked over the sugar bowl my date swore at him and aggressively demanded an apology. I was embarrassed. I suggested his response had been a bit over the top, as indeed was his to me. 'You're questioning me? You dare to question me? You are clearly not an organic Tory or you would understand that a woman, like a waiter, doesn't question the authority of a man – especially if he is paying the bill.'

Given that I had paid for our previous dinner this seemed a particularly cheap jibe. Also I was not convinced that this former Thatcherite would have tried out his spirited defence of masculine superiority on Maggie. But I was at least grateful that it had taken only two dates to reveal his nineteenth-century sensibilities. Needless to say we did not continue to date and I was left wondering how I could share a political allegiance with such a dinosaur. It would be easy to dismiss this as an extreme case and I know that misogyny knows no party boundaries, but the incident encapsulated an attitude towards women, and indeed towards modernity, that many have come to associate with the Tory Party in general. Perhaps Bridget Jones bridled at the thought of a Tory boyfriend because she thought he might be a bit of a drip but she may also have assumed, as I think most of my female friends do, that his attitudes would be antediluvian.

Looking at the evidence, there is no doubt that the early

popularity of New Labour was boosted by its appeal to young women, exactly the group who most readily abandoned John Major in 1997. Just as Wetherspoons, the enterprising pub chain, had deliberately targeted their pale-carpeted, Chardonnay-serving hostelries at the burgeoning spending power of women, so New Labour had deliberately 'feminised' their styling. In contrast to the stiff suited, old-school-tied Tories we had Armani and rows of female role models, dismissed as Blair's babes, symbolising and emphasising the 'newness' of New Labour. And across the pond their spiritual soulmates the 'new' Democrats had at their helm a charismatic leader with a strong, vocal and high-profile wife who controversially admitted that staying home and baking cookies was not her thing. Central to the Clintons' early plans (soon abandoned in power) was their rather vague platform about improving the lot of women. So, explicitly and implicitly, the new politics was deliberately aimed at appealing to the increasingly sophisticated female voter. Many have seen through this approach where it has tended towards sheer tokenism, but in looking for a more sober, grown-up alternative from the Conservatives the signals have been confused.

I winced after 1997 when boyish Tory MPs barracked New Labour's new female members. Sure, many may never have been selected without the illegal single-sex shortlists but the childish braying across the floor of the House of Commons hardly drew attention to the inherent weaknesses of positive discrimination. Instead, it only served to reinforce the impression already long established that the Tory Party is a cultural extension of the single-sex public school and the gentleman's club. I was not alone in noticing this and so we heard briefings from Central Office about the new regime that Hague, as moderniser, would sponsor and later that IDS would also champion. The good intentions were there, the problem acknowledged, but the Tories' aesthetic remained resolutely unaltered. William Hague's educated, articulate, and independent wife was rightly judged an asset and often pushed centre stage because she was also attractive and photogenic. But

when it came to her biggest role on the political circuit, as his supportive partner throughout the general election campaign of 2001,
she was advised to keep mum. Her studied silence throughout the
gruelling national tour just made it look as though she was there on
sufferance – although I am sure from what I know of the Hagues
that that was not the case. Worse, the impression given was of an
anachronistic model of marriage – somehow the Tories had managed to reduce a vibrant, clever and impressive woman to the role
of 'totty' on the arm of her adored hubby. 'Ah' I can hear the Tory
purists cry – these matters are so superficial – 'They shouldn't
matter.' Well, yes, at one level they are superficial but even at that
level they do matter. These faux pas alienate people at the critical
subconscious level – they feel repelled even before they have a
chance to look beyond the presentation.

Taking a leaf out of New Labour's book, the party eventually
appointed a capable and telegenic female chairman. We had, of
course, most importantly broken the male mould of politics several
decades previously with Margaret Thatcher, but many men – in
and out of the party – remained so averse to change that they had
somehow imagined her a token man. Iain Duncan Smith's choice of
Theresa May as chairman was timely and reassuring, indicating
that he would defy his unreconstructed supporters. Some feminist
observers argue that Theresa May's refusal to redesignate herself
'chairwoman' undermined her potential role as a female champion
from the start. But the sort of activist who would take against
Theresa May because she refuses to play semantics will doubtless
never a Conservative be and there is no reason to patronise that
constituency pretending that word games will make all the difference. Far better to acknowledge, as her appointment did, that a
high-profile role for an articulate, professional woman can in
itself – over time, contribute to a realignment of the Tory image –
assuming that she does a good job.

But poor, poor Theresa. How unfortunate to have to make her
chairmanly debut to a party conference during the week in which
the worst of Tory bedroom politics dominated the headlines.

Neither sex emerged well from Edwina Currie's revelations of her affair with John Major and the news of it provoked the sort of bitchy comments from all sides that truly befitted a 'nasty party'. What struck me was the image yet again conveyed of the party's preferred model of wife – silent and subservient where loyalty is reduced merely to contractual obligation. Twenty years previously, when my journey through the party was just beginning, I was flushed with early enthusiasm and an instinctive belief in the fundamentals which stir me still now. The choice between left and right was then absolutely clear and I was prepared to overlook my distaste for the chauvinism I encountered among the spotty Tory Boys because we shared a bigger aim. But even then I remember feeling rather uncomfortable about joining a party that had so recently shown such blatant double standards in the matter of the Cecil Parkinson/Sarah Keays affair. Where he was shown understanding and compassion, she was condemned. His rehabilitation was assured as long as he returned to his wife. The rights and wrongs of such situations are necessarily complex – the greyest of grey areas, but making a scapegoat out of the so-called 'mistress' is a crude attempt to cast judgement in one direction only. It's been the same pattern with every marital indiscretion that has beset the Tories over the years. Women are either the angelic loyal wife, or the whorish corrupting lover and the poor hapless, helpless man has just found himself caught in the middle. So much for a philosophy centred on individuals taking responsibility for their own freely made decisions. John Major's odious statement in which he quickly dismissed a four-year relationship as the biggest regret of his life (if so why did it last so long?) sadly revealed him as a man who shared the least attractive values of an establishment class he had purported to challenge.

Perhaps it is a bit fanciful to surmise that the success or otherwise of one Tory MP's love life bears any relation to the wider state of his party? And I should apologise to Mr Flook, who even as I write may be happily married and engaged in producing the urgently needed next generation of Conservative activists. But presuming that he, or others like him, are still searching for their perfect 'totty' it's probably time they drew some personal conclusions from their malaise. The shame is that the negative cultural associations that continue to blight us Conservatives do prevent many people from making an objective assessment about the party's policies. While my conflation of the dating issue and the decline of the Tory Party may seem merely frivolous it's worth considering the research potential of an active social life in this age of the focus group. After all, when looking to attract a new lover, it's only natural to want to present oneself in the best light, so it is significant that so few people are prepared to describe themselves as conservative or right-wing.

For the sake of this book, and strictly in the spirit of research, I have carried out my own blind survey of eligible single men in London and found that generally, regardless of their actual views, they will almost always describe their politics as moderate left wing. One such friend favours restoring the death penalty, another privatising all schools, a third thinks the asylum system is too lax and tax is too high but all cling resolutely to their leftish credentials, even though I would say they were probably to the right of me. If I were being defeatist I might have to advise the 'Flookies', that for the sake of their sex-lives they should conveniently redefine their politics. Far better that they should jettison the aspects of their Conservatism that leave them unattractive to the contemporary single female. Then the more positive aspects of their philosophy can emerge untainted by the worst excesses of those Tories who remain unable or unwilling to capture the Zeitgeist — think *Sex and the City* rather than sects and the shires.

In the days when I was still at the BBC the post-work, post-gym wine-bar excursions with female colleagues confirmed the resonance of the Bridget Jones phenomenon. For though we all wanted to distance ourselves from such a flawed heroine, it wasn't hard to see ourselves in the calorie-obsessed, Chardonnay-quaffing, resolution-breaking, man-chasing stereotype that made her such a vivid and timely character. I suspect she would be far more likely to consider romance with a Tory if he were to follow some of the advice I have offered. But I'm not so naive as to think that it is solely a matter of presentation (or that she will still be fertile by the time the Tories have smartened up their act). If beneath her apparent enjoyment of the consumer society there lurks the heart of an anti-globalisation, anti-American, anti-capitalist activist then I admit defeat and recommend she should look to the Liberal Democrats for a perfect partner. If Bridget is a non-aligned floating voter who could in time be persuaded that not all Tories are narrow-minded misogynists or bad lovers, it's up to the party to woo her. There is some positive news. IDS may not have been a natural hit with this demographic group, as like William Hague he is not an immediately seductive figure, but contrary to general expectations he did make some encouraging moves towards modernising the party's appeal. On a totemic level he broke links with the men-only Carlton Club, perhaps the last formal vestige of the culture of the gentleman's club. He appointed the first woman chairman and more importantly set about the most thorough review of the selection process, instituting professional recruitment techniques in what has been a largely amateur procedure. None of these are earth-shattering moves but they are significant incremental changes that help to change the culture without riding roughshod over it and they are established practice now which Michael Howard is building on. But it is not just a job of identifying female role models. Perhaps IDS made his most effective contribution towards discarding the despised posturing of politics by promoting Oliver Letwin, a man who eschews the machismo of 'yah boo' debate for a more thoughtful type of engagement. Treated with near reverence by the BBC, Letwin's frequent media interviews proved that the mode of discourse, as much as the content, can re-engage an audience, perhaps even attract a new one – from both sexes.

Of course, the irony is that it is young professional women who have lost interest in the Conservatives; in the past they were the party's keenest supporters. And that support was registered long before the fashionable concept of 'feminising' political parties was considered important. Thatcherism and Thatcher herself, much derided for rejecting the feminist agenda, was nonetheless as popular with women as with men for all sorts of reasons that defy gender-specific attribution. Her stress on 'housekeeping' values may seem outdated now but it endeared her to the practical female voter. Similarly John Major was popular with women as long as his government maintained its reputation for economic competence. If the Conservatives were able to regain their credibility on this and other such 'bread and butter' issues they would again score points with women voters even without having to address any specific so-called 'women's issues'. Many Conservatives argue with considerable merit that appealing to a specific group is patronising and counter-productive. As a woman who clearly defies many of the categorisations political scientists assume of my gender I do sympathise with that view. But those Conservatives do their wider cause no good if in parroting that line apparently unthinkingly they resemble too closely their dogmatic *Spitting Image* cousins who dismiss any such considerations as 'political correctness gone mad'.

Conservatives do not need to take on the agenda of the Left to appeal to women, or indeed to any other specific group. If I thought that, I would not be a Conservative. But if I can momentarily indulge in a generalisation about my own sex, and particularly my immediate peer group, it is to acknowledge that all women are increasingly likely now to be busy, to have complicated lives and to want to identify clear, practical, effective and realisable messages from politicians. This should play to some of the strengths of Conservatism, if only its advocates can stop preaching, pandering and posturing. The Tory Party is perhaps now realising that wooing today's independent woman voter requires as much intelligence and subtlety as seducing her over dinner, and that, like it or not, the mood music plays a significant part in deciding whether the relationship moves up a notch to the respective ballot box or bedroom.

14

Into the Wide Blue Yonder

London–Blackpool–London, October 2003

This most recent stage of my Conservative odyssey began last October. In the days running up to the annual conference the morning chorus was sounding painfully familiar once again. Yes; it was return to Tory 'Groundhog Day', the umpteenth sequel. My alarm clock goes off, the *Today* programme eases me into consciousness, Tory grandee or, as in this latest version, nameless Tory backbencher denies splits in the party, another nameless Tory backbencher confirms splits in the party. Sure enough a leadership campaign is underway.

Allegations concerning Iain Duncan Smith's expenses and the circumstances of the employment of his wife had begun to filter out of Westminster in the week before the Party's bi-annual outing to Blackpool. Iain's leadership was already much sniped at and this particular rumour, even if none of it stuck, was hardly likely to have improved confidence in him. It also proved to be a big distraction from events at the Labour Party conference in Bournemouth where the government was busy revealing its own fissures. Gordon Brown's lurch to left speech might have been headlined 'Old Labour is the new New Labour'. That seemed to be his manifesto in a not so subtle campaign to make Brown the new Blair and it certainly should have been enough to invigorate unity of purpose among Tories. But despite the high profile return of 'tax and spend' and brooding leadership tensions in Downing Street the Tory Party still seemed stubbornly unwilling to relinquish its monopoly on self-defeating publicity. If there were stories of leadership crisis to be told the Conservatives were as determined as ever to stamp their own particular brand of self-flagellation on the conference season.

And so to Blackpool, the conference destination that strikes fear and loathing into the hearts of even the most hardened Westminster hacks. For most the prospect of a good Tory bust-up is at least an incentive to make the frustratingly lengthy trip on the infamous Virgin West Coast line that, true to its name, never seems to go all the way. But I wasn't relishing the week at all. In fact I found the spectre of yet another Conservative disaster depressing and uninspiring. Despite the ongoing Hutton inquiry this instinctive Conservative could not help but be impressed with the prime minister's Thatcher-like Atlanticism and his resolve over the war in Iraq. And on university funding and foundation hospitals Blair was showing admirably long-term and appropriate market and decentralising tendencies. I wanted to see some similar resolution from my own team. Even though the Tories had recently produced a very good analysis of the government's many weaknesses in their 'Total Politics' document it was still their own weaknesses that threatened to dominate their week in the north's premier seaside resort.

I made the journey mid-week. The conference had already started but I planned a lightning visit to see friends, gauge the mood and most importantly catch the leader's make or break speech at first hand.

On the train I overheard a businessman chatting. 'There are two types of Tories,' he said, 'the nice ones, and,' then he added rather ominously, 'the others.' I was relieved that he had acknowledged the 'nice ones'. Perhaps there had been some progress over the years? But I feared the power of the 'others' was still able to dominate the agenda. His comments had been provoked by the day's newspaper reports in which the ghost of YCs past had flavoured the coverage with more than an unhealthy dose of 'otherness'. A young hanger and flogger had called for a return to both and in vivid terms had reminded us all of those worst incarnations of Tory Boy that bedevil 'nice' Tories. How ironic it was that the very 'nicest' of the nice Tories, Oliver Letwin, urbane, liberal and conciliatory, who had used his brief as Shadow Home Secretary so effectively to challenge negative perceptions of the Tories, had had to play host to this throwback reactionary during his otherwise innovative debate on policing.

Given that Letwin had successfully wooed large sections of the liberal media he was likely to emerge untainted from his conference encounter with the not-so-liberal margins of the party. But even as Radio 4's token acceptable face of Conservatism Letwin still had his work cut out if he were to clothe the rest of his party with similar acceptability. Elsewhere in the newspapers that week polling evidence supported the idea that perceived 'nastiness' remained an electoral liability for Conservatives. A year previously Theresa May had made herself just about the most unpopular Party Chairman ever by telling the truth. In pointing out that many people had come to see the party as nasty she had raised the ire of those who were simply too blinkered or self-righteous to listen to the logic of her argument. She did not say it was fair or accurate that Tories were labelled nasty, simply that it was unfortunately the case. But this was not the morale-boosting message expected from a chairman's conference speech and she was pilloried for it. Perhaps in the aftermath of the 1997 defeat the message would have been better received? More worrying, though, than the fuss caused within the party was the reality of its enduring image problem.

Unlike those who continued to argue that the party would automatically come back into favour once New Labour was on the ropes I was convinced by the negative logic of polls in *The Times* newspaper at the start of conference week. These showed that a large majority of the middle and professional classes considered themselves 'right of centre'. The party with which they most closely identified was New Labour, not the Conservative Party. The Tory Party could never win a general election without securing a majority of AB votes. As it bore out my instincts and the experience of my peers this was depressing evidence. Of course the party still had to prove it was capable, tough and combative in opposition, as those who resented Theresa May's analysis had rightly argued. But it also remained the case that to reassure my businessman and overcome the persistently off-putting effect of the 'others' we have first to convince people we are 'nice'. Nice doesn't have to mean 'cuddly', but it does have to mean fair-minded and, most of all, trustworthy.

Blackpool, in its favour, has none of the pretensions of Brighton – which no longer welcomes the Tories for ideological reasons – but the price for this sobering northern authenticity is, well, sobering northern authenticity. The view from the train as it eventually pulled into Blackpool North station seemed to be another fitting metaphor for the state of my party. A shop selling walking frames, stair lifts and other mobility devices for the elderly and the infirm looms large on the horizon, a horizon which I found, as usual for Blackpool in October, cloaked in swirling grey clouds and drizzle. Perhaps it was touching that the party constantly eschewed metropolitanism and elitism by insisting on hosting its conference at a venue long since deserted by New Labour but I thought it was just naff. Many others simply would not bother to come at all as indicated by the frequent 'vacancies' signs in the lace-curtained B and B windows and the two-for-one offers in the 'lap of luxury' table dancing clubs.

Once inside the decaying and Byzantine Winter Gardens conference centre there they were – the decaying and Byzantine

Conservative visitors. Though there were younger faces on the fringes and interesting policy announcements from the floor, the impact of these was muted by the frenzy of speculation about possible challenges to the leadership. I had come partly to see whether this was merely media speculation or whether MPs were really lining up to add their names to calls for a leadership election. An answer came swiftly and in some style. Comfortingly, although the Tories seemed no longer able to run a party, there were still some who even at their most beleaguered knew how to throw one. That was a reassuring thought as I was whisked backstage for the treasurer's champagne reception.

My host was a shadow cabinet member whose role was pivotal to Iain Duncan Smith's fortunes. If anyone would know the state of things he would. Yes, he admitted, things were very bad but they did not know how close to collapse they were. The malignant insecurity rested on the rules which William Hague had introduced which required a vote of confidence in the leader should 15 per cent of MPs call for one. The leadership knew that a number of MPs had called for a vote but not whether or when the numbers would tip over the 15 per cent marker. Threats and gossip were adding to the impression of Iain's vulnerability and increasing the likelihood that more MPs would feel honour bound to ditch a discredited leader. The best way for Iain to halt this vicious cycle was to stamp his authority on the party with a confident and inspiring conference speech. But oratory had never been his forte. I could see why party officials were trying to keep their spirits up by downing bubbly at three in the afternoon.

The most dispiriting aspect of the conversation was the extent to which it confirmed the worst stories leaking out of Central Office. When Iain had stood for the leadership I had thought it unlikely that he would grow into an inspiring figurehead, but I had hoped he would be at least a competent one. Since then, however, even the impression of competence had been at best mixed. And I was being told that in private the reality was worse. Hence the party had been close to this point of crisis at least twice before under Iain's leadership. His mishandling of votes on Clause 28 and gay adoption had sounded a particularly negative note for me. They had been emblematic issues on which I had hoped he would surprise his detractors by doing something counter-intuitive. Instead he had lived up to his conventional image and whipped the vote, forcing liberals to rebel or even resign if they wanted, as the government did, to reform the troublesome and much-hated legislation.

I had worried about that but on the plus side there had been some very positive signs during the first few months of Iain's leadership. His shadow cabinet team was capable and the direction of policy more coherent and attractive than it ever had been under William Hague. It was beginning to challenge negative stereotypes about a Conservative agenda, championing public services and the poor, advocating smaller and devolved government. Europe had taken a back seat. The tone had been less shrill, the public face more caring. And so it was particularly frustrating to follow the two steps forward, four back routine that had become the pattern of IDS's leadership. As much as progress was being achieved with the slow, sober approach to policy it was all too easily undermined by the rows emanating from Central Office. Yet again it seemed to me that mismanagement, human error and amateurism were preventing the party from moving on.

I was disappointed, although not entirely surprised, to note that Iain had repeated mistakes made by William Hague in surrounding himself with too narrow and uncritical a cabal. The highly public and misadvised sacking of key 'modernisers' was a very bad sign. The appointment of Barry Legg, a close friend of the leader's, as the party's chief executive, had been a disaster. According to legend, when Iain had asked a colleague what was wrong with his choice he had been told that half the party disliked the man he had unilaterally appointed, while the other half just couldn't stand him. It had provoked the second crisis of confidence in Duncan Smith, this time throughout all sections of the party. But on these previous occasions he had survived. Many colleagues would have liked to see him go but calculated that the cost to the party of yet another lengthy leadership election so soon after the last would have been dear. And it was hard not to agree with that analysis. Until they could figure out a way round that dilemma Iain's position was bolstered, as had been John Major's and William Hague's, by the complications of replacing him and the lack of an obvious alternative.

With champagne-enhanced candour I was being told that my gloomiest assumptions were appropriate. The media speculation was accurate, the stories about plummeting morale in Central Office true. And yet even here at this doomed conference there would be other signs, more positive signs that told a different story.

This was the tenth annual conference I had attended. When the Conservatives had been in government the excitement of these events was tangible. The opportunity to rub shoulders with cabinet ministers, the allure of an exclusive late night party (Lord Strathclyde, Tory leader in the Lords, had long since taken over from Jeffrey Archer as the dispenser of the must-have invitation) and the sense that despite the stage management there was real power-brokering going on behind the scenes had always given the week a certain thrilling quality. And from a journalistic perspective the conference had offered the chance to observe aspects of the party's culture that a Westminster-based correspondent might never see otherwise.

The activists and their priorities found a voice in the fringe events. It wasn't always pretty but it was revealing. In past years these fringe meetings had been a hectic, well attended and dizzy round of events where the various splinter groups of Euroscepticism always drew the biggest crowds: Conservatives Against a Federal Europe, The Bruges Group, The No Turning Back Group, Conservative Way Forward, The Freedom Association. These had been the big names on the fringe offering disgruntled peers a platform for subversive politicking, activists the opportunity to vent a bit of spleen, and journalists the excuse to write once again the story of the disunited party. When the party was out of power the drama of these events was necessarily less piquant but if in the early years of opposition the conference fringe had been less explosive, it reflected a party lost in its own uncharted wilderness. This year the conference attendees were well down on previous events and yet there was a certain freshness to the fringe. Gone were the guaranteed bust-ups over Europe and instead more emphasis was on finding solutions to public policy problems and delivery of health and education. Gone were the arcane lectures about tax and morality, instead discussions were about how to cut tax without endangering public services. And alongside the established old names of right wing think-tanks, the Adam Smith Institute, the Centre for Policy Studies, there were new, younger organisations – Reform, Policy Exchange and Civitas, all looking for innovative solutions, less hidebound by Conservative tradition. These were positive signs in an otherwise grim week.

Dinner that evening was with a group of prospective candidates. In a cavernous and otherwise empty Chinese restaurant we ate a 'banquet' of egg-fried rice and various dishes à la monosodium glutamate. Though the conference experience might be a feast for the mind, it is never one for the stomach. But fortunately the company needed no flavour enhancement. Our group told a different story about the Conservative Party, one that was barely filtering through this latest round of public antagonism. A funky northern businesswoman, a trendy journalist, an articulate female magistrate, a disabled PR executive, an entertaining young entrepreneur – all under forty, all more concerned about getting rid of the Labour leader than getting rid of their own. All would pass the 'Notting Hill bar test'. If these were the faces of a renewing Conservative Party things were not as bad as they seemed, and for all that he lacked IDS deserved credit for having instituted a desperately needed widening of the candidates list.

At the previous year's conference Iain Duncan Smith had decided to sell himself as the honest straight guy alternative to Tony Blair. In contrast to slick Mr Blair, Iain had emphasised his own studied determination. He styled himself the 'Quiet Man' of politics. Unfortunately a year later large sections of his own party wanted to see him quietened completely.

The finished product of a leader's conference speech evolves over several weeks with the constant finessing reaching something of a fever pitch during the days before it is delivered. Given that IDS was going to have to make the speech of his life the frenetic last-minute processing of his opus was perhaps more intense than usual. As much as many of the party members, who had after all voted this man their first elected leader, wanted to see him shine, there were others, and of course many of the waiting journalists, who hoped his performance that day would hasten his downfall. So the atmosphere in the expectant conference room was positively gladiatorial as the lights were lowered in the build-up to Iain's entrance. A short film painted a picture of 'Iain's journey' that, ironically, echoed the most famous political broadcast of his nemesis John Major. And then there was IDS in person, trying before our very eyes to recreate himself in a different image. Explicitly he said, 'The quiet man is turning up the volume.' This seemed odd to me. Whether or not the quiet man moniker is the best choice for a media age politician, it had worked for Iain Duncan Smith because at least it had the advantage of being credible. It matched what people thought they knew about the man. So why, against the advice of his colleagues, draw attention to an image U turn? I couldn't help wondering if the message was aimed not at the government, but at his own party. Perhaps he was really saying 'I'm not going to go quietly.'

And there was some evidence in this very mixed speech that he shouldn't have to go. But paradoxically that evidence was at its most obvious in the 'quietest' parts of the speech, the sections that were true to the earlier construction of IDS as a thoughtful, earnest politician, uncomfortable with grand gestures, looking instead for practical, incremental change. These sections of the speech, quietly and conversationally delivered, were easily the most engaging and persuasive. Here Iain outlined his personal agenda with its commitment to using the market to deliver the aims of one nation. For all his emerging faults Iain Duncan Smith had given this agenda a higher profile than any Conservative leader of my lifetime. I welcomed it. Less welcome though were those parts of the speech where the 'volume' had been turned up. A very personal attack on Charles Kennedy, an un-parliamentary assault on the prime minister and a clumsy reference to asylum problems were distinctly ungentlemanly. Prejudging Hutton and branding Mr Blair a liar seemed less passionate than opportunistic. The person made to look smaller was not the prime minister but the hitherto 'decent' IDS. What a mistake to structure a speech in this way, ensuring that the only parts that would receive wide coverage would be aggressively delivered soundbites that did not begin to communicate the strongest sections of a very mixed offering.

Much was made afterwards of the curious Mexican wave that punctuated the flow of the leader's speech. Standing right at the back of the hall I had been less aware than observers on the balcony of the careful choreography of these apparently spontaneous standing ovations, but even so the sheer number certainly suggested a contrivance. Barely had Iain managed to emit another sentence before the audience had once again risen to its feet, cheering and clapping. For one of the country's best-known Catholics this was a bizarrely evangelistic spectacle. But of course the real point of all of these theatrics was to whip up a frenzy within this very particular congregation. Iain must have hoped that renewing the faith of his strongest supporters, the party members who had overwhelmingly backed him in the innovative ballot two years previously, would count towards his long term survival. At that moment, and given the more lyrical sections of his speech, it seemed he had confirmed his role as their leader. But given the rising whiff of scandal, the increasing image of incompetence and stuttering progress of opposition, Iain's leadership had needed more than an effective sermon. It had needed a miracle.

Back in London it was hardly any time before IDS was looking all too human again. Many of us wanted to believe the best of him and in his passionate defence of his wife it was possible to see a man who perhaps had been wrongly accused. Wrongly accused that is of any corruption or deliberate bending of the rules, but even with the benefit of the doubt I had to conclude that Iain's judgement now seemed fatally flawed. I was less concerned as to whether he had actually done anything specifically wrong, but perplexed as to how a twenty-first century leader could think this nepotistic way of operating was appropriate or advisable. Each leaked memo or revelation that emerged from Central Office pointed to a totally decaying operation, one that was in considerably worse repair than the system I had known ten years previously. A brief encounter that I had had with Iain's regime had born out this shambolic impression, but my dealings with him had been on his arrival as leader. I had hoped that my experience of cancelled meetings, lost letters, and stolen documents had been 'teething' problems, a consequence of regime change. It seems they were actually symptoms of a malaise that became endemic throughout Iain's two years of leadership. His inexperience had made it hard for him to delegate. From colleagues I was hearing about his preoccupation with minutiae and the subsequent diminution of his authority. He most crucially had not recognised his own weaknesses and made contingency plans. Plots were spotted and plotters accused where there were none – just worried MPs who increasingly had reason to question whether the drastic option of another leadership battle might not be the party's only survival option. The word in Westminster was that one man dominated shadow cabinet meetings. And it was not Iain Duncan Smith.

Enter stage right: Michael Howard.

If my account of the Tory Party was fictional, another *House of Cards* or suchlike, the dramatic re-emergence of Michael Howard in the closing act might seem too unlikely, a plot twist too far. After all, whether fair or not, this man had become a potent symbol of the *ancien régime*, something of a hate figure throughout the Major years. To my generation of voters he was the man who had introduced the Poll Tax and perhaps more damningly called time on the rave culture of the early 1990s. The Criminal Justice Act, clamping down on 'new age travellers' and illegal raves had seemed to some the ultimate Tory project and spawned a wave of popular protests. Mr 'Prison Works' had taken over from Norman Tebbit as a sort of pantomime baddie, a role burnt on to our consciousness by the bitchy but pithy 'something of the night' summation of him. Six years previously Howard had failed to get off the starting blocks in his rather lacklustre bid for leadership after the party's 1997 defeat. Having been knifed in the back by William Hague, who in deciding to run for leadership himself had reneged on his agreement to run as Howard's mate, and in the front by Anne Widdecombe, it was reasonable to conclude that his leadership ambitions had passed their sell-by date. Perhaps Duncan Smith had revived them by bringing him back on to the front bench as Shadow Chancellor but the decision had looked risky at the moment that IDS was trying to fashion a new team to back up his new leadership. No doubt Howard is a brilliant mind, a great operator, but he was hardly the new face of the Tories . . . but then again, such faces were scarce and after a second election defeat, substance, as much as style, was needed more than ever.

Two years on, if Iain was to lose a vote of confidence, I couldn't see that, of the likely contenders to replace him as leader, there was a stronger candidate than Michael Howard. Excepting though, if he were to stand, perhaps the time had come for Ken Clarke? As much as I personally resisted his position on Europe this no longer seemed the time to quibble and I suspected that contrary to press conclusions many of the party members would see it the same way. If the party really was on the brink of another lengthy leadership battle it had to emerge with a leader who could command respect. Despite my personal reservations there is no doubt that Clarke would do that and would certainly re-engage public interest. The other wild card was of course Michael Portillo, but I had long doubted he had any intention of standing again as leader. It was no surprise when he confirmed that in media interviews. More plotted against than plotter it was not hard to see why Portillo had lost his enthusiasm for Westminster and had succumbed to the amazing privilege of a media life.

Since party rules required that leadership elections be decided by a ballot of party members the stakes were very high for MPs deciding whether or not to add their names to those who had already requested a motion of no confidence. It might be better to pull together behind IDS at least until a general election, after which – assuming another Tory defeat – he could stand down, causing less collateral damage. The prospect of a drawn-out series of ballots as candidates appealed first to MPs and then to party members was not an enticing one, particularly when the Conservatives had the ever more vital job of opposition to prosecute. The government and much of the media must have relished the revival of Tory Groundhog Day but any Tory with half a mind would have realised that the net effect of such a spectacle may cause more harm than good. Yet again the Tories would appear disunited, petty, self-obsessed just as the government was about to enter its most testing time under the shadow of the Hutton Report and likely rebellions over top-up fees. A year previously during a former outbreak of insecurity IDS had effectively neutered a rebellion with the vivid warning that the Tory Party must 'Unite or Die'. That choice seemed no less stark when news did eventually break on October 28 that MPs had decided to call a vote of confidence in their leader.

I had observed the Conservative Party, as active member, party insider and disinterested hack, for a quarter of a century. Its ascent and descent had been equally pronounced. In my teenage years it seemed unassailable, and now in opposition it seemed all too close to extinction. In government Tories had been deemed nasty, in opposition irrelevant. The truth of course was never quite so absolute but it was fair to say that having lost the responsibility of government the party seemed also to have lost the ability to govern itself. And now after years of drift this, more than any previous crisis I could remember, was a pivotal moment. Would they unite? As New Labour continue to be a moving target, an indistinct melange, a political chameleon, the Tories still seemed befuddled as to how to unite against it. Might they die? The end of the Conservative Party, though not inevitable, remained possible. Iain Duncan Smith had told colleagues that he had earned the right to lead his party. But Conservatives should scorn the random claim to rights. If he could not command respect he could not demand the right to lead. And so for his party, if it could not command respect it had no absolute right to survive. As much of a Conservative as I am, even I was beginning to wonder how I could carry on backing it if it were to come out of this imminent leadership battle weaker than it had gone into it. Perhaps in sympathy with the times it had become seduced by the victim mentality? Perhaps it might never sort itself out and in its place Britain would evolve a new libertarian party to oppose a post-Blair social democratic alliance and some hard left splinters?

At that moment any number of scenarios seemed possible. The one that by now seemed least likely was that this fractious, fratricidal bunch would actually pull itself together.

Back to Groundhog Day and back once again to the Pugin-papered committee room corridor where so many Tory leaders had had to face the judgement of their parliamentary colleagues, and now Iain Duncan Smith was making history in the most ignominious fashion. On 29 October 2003 the party's first 'elected' leader became the first forced out by a vote of no confidence. The result, although closer than many had predicted, had nonetheless become something of a foregone conclusion during the hours in which IDS had campaigned to save his leadership. Journalists jostling in the cynical waiting crowd added the voting figures to stories they had already written. But even so there was a surprise to come. Emissaries for David Davis rustled through the throng with news of his imminent press conference. I, like all my colleagues, anticipated a speech in which the party's most ambitious wannabe leader would be first to announce his candidacy. We were wrong. Outmanoeuvred. Instead as we strained to hear the 'impromptu' announcement on the steps of the Common's main entrance we heard a declaration of delayed leadership intent. No, Davis wouldn't be running for the leadership now but backing the only man who could unite the party, Michael Howard. Very classy. In one deft move Davis became the man who united the party, leading the way for an outbreak of solidarity behind Howard, enhancing his own statesman-like credibility and scoring countless points for a future election. Here was a politician's politician in action. And regardless of the tactical advantages it was also the right thing to do. Full points all round.

All this sensible, adult behaviour was curiously bewildering. Had we really gone from backstabbing to backbone in one fell swoop? As close of nominations loomed, the warm wishes for Michael Howard glowed ever more intensely, bestowing on him at first a ring of confidence that by the time of his confirmation as unchallenged leader seemed transformed into a halo. Relieved of uncertainty Iain Duncan Smith also underwent something of trans-formation, sounding once again relaxed and charming as he toured radio studios to promote his novel. Colleagues were relieved that he had this distraction while they planned to, as one put it to me, 'airbrush him out of history'.

And what of Michael Howard's history? Would the Conservative Party of 2004 find new life with a relatively elderly leader, one whose reputation spoke of a different era? The first signs were greatly encouraging with all the newspapers praising his professionalism, his brain and his unquestioned authority. A supportive press was in itself a very welcome change, a chance to reverse years of morale-bruising headlines and ever-perpetuating cycles of bad publicity. If Tories could regain confidence in their leadership they might yet rediscover their sense of direction and purpose. And the burst of positive momentum that followed Howard's first parliamentary outings as leader was tangible. Suddenly the impression of haphazard decay was replaced with discipline and order. If Michael Howard was to do nothing else but install a successful operation at the heart of the Tory Party he would have done it an invaluable service. The news of serious heavyweights recruited to run Central Office was long over-due and a welcome relief. Rumours about abandoning the by-now-fated Smith Square HQ, with its own special version of sick building syndrome, also showed common sense and determination. Within only a week of his accession it seemed to me, and to returning donors and renewing members, that the Conservative Party was back in business. This was pretty miraculous – the halo, it seemed, was well deserved.

It was Michael Howard's history in government that would preoccupy the attentions of the press and New Labour, looking for embarrassing stories and hoping to 'smear' him with Thatcherism. While I had had my reservations about some of his less liberal pronouncements as a minister I had nonetheless always admired Howard, probably because I knew that the genesis of his conservatism was not so different to my own. It was his family history that had endeared him to me even though I knew that he could appear an unsympathetic public figure. Before my interest in Tory leadership elections had grown jaded I had followed the events of the contest of summer 1997 with close attention. Although Howard's first attempt to run for the leadership ended almost as soon as it had begun it did leave a lasting impression on me.

Apart from winning the fewest votes in the ballot of MPs, Howard's other notable contribution to that election was a little reported speech he made while still plying his candidacy. It was moving and personal and told of a family that had chosen Britain for many of the same reasons as my father had. Of course it struck a chord with me and of course I understood why Howard had also seen an inevitable connection between his family's journey and his perception of the Conservative Party as a force for decency and a bulwark against extremes. Listening at the time to that speech I was struck also by the very different image it gave of a man whose persona could seem uncaring, patronising and even at times shifty. I hoped then for his sake and for the party's that that speech could have had a wider audience but in the wake of his failure to make the second round of the election it seemed consigned to the shredder. I never imagined that I would hear the same speech, or at least another version of it, delivered when Howard himself became leader. But six years later amidst the oak-clad walls of the new Saatchi gallery, itself a testament to modernity and tradition

combined, there was Michael Howard reviving that former election speech now as an introduction to the man as leader.

Listening to it and his later 'British Dream' speech, I could easily
have been a teenager again, idealistic and optimistic, which after
years of disenchantment and scepticism was a pleasure. But a selfish pleasure of course, because having my political buttons pressed
is hardly the point. In a very few days Howard had clearly
succeeded where at least three of his predecessors had not. He had
managed to make his party feel good about itself again but vital
though it was to inject a sense of positive momentum, it was only
the start of a process, until then only ever half-heartedly applied,
to make the public feel good about it. Nevertheless, so unexpected
and honeymoonish was this outbreak of positive feeling last
November that it momentarily seemed hard to imagine what
next spoke would fall into the Tory wheel. An embarrassing episode
of self-recrimination had been kept to an efficient minimum, a
sensibly streamlined shadow cabinet representing all shades of
opinion was united in purpose, a newly sanguine and comparatively
modest leader was successfully belittling a comparatively smug
prime minister. Good heavens, at this rate it might be possible
that instead of being pilloried for my allegiances at Islington
dinner parties I'd be congratulated for them. I was starting to
imagine a whole new social life opening up when my fantasy
was rudely interrupted by the newly appointed shadow home
secretary backing a return for the death penalty. David Davis, it
seemed, had more in common with the party conference speaker
who had called for a return to hanging and flogging than his
predecessor Oliver Letwin. Just as Michael Howard was working
hard to soften the hard edges of his own previously unsympathetic image, here was Davis trying to outflank David Blunkett in
a bid for the nasty vote. Oh well, I guess you can't have it all.

At several stages in the recent history of the Tory Party 'having
it all', or at least coming close to it, might have meant a Michael
Portillo leadership. I couldn't help but remain fascinated by the
former minister I had encountered and been so impressed by at

first-hand during my early green days as a party official. While many had seen his evolution as suspicious or contrived I prefer instead to see the eventual emergence of Portillo the liberal, creative cosmopolitan as a return to form, a realisation of his early promise. And neither do I think these qualities were in any way inconsistent with Thatcherism or Conservatism, only that during the worst excesses of 1980s and 90s rhetoric the party and Portillo had, made arrogant by its own successes, lost perspective and the ability to communicate. Portillo had appeared to repudiate too much of his past for the tastes of his own party, hence not making it to the leadership in 2001 and now his imminent departure from parliament altogether. But although he has been unable to realise his very particular ambitions for the leadership there is no doubt that his most public of personal reassessments has and will shape the party's future direction. Portillo's post-defeat renaissance graphically pointed to the necessary change in public perception that his party also needs. To put it crudely he went from being Mr Nasty to Mr Nice – possibly in the end too 'nice' to be a Tory leader, but proving nonetheless that even the driest and apparently most unreconstructed of right wingers can emerge as sympathetic, attractive and possibly most important, media friendly personalities.

It is the same journey that Howard has to complete if he is really to turn round the fortunes of the Conservative Party. During his pitch for leadership Portillo said that Conservatives must tell people 'what they are for rather than what they are against'. Some old timers found that kind of advertising speak risible but very soon after Michael Howard became leader he paid his own homage to Portillo's advice by issuing his own credo. 'Howard's Way', as his fifteen beliefs soon became known, was exactly a positive statement of Conservative ideas, a high profile effort to say what the party is for. Some criticised the statement for being too impressionistic, but that is what, it seemed to me, was its strength. Accepting the need to create the right impression showed that Portillo's logic had got through and with Howard at the helm there was no need for traditional Conservatives to fear that their agenda would be lost completely in a lurch to the left. It seemed as though an unlikely but effective compromise between style and substance may indeed have emerged and that as leader Michael Howard had something of the all right about him.

Over the longer term Howard's test would be more demanding and along with appropriately refashioned 'niceness' (lifestyle interviews, love of the Beatles, hatred of discrimination etc.) he would have, more importantly, to show determination, consistency and credible policy development. But sticking with all the policies inherited from the former leader sounded one note of warning for those of us anxious and keen for Howard to succeed. Conservative opposition to top-up fees had seemed merely inconsistent under IDS, but under Michael Howard, a more intellectual figure, it seems more blatantly opportunistic. Had it not been for the potential to score tactical points at the government's expense Conservatives would normally be expected to back the principle of top-up fees, or some similar market solution, to solve the impending crisis in university funding, and voters should be considered bright enough to realise this. Howard explained his opposition to the fees in 'touchy feely' terms; a similar scheme would have deterred him from becoming the first member of his family to have a university education. But much though I had previously enjoyed Howard's family revelations I wasn't pleased to hear this resort to emotion despite my campaign for the elevation of the 'nice' Tory. Used in that way it seemed not so much nice but insincere. The danger was that to a sceptical public it was likely to appear not so much counter-intuitive as contrived.

When New Labour had won not only the heads but the hearts of former Tory voters they had exploited a very real revulsion that many had developed for their former political sweethearts. But rather than raising the game in government New Labour have proved as duplicitous and unpleasant as the Tories had been perceived to be. So while it is certainly true that Tories no longer have a monopoly on nastiness this is hardly good news for us Conservatives. Instead it means that faced with the cynicism that now greets politicians from across the spectrum it's more than ever the case that the Conservative Party will only recover if it regains trust and respect. Disillusion with Labour will not be enough to save the Tories: there must be positive reasons to vote Conservative, and these will depend both on the messengers and the credibility of their message. And this does not mean soft soaping the electorate. Challenging New Labour on their own territory gives contemporary Conservatives the opportunity to be bold and to champion long term, radical reform where necessary. There is plenty of scope to offer a distinctive and sympathetic right of centre agenda on education, where progressive teaching methods are still to be defeated, on health, which can remain free at the point of use, and on transport just as much as there is on tax, Europe and crime. After all if the Conservatives cannot be ambitious in opposition then when?

Now I'm looking forward with some renewed optimism to the alarm going off and the *Today* Programme waking me with news of a Conservative revival, meaning that the Tory Groundhog Day is over. In the film the main character, a hapless TV weatherman, finds himself stuck in the same day over and over again. Each day he relives he learns a little more about the reasons for his stasis until he is finally sufficiently aware of his mistakes to move on to another day. Michael Howard may not have the Hollywood appeal of Bill Murray but he is the Tories' strongest leader for a good while. He may not have been the obvious solution for which I was searching but I'd like to forecast blue skies ahead for the possibly rather nice Mr Howard.

INDEX